D1349160

This is an original, deliberately controversial and, at times, disturbing appraisal of the state of comparative law at the beginning of the twenty-first century: its weaknesses, its strengths, and its protagonists (most of whom were personally known to the author) during the preceding 35 years. It is also a reminder of the unique opportunities the subject has in our shrinking world. The author, the holder of chairs and visiting chairs in 25 universities and a fellow of five academies, including the British Academy, brings to bear his experience of 35 years as a teacher of the subject to criticise the impact the long association with Roman law has had on the orientation and well-being of his subject. With equal force, he also warns against some modern trends linking it with variations of the critical legal studies movement, and urges the study of foreign law in a way that can make it more attractive to practitioners and more usable by judges. At the end of the day, this monograph represents a passionate call for greater intellectual co-operation and offers one way of achieving it. A co-operation between practitioners and academics on the one hand and between common and (modern) civilian lawyers on the other, in an attempt to save the subject from the marginalisation it suffered in the 1980s and from which the globalisation movement of the twenty-first century may be about to deliver it.

By the same author and also published by Hart Publishing

Foreign Law and Comparative Methodology
Always on the Same Path
The German Law of Torts (4th edition) with Hannes Unberath
The Tortious Liability of Statutory Bodies

About the author

Basil Markesinis is an honorary QC and holds doctorates or honorary doctorates from (in alphabetical order) Athens, Cambridge, Ghent, Munich, Oxford, and Paris I (Panthéon-Sorbonne). After holding successively the Chairs of European Law and then Comparative Law at the University of Oxford, where he founded the Oxford Institute of European and Comparative Law, he then moved to University College London to the Chair of Common and Civil Law, which he holds simultaneously with the Jamail Regents Chair at the University of Texas at Austin. He has authored or co-authored 25 books and over one hundred legal articles, which have been published in leading law journals in America, Belgium, England, France, Germany, Greece, Italy, and the Netherlands. He has lectured extensively in 25 different law faculties including Cornell, Ghent, Leiden, Michigan, Munich, Paris I, Paris II, Rome, and Siena, where he has held visiting professorships. He is a Fellow of the British Academy, a Foreign Fellow of the Royal Belgian and the Royal Netherlands Academies, a Corresponding Fellow of the Academy of Athens, and a Member of the American Law Institute. In 2002 he was appointed Conseiller Scientifique du Premier Président de la Cour de Cassation on matters of European law. He has received high decorations for his work on European law and integration from the Presidents of France (three times), Germany (twice), Greece, and Italy (three times) on the last occasion (2002) being promoted to the rank of Knight Grand Cross of the Order of Merit.

Comparative Law in the Courtroom and Classroom

The Story of the Last Thirty-Five Years

BASIL MARKESINIS

Foreword
by
The Rt. Hon. The Lord Phillips of Worth Matravers,
Master of the Rolls

·HART·
PUBLISHING
OXFORD – PORTLAND OREGON
2003

Hart Publishing
Oxford and Portland, Oregon

Published in North America (US and Canada) by
Hart Publishing c/o
International Specialized Book Services
5804 NE Hassalo Street
Portland, Oregon
97213-3644
USA

© Basil S Markesinis 2003

Hart Publishing is a specialist legal publisher based in Oxford, England.
To order further copies of this book or to request a list of other
publications please write to:

Hart Publishing, Salter's Boatyard, Folly Bridge,
Abingdon Road, Oxford OX1 4LB
Telephone: +44 (0)1865 245533 or Fax: +44 (0)1865 794882
e-mail: mail@hartpub.co.uk
WEBSITE: http//www.hartpub.co.uk

British Library Cataloguing in Publication Data
Data Available
ISBN 1–84113–398–1 (hardback)

Typeset by Hope Services (Abingdon) Ltd.
Printed and bound in Great Britain on acid-free paper by
Biddles Ltd, www.biddles.co.uk

I am acting on behalf of later generations. I am writing down a few things that may be of use to them; I am committing to writing some helpful recommendations, which might be compared to the formulae of successful medications . . . I am pointing out to others the right path, which I have recognised only late in life, when I am worn out with my wanderings.

(Seneca, Epistulae Morales ad Lucilium, letter VIII, trans. Robin Campbell)

Foreword

For more than 30 years Professor Basil Markesinis has been conducting a crusade. He believes passionately that the primary role of the comparative lawyer is to assist the practitioner, and above all the judge, in the development of the law. Neither the practitioner nor the judge has the time to research, analyse and digest the law that is developing in jurisdictions other than his own. That is the task of the comparative lawyer. The law provides the rules for resolving the problems that arise out of factual situations. The last 50 years have seen radical changes in these factual situations and in political and economic attitudes and practices. The law has to accommodate and reflect these changes—European integration, world trade, the global recognition of human rights, information technology, the power of the media, social security and modern insurance practices are some that Professor Markesenis identifies. In the different jurisdictions the judges are applying, and developing, the legal principles of their own systems to resolve the new problems that are thrown up by these changes. Principles of law, which on their face appear to differ from one jurisdiction and legal system to another, are seen by Professor Markesinis as no more than the tools for resolving common problems. Those tools are shaped—the legal principle developed—by the judges under the influence of considerations of policy in a manner which is largely latent in the civil law systems, but expressly recognised by the reasoning that is typical of the judgments of the superior courts of the common law jurisdictions. A judge in one jurisdiction, grappling with the issues, including policy issues, that are raised by a novel factual situation will be assisted by consideration of how colleagues in other jurisdictions have resolved the same issues. The comparative lawyer must first stimulate the judge to seek such information and then provide it to the judge directly or through the practitioners, who will wish to be in a position to satisfy the judge's quest for information. This will result in a fruitful process of cross-fertilisation under which judges will begin to borrow each other's tools so that their laws are drawn closer together: 'bridge building between systems and even cultures is a complex and noble task'.

Some of these propositions are controversial and Professor Markesinis has deliberately set out to write a controversial book. He starts with a survey of the field over the last half century: a comparative study of comparative lawyers. The sixties he identifies as a golden era of comparative law, graced by a number of 'heroes, if not gods', but most left no legacy to be built on by those that followed. This was because of shortcomings in their approach to their subject. They were obsessed with the pedigree of legal principles, delighting in tracing these back to Roman law. They wrote for the delectation of each other, rather than for a wider audience, incestuously citing each other's works. This backward-looking learning was of no assistance to the practitioner or the judge and obscured the understanding of the development of the common law. The comparatists brought about their own neglect by those shaping the law.

In a remarkable, indeed unique chapter, Professor Markesinis explores the 'science of reputology', carrying out a statistical survey of citations of comparatists in academic works and contrasting these with their citation by the courts. He comments that the results produce a measure of reputation, but not of scholarship and that publications make no significant mark if not written in English. More pertinently, he finds that the figures support his thesis—the comparatists had only a tiny impact on the world of practice.

The latter part of this work is devoted to an exposition, by concrete example, of the methodology that Professor Markesinis advocates and applies to the study of comparative law. He takes as his building blocks specific decisions of the courts and analyses the policy issues raised by the particular facts and the manner in which the legal principles of the particular system are deployed to resolve those issues. Comparison with a case of similar facts raising similar issues resolved under a different legal system, demonstrates that judges apply similar policy considerations to reach similar results by the manipulation of apparently dissimilar legal principles. A case-based study of a foreign legal system enables a student to build up a true understanding of the working of the system, illuminated by his knowledge of how his own system tackles the same problems.

Professor Markesinis leaves us on a note of optimism. Where foreign law is presented in accordance with his methodology, judges are prepared to take note of it, and are increasingly doing so. The recent decision in *Fairchild v Glenhaven Funeral Services Limited* [2002] UKHL 22 provides a powerful illustration of this trend. In making this significant development of the law of causation in negligence, four members of the House of Lords drew on contemporary foreign jurisprudence, though it is fair to observe that one also made extensive reference to Roman jurists.

This vigorous and erudite work makes out and advances Professor Markesinis' case that if comparative lawyers provide concrete, focused and detailed studies of the decisions of foreign courts, packaged to meet the need of practitioners, they have a valuable role to play in the development of the law.

I would strongly endorse his exhortation to practitioners not to ignore the jurisprudence of the other European courts, including those at Luxembourg and Strasbourg.

Lord Phillips of Worth Matravers
Master of the Roles

Royal Courts of Justice
October 2002

Preface

Aristotle regarded politics as the supreme science. In one way or another, academic life has nowadays become the lowest form of politics, where low stakes surprisingly provoke strong antagonisms and, at times, even petty human behaviour. Low pay and a declining social status may be part of the reason. The hypersensitivity that often comes with political correctness, is another. Begging—nowadays euphemistically called fund-raising—for one's living is a third distraction from teaching and research; and for better or for worse, it is having a growing impact on what is taught and how it will be taught. The entre-preneurial atmosphere is made worse by the fact that so much of modern university administration is left to amateur dons and not entrusted, as it is in the USA, to trained professionals. There is little doubt that the post of professor today bears little resemblance to the German or French professoriate of the turn of the twentieth century, which set the ideal for so many coun-tries including the USA one hundred years ago. The decline is visible to all except those who have recently acquired the title.

But there is also a higher level of legal politics, which those particularly involved in the international side of law can per-ceive and pursue. It involves building bridges between sys-tems, which the nineteenth century sovereign state made appear more different than they were or, at any rate, have become. Bridge building between systems and even cultures is a complex and noble task, for the search for the common ground can help create an open mind and foster tolerance at a time when intolerance is again on the increase. It is also intel-lectually challenging; for bringing down barriers, erected by years of nationalism, calls for ingenuity and perseverance—legal as well as political. In this country, finally, there is the practical need to encourage a closer working relationship between the different agents of law-making. This offers a new dimension to English law since the co-operation of academics and judges, though a tradition with a venerable history on the continent of Europe, is a relatively new phenomenon in England.

Teaching a subject can never be undertaken in isolation of its times. It is at its most effective if it is part of a wider scheme of things and fits in with the world around us. In my view it is fitting that the College, which in the mid-nineteenth century challenged the Oxbridge view that the university curriculum was complete with classics and religion, should, again, take the lead and challenge the continued utility of Roman law, arguing, instead, for the centrality of contemporary foreign law. Those who know my work will, of course, realise that I have been slowly developing this creed over the last 35 years in academic life. If in this, the latest of my works, my thesis prompts wider debate (perhaps because it is supported by cruel statistics), it will have scored one of its aims. For the time to stir (if not drain away) stagnant waters is well overdue.

BASIL MARKESINIS
Bentham's College, London
3 October 2002

Acknowledgements

Chapters one, two, and six are entirely new. So is chapter three, though it is not entirely mine since in its writing I was greatly assisted by Dr Jörg Fedtke, formerly of the University of Hamburg and currently University Lecturer in Law at UCL, and Jon Pratter, Foreign and International Law Librarian at the Law School of the University of Texas at Austin. Chapter four, always conceived as an integral part of this book, also comes from my pen but has already appeared (in a slightly different form) in the July 2002 issue of the *Cambridge Law Journal*. Chapter five is, likewise, a modified version of another recent essay—my inaugural lecture at UCL, first published in vol 54 of *Current Legal Problems 2001*—and does for public law what chapter four attempts for private law. Chapter six rounds up the treatment, setting the whole raft of ideas and proposals presented in this book against the context of my 35 years in English and international academic life. Like the rest of the book, it not only looks back but also looks forward into the future with ideas of wider import. Appendix 1 reproduces a brief correspondence between Lord Atkin and Harold C Gutteridge QC (the first holder of the Chair of Comparative law at the University of Cambridge). The two letters, which first appeared in Geoffrey Lewis' excellent biography of Lord Atkin (published by Butterworths in 1983) and are reproduced here by kind permission of the author and the publishers, were exchanged 70 years ago. Yet they are more topical today than when they were written; and they are also in perfect harmony with the philosophy of this book. The two translations of the German cases in Appendix 2 are by Tony Weir and Raymond Youngs, while Appendix 3 explains the method followed in the very extensive electronic searches made for the writing of chapter three. Professor Fred Shapiro, of the Yale Law School, generously gave his views on the use of statistics, but bears no responsibility for them. My good friends Professors Wulf-Henning Roth (Bonn), Michael Coester and Dagmar Coester-Waltjen (both Munich), Giovanni Grottanelli de' Santi (Siena) and Guido Alpa (Rome, *La Sapienza*) read, discussed, advised on and sometimes disagreed with parts of the manuscript. Dr Hannes Unberath, once a pupil and now a young colleague at the University of Munich, read, listened, and reacted as I developed my views in and outside the classroom. He was well qualified to do so since, like me, he had studied in the Two Worlds I am describing and, again like me, loves them both. The Jamail Research Centre of the University of Texas at Austin tirelessly provided bibliographical assistance; and it is, of course, Joe Jamail's munificence which made my link with that great University possible. Finally, the Master of the Rolls, the Rt Hon the Lord Phillips of Worth Matravers, lent the gravitas of his authority to a deliberately controversial book whose greatest redeeming feature is its sincere belief that judges are still at the centre of the legal universe. To all of the above I am immensely grateful, as I am especially to Jörg Fedtke for casting his eagle eye over the entire finished manuscript with the care and discernment I have come to expect from German friends. Naturally, I release them all from liability arising from ideas contained in it, often very personal, and developed in a teaching career which took me to 25 leading law faculties over a period of 35 years and was really great fun. In this peripatetic life I was (metaphorically) constantly accompanied and supported, by Guido Calabresi, Keith Clark, John Fleming, Gibson Gayle Jr, Sir Roy Goode, Jack Hamson, Professor Tony Honoré, Tim Koopmans, Harry Lawson, Professor Werner Lorenz, Henry Schermers, André Tunc, David Williams, and Charlie Wright. Towards them I truly feel the gratitude that Dante must have felt to Virgil for enabling him, at the end of a long journey, 'to see the stars again.' Last but by no means least, I thank Amy Brown for being as loyal and invaluable a secretary as her marvellous predecessors, Pam Celentano, Pat Gibb, and Pamela Harries. I could not have written as much as I have in my life and also founded and run three Institutes without their constant help.

The book is dedicated to the late Jack Hamson, formerly Professor of Comparative Law at the University of Cambridge and one-time Treasurer of Gray's Inn. Hamson was a teacher who cared about his students more than anything else in this world, apart from the 'beautiful Isabella,' his charming wife. If I rendered any real service to education, it must be found in my efforts to be of assistance to my many pupils in many countries. I learnt this lesson, if nothing else, from Jack. I am by no means the only one who remembers Jack with deep gratitude; but few can miss him more than I do.

BM

PS: In the book I have used the title of Professor only for living colleagues and, again, only the first time their name appears in the text; after that, to save space and avoid making the text too heavy, they are referred to only by their surname.

Contents

Abbreviations

A. 2d	Atlantic Reporter (Second Series)
AC	Law Reports, Appeal Cases (House of Lords and Privy Council from 1891)
All ER	All England Law Reports
Amer J Comp L	*American Journal of Comparative Law*
AöR	*Archiv des öffentlichen Rechts*
BCLR	Butterworth's Constitutional Law Reports (South Africa)
BGB	Bürgerliches Gesetzbuch (German Civil Code)
BGBl	Bundesgesetzblatt (German Government Gazette)
BGH	Bundesgerichtshof (Germany's Federal/Supreme Court)
BGHSt	Entscheidungen des Bundesgerichtshofs in Strafsachen (Decisions of the German Supreme Court in criminal matters)
BGHZ	Entscheidungen des Bundesgerichtshofs in Zivilsachen (Decisions of the German Supreme Court in civil matters)
BR-Drucks	Bundesrats-Drucksache (printed matter of the German Bundesrat)
BT-Drucks	Bundestags-Drucksache (printed matter of the German Bundestag)
BVerfG	Bundesverfassungsgericht
BVerfGE	Entscheidungen des Bundesverfassungsgerichts (Decisions of the German Federal Constitutional Court)

BVerwGE	Entscheidungen des Bundesver-waltungsgerichts (Decisions of the German Federal Administrative Court)
Ca App	California Court of Appeal
California L Rev	*California Law Review*
Cambridge LJ	*Cambridge Law Journal*
Can Bar Rev	*The Canadian Bar Review*
Cardozo L Rev	*Cardozo Law Review*
CC	Constitutional Court (South Africa)
CE	Conseil d'Etat
Ch D	Law Reports, Chancery Division (1875–90)
Chi-Kent L Rev	*Chicago-Kentucky Law Review*
CISG	United Nations Convention on the International Sale of Goods
Civ Just Q	*Civil Justice Quarterly*
CLJ	*Cambridge Law Journal*
CLP	*Current Legal Problems*
Colum J Eur L	*Columbia Journal of European Law*
Columbia J Transnat'l L	*Columbia Journal of Transnational Law*
Colum L Rev	*Columbia Law Review*
Copyright Rev	*Copyright Review*
Cornell L Rev	*Cornell Law Review*
Denning L J	*Denning Law Journal*
EGBGB	Einführungsgesetz zum BGB (introductory law to the BGB)
European Rev of Private Law	*European Review of Private Law*
Fam L Q	*Family Law Quarterly*
FED App.	Federal Appeal
F. Supp.	Federal Supplement
GRUR Int	*Gewerblicher Rechtsschutz und Urheberrecht, Internationaler Teil*
Harv L Rev	*Harvard Law Review*
Hastings Int'l & Comp L Rev	*Hastings International and Comparative Law Review*
Hastings L Journal	*Hastings Law Journal*

ICLQ	*International and Comparative Law Quarterly*
ILJ	*Indiana Law Journal*
Ill App	Illinois Court of Appeal
ILR	*Iowa Law Review*
JBl	*Juristische Blätter*
JCL	*Journal of Comparative Legislation and International Law*
JCP	*Juris-Classeur Périodique* (also referred to as *SJ—La Semaine juridique*)
J Legal Stud.	*Journal of Legal Studies*
JSPTL	*Journal of the Society of Public Teachers of Law*
JZ	*Juristenzeitung*
KB	Law Reports, King's Bench
Law Com No	*Law Commission Paper* (number)
LG	*Landgericht*
LMCLQ	*Lloyds Maritime and Commercial Law Quarterly*
Lloyd's Rep	*Lloyd's (List) Law Reports*
LS	*Legal Studies*
LQR	*Law Quarterly Review*
Maryland L Rev	*Maryland Law Review*
MLR	*Modern Law Review*
NCL Rev	*North Carolina Law Review*
NE 2d	North Eastern Reporter (American law reports)
NJW	*Neue Juristische Wochenschrift*
NLJ	*New Law Journal*
New York University L Rev	*New York University Law Review*
Northw J Int'l L B	*Northwestern Journal of international Law and Business*
NW 2d	North Western Reporter (Second Series)
NYS 2d.	New York Supplement (Second Series)
OGH	Oberster Gerichtshof (Austrian Supreme Court)

OLG	Oberlandesgericht (German Court of Appeal)
OJLS	*Oxford Journal of Legal Studies*
OUP	Oxford University Press
OVGE	Entscheidungen der Oberverwaltungsgerichte (Decisions of the German Administrative Courts of Appeal)
PL	*Public Law*
P. 2d	Pacific Reporter (Second Series)
QB	Law Reports, Queen's Bench (1891–1900; 1952–)
RabelsZ	*Rabels Zeitschrift für ausländisches und internationales Recht*
RdA	*Recht der Arbeit*
Revue dr unif	*Revue de droit uniforme*
Rev int dr comp	*Revue international de droit comparé*
Rev trim dr civ	*Revue trimestrielle de droit civil*
Rev trim dr com	*Revue trimestrielle de droit commerciale.*
RGZ	Entscheidungen des Reichsgerichts in Zivilsachen (Decisions of the German Imperial Court in civil matters)
RVO	Reichsversicherungsordnung (Imperial Insurance Act)
SAJHR	*South African Journal on Human Rights*
SJ	*La Semaine juridique* (also referred to as *JCP* = *Juris-Classeur Périodique*)
RLR	*Restitution Law Review*
SLT	*Scots Law Times*
Tul Eur & Civ L Forum	*Tulane European and Civil Law Forum*
Tulane L Rev	*Tulane Law Review*
UBCL Rev	*University of British Columbia Law Review*
UCL	University College London

UNIDROIT	L'Unification du droit
Va L Rev	*Virginia Law Review*
VersR	*Versicherungsrecht*
Wall St J	*Wall Street Journal*
WLR	Weekly Law Reports
Yale L J	*Yale Law Journal*
ZaöRV	*Zeitschrift für ausländisches öffentliches Recht und Völkerrecht*
ZEuP	*Zeitschrift für Europäisches Privatrecht*
ZfRV	*Zeitschrift für Rechtsvergleichung, Internationales Privatrecht und Europarecht*
ZGR	*Zeitschrift für Unternehmens- und Gesellschaftsrecht*
ZIP	*Zeitschrift für Wirtschaftsrecht und Insolvenzpraxis*

Table of Cases

South African Constitutional Court

United States

MODERN CIVIL LAW

Austrian Supreme Court

Dutch Supreme Court

France

Conseil d'Etat

Cour de cassation

Germany

Reichsgericht

Bundesgerichtshof

1

Reflections on the State of Comparative Law I: The Twilight of the Heroes

'Tell the King, the fairwrought hall has fallen to the ground. No longer has Phoebus a hut, nor a prophetic laurel, nor a spring that speaks. The water of speech even is quenched.' The last Delphic prophecy delivered to the Byzantine Emperor Julian, known as the Apostate, when he sought the Oracle's advice about his attempt to revive the old, pagan world. (H W Parke and D E W Wormell, *The Delphic Oracle* Oxford, Basil Blackwell, 1956, vol I, 290; vol II, 194)

1. OF GHETTOES AND SMART NEIGHBOURHOODS

As one enters the final stretch of one's professional life as a law teacher one is tempted to ask, with a considerable measure of self-doubt, the question 'what value have I added to my product (for which read subject) during the years I ran the shop?' For, as Montaigne rightly stressed,[1] 'it is a misfortune that wisdom forbids you to be satisfied with yourself and always sends you away dissatisfied and fearful.' To his list of epithets, I would add 'frustrated.' For comparatists more than others, forced by the nature of their subject to keep looking at different systems and sources of ideas, realise, I think full-well, that in the realms of the arts (rather than the sciences) it is very difficult to be truly original. At best, one is thus only likely to modify or improve an earlier idea and, occasionally, because of a change in circumstances, be in a better position to implement it.[2]

Not all academics are prone to self-doubt. In his Francis Mann Lecture Professor Peter Birks,[3] a keen and eloquent advocate of an enriched legal curriculum, had no doubts that one of my subjects—comparative law—remained 'in the ghetto.' Referring to me, he added, that this was despite 'all my energy'—a compliment he had paid me some five years earlier when he gave a different lecture[4] (but one in which he also touched on the same subject) at my Institute of Anglo-American Law in Leiden. Since one of his own subjects—Roman law—would appear (for different reasons) to share the same fate, he knows how it feels to try to operate from an (apparently) disadvantaged neighbourhood. More importantly, however, if he was right to say what he said about the state of affairs in 1997, one wonders how he would have described the 'neighbourhood' of comparative law at the time I embarked on my career in England exactly 30 years earlier? Was it then Chelsea or was it always Brixton? And if it was in a better condition than it is now, am I one (of many) who, having inhabited it for 30 years, contributed to the decline? He did not suggest that; but I must ask the question.

In many respects the late 1960s were, I think, a golden era inhabited by heroes if not gods. Professor René Rodière and André Tunc held the relevant chairs in Paris while René David, with his best years by now behind him, had retreated to Aix after '*les événements*' of 1968 had broken his favourite faculty into fragments. Konrad Zweigert, Professor Hans Stoll, and Professor Werner Lorenz were, among others, active in Germany; and so was that meticulous polymath, Professor Ulrich Drobnig. Gino Gorla, that finest of Italian minds, was reigning undisputed in Italy. Sir Otto Kahn-Freund was displaying his pulverising personality[5] to the Oxford Law Faculty, which was not only putting up with it but also, apparently, liking it! The late Jack Hamson—a man endowed with a subtle (and mischievous) mind and a unique turn of phrase (alas, rarely committed to paper)—was on the verge of passing on the baton to the mild-mannered and self-doubting Professor Kurt Lipstein, the last of the learned émigrés bequeathed by the Hitlerian madness to the Anglo-Saxon world. Last but by no means least, a young Tony Weir had just completed with Professor Pierre Catala of the University of Paris one of the most stimulating pieces on foreign law and comparative methodology ever to be written. I say nothing of the scene across the Atlantic. Though how can one ignore recalling that Max Rheinstein, in my view the civilian who most penetrated the common law mind, was still teaching at Chicago and Rudi

Schlesinger was captivating successive generations of law students at Cornell, having just completed his most unusual scholarly endeavour on the common core of legal systems (to which I will return later). And then there was Jack Dawson and John Fleming—the latter, after some hiccups, having managed in 1960 to transfer to Berkeley the talent that has earned him such renown in the antipodes (and, later, in Canada). The first was a truly erudite comparative legal historian; and both he and Fleming were interested—mainly—in the common law of obligations. But they also kept weaving into American law Germanic ideas with learning and effect surpassed, in my view, only by the more open efforts of Karl Llewellyn and Roscoe Pound some 50 years earlier. It would thus be a mistake to regard Dawson and Fleming purely as 'national' lawyers though, as we shall note in chapter three below, their work poses some problems of classification.

In terms of *personalities* this was, indeed, a unique era; and I was privileged to have grown up in such an environment and to have met the above and worked with most of them. I have such vivid memories of most of them that I appreciate more fully than most of the current generation of comparatists the full meaning of a statement made by Goethe to Johann Eckermann at the end of the former's long life.[6] For it reflects on the value of the poet's *first hand exposure* to important events and people, which subsequent generations can only attempt to understand through books.[7] The experience is simply not the same.

So whatever the value of Birk's ghetto theory for the mid-1990s, clearly it was inapplicable to the situation that existed in the mid-1960s, as those who lived through it can attest. And if decline followed, what brought it about? The search for reasons stems not only from a wish to test the veracity of a provocative statement but from suspicions about some structural weakness of a university system in which I have served for 35 years and which may have contributed to the undoubted problems. If some of these problems can be identified and exposed, this enquiry may even hold lessons for the future. What follows in this and the ensuing chapter, inevitably contains, to quote Goethe again, 'fragments of a great confession.'[8] But they may also help explain my views and even the state of comparative law in our times. For one of the themes of this book is the idea that it is precisely these types of contacts and background that help shape one's work in later life.

2. DECLINE

Let us look at the scenario under three headings, bearing in mind that the ideas they contain cannot be kept strictly apart. *Indeed, the overall message of this book will only be fully grasped if all its six chapters are digested together.*

(a) The Absence of the Defining Treatise, the Inspiring Thesis, the Invention of a New Methodology

Any account of textbooks, treatises, or influential monographs of that period must start with David's *Les grands systèmes du droit contemporain*, even though it dates from an earlier time than that which I am taking as the starting point of my enquiry. The way this book came about reflects the personality of its author: larger than life, full of charm and *bonhomie* (which his photographs reveal, in contrast to the austere Ernst Rabel), but no less tough and ambitious for that inviting appearance.

Yet, with all its originality David's book suffered from a number of defects, which time, I think, has magnified not diminished. First, its attempt to divide systems into legal families—though original at the time—was and has remained fuzzy at the fringes. Secondly, his groupings always struck me (and others) as defective, since they were entirely devised on the basis of private law and ignored the different arrangements that might result if public law had served as the yardstick. Thirdly, some of David's aims were questionable or so, at least, I have always felt. For instance, vis-à-vis the then Soviet block, they prompted ideas, which had to be revised with subsequent editions. Towards the rest of the world, they hardly concealed his attempts to place French law in a pre-eminence that was neither easily acceptable to all, nor likely to prove correct with time, despite its many merits. Both these undercurrents allowed his position as a citizen to cloud his judgement as a scholar. Finally and most importantly, his book treated comparative law at such a level of generalities that it slowly became unappealing in the classroom while never being useful in the courtroom. But not before it managed to dominate during the 1970s and part of the 1980s the reading lists of most law schools which taught comparative law. Thus, marvellous in the 1950s, the book and the 'method' it stood for began to age by the time the last decade of the last century began. For in the 1950s the book addressed a gap—as David rightly sensed and intended to fill.[9] Thirty years later it became an obstacle to new thinking, especially in France, as David's reputation was by then so unshakeable in his own country that few had the guts to rebel. Even my mentor and friend Tunc, who was at the time so skilfully laying the foundations of his great crusade on traffic accident law, ignored his own prescription when it came to teaching his general class on comparative law at Paris I. For whereas in his own research on specific topics he made skilful use of detailed foreign and interdisciplinary information, in his main course with his students, which I attended avidly in the early 1980s when working in Paris as Visiting Professor, he substantially followed the David method. And this, at least in so far as it was encapsulated in David's best-known work, was happy to present the 'great lines' of foreign laws and ascribe to the subject primarily a *'mission civilisatrice'*—and content to leave matters at that.

These attitudes spread to the common law world. This was inevitable since for a long time there was no other book to recommend to students able and willing to develop an interest in foreign law. This grip even strengthened for a while after Professor David Brierly produced in Canada in the mid-1980s an English version of the text. For a period of 30 years before Birks made his ghetto speech, English students (and more advanced lawyers) had thus little to consult that came from British pens even though, as we noted, there was no shortage of great names.

Apart from David's book, there were, in fact, only three other general works. The first was by Sir Morris Amos and F P Walton and was entitled *French Law*. The second was by the late Ernst Joseph Cohn—a German, not an Englishman—entitled *Manual of German Law*.[10] Both were good books, the latter in my view more perceptive than the former, but too cursory to be of any real practical value. Moreover, neither was really a work on comparative *methodology*, both books being content to offer readable descriptions of the basic branches of two major foreign legal systems with only the occasional reference to English law. Indeed, on reflection, both these books, and the bulk of the periodical literature of the time, give the impression that the French terminology of *droit comparé* had prevailed over the more accurate German *Rechtsvergleichung*. For, in reality, these (and most of the articles of that period) were not works on comparative law at all but small textbooks or essays describing one of two foreign legal systems: the French and the German. It would thus appear that comparative law was seen as a medium for providing elementary knowledge of a foreign legal system and little more. This was and still is more than a point of mere terminology. For it reflected and reflects a conception that was destined to have an effect on the way the subject was researched, taught, and used in this country. Thus, the only truly English comparative *textbook* that I recall from this period was William Buckland and Lord MacNair's *Roman Law and Common Law*. And it was no coincidence that its last edition was brought up to date by England's foremost comparatist, the late Harry Lawson. Common lawyers of my generation thus had no books on comparative law, since the ground-breaking *Einführung in die Rechtsvergleichung auf dem Gebiete des Privatrechts* of Zweigert and Kötz had not yet seen the light of day even in its homeland.[11]

Across the Atlantic the picture was somewhat different for there German émigrés propagated their subject differently than they did in England. For present purposes the account must start with Schlesinger. Schlesinger shared Rabel's interest (and more about Rabel later) in the 'real world.' This was a most fortunate predilection given that he had been forced, because of his Jewish background, to settle in the 'New World.' And the professional nature of the American law curriculum would not (and in my view still does not) easily tolerate philosophising or generalities in its courses. Schlesinger perceptively gave his subject his own, *practical* twist. His book, though entitled *Comparative Law*,[12] is really and in the main a work about foreign law as pleaded and used in American courts and not a 'theoretical' or 'philosophical' work on comparative law nor a fully fledged thesis on comparative methodology in general. These attributes made *Comparative Law* the only textbook-cum-casebook of its kind. They also enabled its charismatic author to draw the crowds into the classroom in a way that no other comparative law teacher in the USA (or come to that in England) has since managed to achieve. But the book's strength was also its weakness. For, on the whole, it had little that could be of use to an English teacher,[13] and even less to an English (or non-American) practitioner or court. And as one moved further eastwards onto the Continent, its relevance became minuscule. The impact, which the book has thus had in England, and on the European Continent more generally,[14] has thus been much, much smaller than that which it had on its home turf. The statistics given in chapter three below, attest to this.

The same, I think, can also be said of Schlesinger's other undoubtedly great venture, his *Formation of Contracts: A Study of the Common Core of Legal Systems*,[15] though here one must adopt a more nuanced approach. Once again the idea of assembling a distinguished team of foreign lawyers to discuss common factual situations in a way that would bring out the common threads that ran through the various legal systems was brilliantly conceived and meticulously executed. But though it was rightly praised for its many innovations, its basic premise—a fact-oriented analysis—appears much more original to Europeans unaccustomed to their law being presented to them through decisions dealing with narrow factual situations than it does to common lawyers. Other, 'lesser,' objections were levelled against it at the time, mainly by some (French) reviewers.[16] But in my view, by far its greatest weakness was the fact that, though it produced some immensely useful information gathered by its carefully drafted and fact-oriented questionnaire, the project never tested its main premises beyond the easiest part of contract law—offer and acceptance. For it avoided[17] grappling with some of the doctrinally nightmarish issues (such as consideration, reliance, mistake, and breach) which have really separated common and civil law of contract. The future of the so-called Trento project, which is animated by former pupils of Professor Rodolfo Sacco and borrows largely from the Schlesinger approach, will show how broad and how usable is the methodology which it (partly) invented. But in my own view the influence which Schlesinger's work on the 'Common Core' had in the American classroom (and periodical literature) was almost as small as was its appeal in the court-room where its impact was, frankly, nil. The statistical informa-tion I provide in chapter three below supports, I think, this contention.

Fleming was another German émigré with a penchant for comparative law and the linguistic ability to satisfy it. Though he was widely respected by the American comparatist world during his Berkeley years he, too, failed to leave a magnum opus on comparative law or a distinct methodology for others to follow. For despite his formidable knowledge of different legal systems (especially the German), which he wove (often imperceptibly) into his tort book, and the incisive case notes he wrote for the *Law Quarterly Review* towards the end of his life, his excursus into foreign law were brief and not connected to any central theme. His name will thus endure mainly through his quite unique textbook. Though this constantly blended the solutions and ideas of at least three major common law systems—the Australian, the American, and the English—*and in that sense was a masterpiece of comparative law in practice*, it gave (understandably) no clues on comparative methodology. What brought this, (often) disparate, material together was Fleming's command of detail that could be displayed to full effect by his pithy language. But the comparatist who is seek-ing to learn from the master just obtains the finished product, but no instructions as to how to get there himself. In my opin-ion, the book was so closely linked to Fleming's genius (and irreverent spirit that surfaces in throwaway lines in his work) that it is difficult to see it surviving his death; and if it does, it will not be the same book for long.

(b) The Comparatists in Britain and the USA

But there were learned comparatists in England, as well; and they wrote with erudition and elegance of style. Did that work not train minds, create schools, secure continuity of interest in what the greats had started, by multiplying contacts with other systems and their lawyers? Over the years, it became increas-ingly obvious to me that these great men fell into two categories;

and—unconsciously—both groups failed to address these questions (except, perhaps, the first) in an enduring fashion.

(i) The Academics

The first group were academic purists, still linked to the dying scholarship of Roman law but unable to shake it off completely and focus on European law in its new incarnation in the form of modern French, German, or Italian law, or comparative methodology. Their German counterparts had made this switch in droves after the end of the First World War; and the Max Planck Institute in Hamburg (founded in 1926, effectively as the successor to the Kaiser Wilhelm Institute) gave them a welcoming home, one might even say a mission. As we have seen, so did their American counterparts, even though most of them were central European émigrés and thus also trained in Roman law. But this did not happen in England. The writings of the best of this group—and here I unhesitatingly include Lawson and his masterpieces *The Rational Strength of English Law*[18] and *A Common Lawyer Looks at the Civil Law*[19]—are classics that still repay reading as much for the pithy style in which they were written as for the originality of their ideas. But otherwise in England the link between comparative law and Roman law as well as legal history was more than kept alive: it remained dominant. Dominant in the texts these scholars produced;[20] dominant in the share it claimed of their total literary output; and dominant in the 'establishment' mentality that continued to control the subject well into the 1970s and treated Romanists almost as the only natural holders of chairs of comparative law.[21] Indeed, it is not just the blending of Roman and modern material, which nowadays seems less accessible or relevant, that is obvious from the writings of this era. One also gets from the writings of these authors the same impression found mostly in legal history: the author is mainly addressing a small circle of acolytes, academics of the purest kind.

The clinging to Roman texts and legal history, though undoubtedly adding enviable erudition to their work, and in some instances explicable by reference to the authors' own past and training did not, however, further the future of comparative law in a rapidly changing world. For one, much of classical Roman law (eg the condition of women, the status of paterfamilias) has been turned on its head. And to the extent that these topics (but not the solutions given by the Romans) are important to us now, they tend to form part of public law as much as private law. Other, lengthy references to Roman law add little to the understanding of the common law, which has developed oblivious to Roman ideas, even when they ran on parallel lines. To the extent that they figure in contemporary writings, they seem—to me at least—to creep in more for (legitimate) extraneous but not 'functional' reasons.[22] In my view, such exercises only help distance their authors and their ideas slowly but steadily from the real world of practice which, in the common law world, is the bloodline of survival and regeneration. Thus, as comparative law (and later European Community law) de facto pushed Roman law aside, the surviving Romanists began to complain, but to no avail.[23] But the change, or so it seems to me, has been brought about by themselves, not least because the English attachment to classical Roman law prevented a shift along the lines of Professor Reinhard Zimmermann's work, which came to place much emphasis on the influence of history on the development of the modern codal structures—and arguably beyond—by providing the foundations of a common European legal culture. Professor David Ibbetson's *A Historical Introduction to the Law of Obligations*[24] is one of the few works that has attempted something similar (though not as ambitious as Zimmermann's magnum opus) for the common law of obligations. Although I suspect more attempts of this kind will be made in the years ahead,[25] as the struggle for survival becomes more desperate, the tide has changed in favour of Community law, comparative human rights law, and European efforts towards codification, to mention but a few.

Not that the attempt to link the study of legal history and Roman law to comparative law has not had a long and understandable history. Indeed, some erudite scholars such as Zimmermann make a valiant attempt to keep them linked. I doubt that this will succeed in England; it may even be doomed in his own country (which, for financial reasons, is experiencing a bigger crisis at the level of higher education than most of us in this country are aware of). The reasons are not just the practical and financial ones, which deliberately form a recurring theme of these first two chapters because I do not wish to allow academic purists to believe that they can wish them away. Nor am I being pessimistic because I strongly suspect that charismatic Zimmermanns are less easy to find these days than in the golden era of legal history and Roman law, which coincides roughly with the turn of the last century. Nor do I invoke the declining interest in Latin, which is rapidly following the disappearance of ancient Greek, even among contemporary classical archaeologists. The real reason is that whatever the beauty and richness of Roman law, it was not expected to cope with some very contemporary phenomena or institutions. I shall return to this theme in this and the next chapters.

Our law is thus increasingly public law in its character, regulation-oriented in its structure and ambit, concerned with the manifold problems arising from the power of the modern press, information technology, patents and copyrights, and deeply affected by social security and modern insurance practices. Add to these some contemporary challenges such as the globalisation of the financial markets and the needs of the modern, multinational law firms, and I think it is easy to understand why the study of the legal past is likely to become less relevant and less prevalent in the future. No doubt, one can imagine ingenious scholars constructing ingenious and ingenuous links between Roman law literature and modern problems. Again, one's mind turns to Zimmermann. He has attempted this most recently in his marvellous *Roman Law, Contemporary Law, European Law: The Civilian Tradition.*[26] There, with his usual enthusiasm, felicitous style and attention to detail, he highlighted with great effect the continuity between the old Pandectist law of the nineteenth century and the way the German courts interpreted their 'new' Code of 1896 in the years after its enactment. The defenders of the old faith will seek comfort in such pronouncements and, no doubt, will find other illustrations to support their view. But the beginning of the twenty-first century is very different to that of the twentieth. My point is that the extent of the changes—which I mentioned above by way of illustration and not as an all-inclusive list—represent a marked departure from the past. Indeed, not just marked but so radical as to render the invocation of the example of German jurisprudence at the turn of the last century as an example of continuity and of what can go on happening in the future, appear weak and unconvincing. For the changes we are experiencing increasingly make the linking with the Roman past as meaningful as referring a modern nuclear scientist to Democritus as the father of the atom theory. The Delphic pronouncement quoted at the beginning of this chapter contains the message that Romanists cannot bring themselves to accept. But it is no less true for being unpalatable. A cultured emperor who could not see the writing on the wall became known as the 'Apostate'; the more opportunistic predecessor who shifted to the new creed was called 'Great' by history and was made a Saint by the faith he did not espouse until he reached his deathbed.

In the midst of this Romanistic vogue just described, one exception stands out in the English Pantheon. The exception is Kahn-Freund; and I shall say more about him in section (c), below, for he, I think an equal of Lawson's in intellectual terms, also managed to create a school and leave a methodology for approaching foreign law. Moreover, and this is little known in this country, he remained influential as a writer in his country of origin, thus being the only 'English' comparatist who played successfully on both tableaux. But he was *neither a Roman lawyer nor an Englishman* but, first and foremost, a German legal sociologist and labour lawyer. The statistical information given in chapter three, below, confirms the view of his broad and enduring influence. In short, he was a scholar who also left a legacy that reached both sides of the Channel and which the others have not matched.

As stated, the British trend of linking comparative law to Roman law and history was not followed in the USA. The little I said about Schlesinger confirms the above; and Fleming—though a long-standing friend—openly attacked my second edition of Lawson's *Negligence in the Civil Law* for retaining unnecessarily and out of sentimental reasons Lawson's section on Roman law.[27] So in the USA, if Roman law survived, it was (mainly) in the history departments; and this separation, undoubtedly, helped comparative law finds its own feet assisted by the fact that it had its own journal. This trend was supported (both in the USA and Germany) by those like Rabel and Rheinstein who helped give the subject the concrete, pragmatic, and contemporary look which I, for one, admire. Though German, and arguably with the best of their work being done during their German years, the impact these two men had on the American comparative law scene of the second half of the twentieth century cannot be underestimated.

For me Rabel, in particular, still stands out as a giant of my subject—as the indisputable creator of an enduring methodology, notwithstanding some (valid) objections which modern authors levy against him. I shall say more about his work and method in the next chapter. Here suffice it to say that his ability to grasp the realities of the new world order of his time is particularly remarkable given his own beginnings. For he started as a pupil of the great Austrian Romanist Ludwig Mitteis, to whom he always remained indebted for the discipline and methodological precision, which he instilled in him.[28] Indeed, during the early part of his career, he flourished as a Romanist. But from 1916 onwards, when he moved to Munich and took over the direction of the Institute for Foreign and International Law,[29] he shifted his attention to modern law as Jhering had, in one sense, foreshadowed by his call to go, with the help of Roman law, beyond Roman law.[30] Unlike his British counterparts, Rabel consciously chose (mostly) not to link his comparative studies to history or philosophy but to the interests and needs of the practitioners of his time; and he saw to it that his disciples did the same. This was a world that he got to know and admire since he, himself, was to act as a judge, as an arbitrator, and as a consultant of big business and which, later in his life, he was to reinforce as a result of studying the common law.[31] Though one finds hints in his work suggesting an interest in legal theory and philosophy, and legal history when it helps put a living rule in its proper context, on the whole these themes take second place in Rabel's work. Instead, the man becomes pre-occupied by the task of focusing on (relatively) narrow topics and presenting them in a way that might be useful to practitioners of all kinds, in pursuit of his wider political agenda. To do this, he pioneered another break with German tradition: he set aside language and concepts and tried instead to focus on the function the rules under study were meant to achieve. It is thus a great misfortune that his work never really became widely accessible to the English common law world, which, by definition, shares with him an interest in specifics and a dislike of theorising. Indeed, I often wonder what the state of comparative law would have been in England had Rabel chosen to migrate to our islands rather than to the USA and created here, rather than on the other side of the Atlantic, the generation of disciples that were to give his German work its common law facet? On further reflection, and judging from the way Oxford of the late 1940s and early 1950s received other great German émigrés, Rabel may have been wise to choose the USA. Martin Wolf and Fritz Pringsheim are obvious examples; but there are others.[32]

(ii) The Practitioners

The second group of the golden era were primarily émigré practitioners and only part-time academics (though no less admirable or learned for that). This group comprised those who practised foreign law in the international field and who made skilful use of the foreign expertise in their daily work, taking full advantage of their linguistic abilities and their indomitable energies. I include here men like Ernst Stiefel in New York[33] and Mann and Clive Schmitthoff in London. Of the English group, the former became, in fact, more recognised than the latter, in part perhaps because he was willing to emphasise his new founded Englishness and remained exceptionally severe towards his German background—something which must have appealed to some of his hosts.[34] But this group confined the use of the knowledge of foreign law to writing specialised legal pieces mainly connected with the law they practised[35] and failed to show their contemporaries and their successors *how* to interest the English in their foreign learning. The way they exploited their Janus-type personalities was thus left to be described anecdotally by those who worked with them, and benefited from (or often had to put up with) their strong personalities and abundant energy, rather than studied through texts that made their expertise and their insights transferable to others.

The inability of the British 'greats' to leave a coherent methodology that could clearly be identified with one of them was not their only omission (one might even call it failure). Both groups did not leave successors to continue their tradition, even though the academics supervised scores of DPhil students. It could thus be argued that their scholarship did not translate beyond fond memories into an enduring legacy. There was thus no Sacco,[36] Professor Mauro Cappelletti,[37] Schlesinger, or Rheinstein[38] among the above. Kahn-Freund, as I have already said, is, in my view, the only exception; but then he was not at all English. His strong Germanic accent, like that of another influential émigré, Sir Leon Radzinowicz (who also left a legacy by creating the Cambridge Institute of Criminology), reminded everyone of that—if any reminding was ever needed! Unlike some of their kind—Hamson, Lipstein and Mann, for example—these two jurists did not even try to blend into the new environment. Their self-confidence preserved their individuality and, ultimately, ensured local acceptance and recognition with the conferment of their knighthoods.

In this sense the British 'greats' differed, as a group, from their German counterparts and what they were consciously trying to do in Berlin at the Kaiser Wilhelm Institute and (from the mid-1920s) in its successor in Hamburg, and in most other institutes in Germany (Frankfurt, Heidelberg, Munich etc).[39] To be sure, Rabel's shaping comparative law into a science, and inculcating the special mentality it needs into the minds of young scholars, was to some extent dictated by his political agenda to make German industry competitive again in the midst of the Weimar depression. No such agenda existed, of course, in England (though, as we noted, something not dissimilar had crossed David's mind since he was always anxious to promote, through law, French influence abroad). But in England even talk about promoting political agendas through cultural means was seen as an un-academic, even vulgar exercise. Yet such statements must be taken with a pinch of salt, for empire-building is a dream that not many British academics have not had. The real reasons for the omission I refer to are much wider; and they go back to the Oxbridge ethos as it was shaped during the golden era of these two centres of learning namely, between the two Wars and until about the end of the 1950s.

(iii) Other Specifically English Reasons for the Decline

So why was there no urge to encourage the creation of schools of thought in England? I am, of course, thinking of comparative law, though parts of what I say may be of wider import. Whatever the reason, it is, I think, undeniable that few of those of us who, at the time of writing, profess an interest in comparative law can be treated as intellectual heirs to Gutteridge, Hamson, Lipstein, Lawson, Honoré, Nicholas or Rudden. I make this point in all honesty and despite my admiration for much of the work of these learned colleagues. For judging from myself, I cannot say how much I owe to the above colleagues in *methodological* terms, even though I undoubtedly benefited from their learning, their company, and the invaluable support which the second, fourth and fifth of the above gave to me throughout my career. On the other hand if I have incurred 'literary debts,' as the Germans so aptly call them, I feel they are towards the Germans, especially to Rabel and his Zweigert and Kötz progenies as well as Lorenz in whose company I spent many hours later in my life. And these debts are as much for what these scholars said, as for the way they put what they thought into writing. This does not mean, of course, that the Rabel School does not have its underdeveloped parts or even weaknesses; I shall, in the next chapter, mention a few and say how I tried to cope with them myself. And it is here that I may have added a stone or two to the edifice of comparative law.

Declarations of intellectual indebtedness serve no wider purpose than to satisfy the personal need of retrospection and reminiscence to which older people are more prone, so I shall say no more on this subject. But speculating why the 'greats,' especially those who operated in England, did not ensure that their subject and the approach flourished after their passing or retirement, may reveal something that goes beyond what was said about their work or them as individuals—something interesting about the wider English academic scene that has to be considered, even if the thoughts here expressed will not, once again, please everyone.

Lord Annan, in the last book published just before his death and entitled *The Dons*, allows many useful clues on this subject to drift to the surface of his oceanic but elegant name-dropping. For in the world he describes, apart from such gigantic personalities such as John Henry Newman, Benjamin Jowett, Lord Rutherford and Isaiah Berlin, one finds the core of the Oxbridge don. His sketches of many of the Oxbridge greats suggested wide-spread homosexuality,[40] sad loneliness, especially at the end of their lives, wit only barely less developed than egos, topped up, in some instances, by a heavy dose of dilettantism. I am emphatically *not* saying that these were features shared by *my* British greats. What I am saying, however, is that this seems to me to have been the mentality in the environment in which they operated and which I experienced during my 20 years as a Cambridge and Oxford don even though I came at the tail end of the epoch which Annan describes as the 'golden age' of the Oxbridge don.[41] And what I saw *and noticed distinctly*—since it stood out so clearly from the different worlds of Germany, and France, and Italy and Greece, which I also know well—was a 'pretended modesty,' a cynical attitude towards the importance of publishing one's thoughts however modest or wrong they might turn out to be, and a self-conscious (but unjustified) superiority complex towards those who were not members of the clan. I write with concrete examples in mind, not figments of the imagination; though names, of course, are better guessed than mentioned. But I write it nonetheless, for this is not the frame of mind that promotes comparative law nor helps gain England friends abroad.

In scholarly terms the mentality and characters I am referring to, and the overall environment (much more prevalent, I think, in arts rather than sciences) tolerated the above characteristics. In my experience, but also from reading auto-biographical works such as Lord Annan's, this far too frequently resulted in unhappy lives being led in the loneliness of one's College rooms once the last glass of port had been consumed in Hall and the post-prandial mirth had subsided. More importantly, and I return deliberately to this point because it is crucial if one wants to understand the international literature on foreign and comparative law, it is reflected in a serious deficit in written work. This last point is really quite striking if one considers some Oxbridge law chair-holders between, say, 1920 and 1970. For, in my opinion, some would never have come remotely close to holding chairs in any respectable

Continental European university while the claims of other, worthier colleagues, were left unsatisfied.[42] But the Oxbridge preference for the teacher rather than the writing scholar, for the wit rather than the disciplined and sombre polymath (though, of course, they had those, too), for the effervescent quip rather than the premeditated response, had, on the whole, I think, an inhibiting effect on writing[43] with the result, I guess, that for most who fell into this category:

> Fama di loro il mondo esser non lassa . . .
> non ragioniam di lor, ma guarda e passa![44]

And to this day this attitude has not entirely been removed. By this, I do not mean that it is still possible to get a chair in a leading university on the basis of a handful of works. What I am referring to is the deliberate killing of the writing ethos—at least until the research assessment exercises shook the foundations of the lethargic existence of the English don. I suspect things were different for scientists, especially those who worked in laboratories and were forced, as it were, to participate in a greater interchange of ideas.

Still more opposed to the creation of a writing ethos and the idea of scholarly continuity has been the exploitative teaching imposed by the Oxbridge 'system' on their younger colleagues. This, again, is linked to the preference for teaching over writing and research. And it has blighted many a young don's career because it resulted in—and at times even cynically encouraged—writing sterility. Thus, my 20 years in Cambridge and Oxford—five spent in Oxford as a holder of two chairs—have still left me aghast at the way the system can destroy young talent. For it subjects these brilliant youngsters to impossible teaching and committee demands (often to discuss matters such as fund-raising for which they are totally unsuited or curriculum reform which always seems to animate old fashioned dons). The amateur and the federalist—by which I mean the College-centred don—thus combine to make the English university less efficient than its American counterpart, which is regarded in the Oxbridge I got to know with a mixture of envy and disdain. In a similar vein, the one-to-one teaching is an amazing experience; but it also has its drawbacks beyond the obvious one: cost. And one which I regret particularly in the light of my own experience in other universities is the fact that one can sail through Oxford—and I know many such young lawyers who have done just that—without ever having sat at the feet of Professors Patrick Atiyah, Ronnie Dworkin, Guenter Treitel or Sir Roy Goode but, instead, having received their legal training from brilliant (in many cases) but inexperienced (in at least as many instances) youngsters. Finally, the English university system is, only in appearances, less hierarchical than the German or the Italian. But what it gains in appearances, it loses in the kind of duties and responsibilities that the senior/junior relationship can impose on both parties.

As far as comparative law is concerned this set-up is very different from the environment that Rabel created at his institute where the search for talent was exceeded only by the effort to bring it out by, among other things, facilitating the interchange of ideas and cultivating an esprit de corps. The Oxbridge system—indeed, more so Oxford than Cambridge—in my view cultivates a different allegiance; the allegiance to the College which, by the way, in these fund-raising days is causing a tension of its own with the university proper.

Another difference from the continental, institute-based development of the young scholar, is the constant encouragement given in the latter to young colleagues to commit their ideas to print. In the beginning, these take the form of a short note, later, perhaps, an article, and culminate in the longer pieces, which earn the candidate his higher doctoral degree and his *venia legendi*. How good this is, not just for the science of comparative law but also for those who are trained in such an environment, Rabel's in particular, can be noted simply by mentioning randomly the names of Henri Batiffol, Ernst von Caemmerer, Andreas Gasis, Professor Gerhard Kegel, Friedrich Kessler, Rheinstein, Potis Zepos, and so many more in so many other countries of the world, from Greece to China and Japan, South Africa, Portugal and even Brazil. For all sprung out of this environment and spread the modus Germanicus far beyond what the German language on its own could have achieved. And before this is dismissed as a Germanic phenomenon—using the term in a pejorative way—let us recall that the same compliment could be paid to Sacco and to a lesser extent Cappelletti. For though their cliquish attitudes have not left many eyebrows un-raised in their native country, the fact is that both these colleagues have done more to establish their subject in their own country than my greats did in mine. This environment still lives on in Germany; and I know this first hand for I have worked for the last five summers at the Munich Institute of Foreign and International Law where, as I have already noted, Rabel and Rheinstein started their comparative law careers.

Finally, mention must be made, I think, of the absence in England of the prolonged partnership between the older and experienced scholar and the young novice, which is fostered in Germany by the doctorate and then the gruelling *Habilitation*, both nurtured, as I have already said, in that uniquely German hothouse environment of the 'Institute.' The same is still true of Italy, less so of France. Thus, the long and systematic imparting of knowledge and the gradual shaping of the mind (through example rather than teaching) has been deliberately sacrificed in England to the altar of dazzling wit, paradox, brief university studies, and the idea that any hierarchical relationship is necessarily exploitative in nature and must thus be avoided.

But that is one side of the coin; and there is, of course, another. Max Perutz, the distinguished Austrian-born molecular biologist who, because of his Jewish background, found himself exiled in this country, thus wrote in later life:[45]

> creativity in science, as in the arts, cannot be organised. It arises spontaneously from individual talent. Well-run laboratories can foster it, but hierarchical organisation, inflexible bureaucratic rules, and mountains of futile paperwork can kill it. Discoveries cannot be planned: they pop up like Puck, in unexpected corners.

This seems to argue against what I have just said. To some extent it does prove that this, too, is a debatable issue. But Perutz' sentences are also a carefully crafted statement. It contains caveats, which suggest that both approaches towards academic regeneration can be dangerous if their key features are taken to extremes. The extreme opposite of Perutz' hierarchically structured laboratory can be the College 'insularity,' leaving everyone to do their own thing, which Oxford even more than Cambridge tolerates (especially in the arts subjects). I have experienced it at first hand and know that it can encourage administrative paralysis and also lead to the kind of extreme form of dilettantism, probably best epitomised by the late Warden of All Souls, John Sparrow.[46] The latter feature is more relevant to the theme of this book than the former. For to oppress a younger colleague (as can happen in Germany) is just as much a crime as it is a sin to allow (as is the case of Oxbridge) a talented one to fritter away his intelligence and end his life lonely if not abandoned.

The final verdict thus calls for a *careful balance*—and I deliberately stress my words. No comparatist, especially no one who has experienced both the English and continental approaches as a student and as a teacher, can thus condemn or adopt outright either model.[47] Instead, he must try to understand both, weigh their respective strengths and weaknesses, and devise a mixture of his own that combines the best features of both systems.[48] But the English model—and this is my conclusion—has not favoured comparative law. For, at the end of the day, the brevity of the teaching relationship in the English law faculty, its emphasis on the tutorial rather than the writing of the dissertation, and its being conducted in an atmosphere of *apparent* equality, have not been conducive to the creation of schools of thoughts, of intellectual heirs or, even, a planned continuity of ideas or inventions. The absence of assistantships, an institution fiercely criticised by English purists conscious of its occasional abuses in Germany, has also come at a price. For at its best this academic relationship fosters a complex set of mutual duties and obligations, social as well as intellectual, which, in the end, works well for the younger colleague whose career is thus promoted. And it also works well for the older man, whose ideas continue to be refined, improved, or altered, but rarely die with his retirement.

All in all, therefore, in England and the USA, the chances of the substance and glitter of the golden age surviving the death of the last émigrés were not good. As we shall note further down, what is bringing the subject out of decline is politics not geniuses; practical needs not academic hothouses; private enterprise, not government-inspired guidance; business-related law, not philosophy; not to mention the gold at the end of the American rainbow which is triggering off a new (and voluntary) westward emigration of foreign talent.[49]

(c) Leaving a Working Method

The 1960s, as I said at the beginning of this book, were popu-
lated by charismatic comparatists; and yet they left us no workable directions as to how to produce the kind of goods they
themselves did.

Am I alone in complaining that whatever the value of their
writing, the works of these masters are inadequate as far as
leaving us a comparative methodology is concerned and
telling us whom to target, how to present foreign law to home
audiences, and how to put it to practical use, to mention but a
few hitherto un-unanswered questions? Professor John C Reitz
recently gave the answer I have been mulling over for a very
long time: 'No.' In fact he put it more elegantly when he
wrote:[50]

> Most of us who teach and write in the field of comparative law . . . were
> not taught formally how to do comparative law. Rather, we have for
> the most part worked out our own methods based on an amalgam of
> the scholarship we thought effective for our particular purposes at that
> time.

Earlier, Sacco, a leading Italian comparatist, had come up
with a similar (negative) conclusion, if only to claim that he
had provided the missing link himself. Referring to the generation of David, Schlesinger, and Gorla, he made essentially the
same point as Reitz when he described, one suspects with a
touch of false modesty, his own contribution to comparative
scholarship as being similar to the:

> act [of a] notary that . . . puts things [thought of by the previous gener-
> ation] in writing, using some neologism when necessary.

Sacco then concluded as follows:[51]

> I have been forced to do so because the three masters who taught me
> what I know curiously, indeed, very curiously, have forgotten to spell
> out at the end of their works the formulas that allowed them to reach
> the magical results of their researches. They never seemed to have
> noticed the work of restating their methodology that I have done.

Sacco's point about David, Schlesinger, and Gorla, and of the
relationship of his own work to theirs, strikes me as ambiva-

lently phrased. If there is an implication in the above statement that none of his masters really devised a transferable methodology, I think he may be correct. And if I am wrong to read such an implication, I think he also is wrong not to make it. More importantly, such an accusatory implication applies with greater force to the English greats—Lawson, Honoré, Nicholas, Rudden, Hamson, and Lipstein. My express extension of Sacco's view to the 'English school,' with which the Italian comparatist—not an English speaker—never seemed to have much affinity, would probably please him. For it makes his contribution through his theory of 'legal formants'[52] even more important (even if one allows for some influence from Schlesinger's work on *Formation of Contracts*).

But if Sacco was right in claiming that his 'heroes' left no prescription as to how to do comparative law, he was wrong not to mention Rabel in his list of 'masters.' On reflection, the omission is not surprising given how different these two men must have been. But whatever the reason for omitting Rabel, the failure to bequeath a methodology for comparative law is not an accusation that can be placed at his doorstep. For Rabel did leave a methodology, with which some contemporary comparatists have sought to find fault, but which, nonetheless, may well be the one that has dominated serious comparative work ever since it was devised in the 1920s and 1930s. It is thus more plausible to suggest that Sacco's greater intellectual affinity with David, explicable on a variety of grounds including their shared use of the French language, almost dictated the omission of the German who was so bent on detail and particularism and seemed to abhor philosophising. I do not see these last two features as prominent characteristics of Sacco's approach; nor is the latter's tendency to invent neologisms something which, I suspect, would have appealed to the German (or, more accurately, Austrian) genius.

But as I stated earlier on, England can boast one exception: Kahn-Freund. In comparative law terms the book of his that breaks the (English) mould just described is his Hamlyn Lectures published under the title *Labour and the Law*. The work had all that is needed to become an instant success. It was small and readable; and instantly got onto the reading list of every labour law teacher. It came at the right time, namely when labour unrest was to become a particularly strong feature of English life and was to remain so until the end of round one of the Thatcher anti-labour reaction of the first half of the 1980s. It was a book with a theme and, what is more, a theme that was relevant to English society at the time when it appeared. Intellectually, the book innovated by bringing sociological (especially German) thinking into English law in general and labour law in particular; but it did so in a way that recognised that law (and not sociology) had to be at the core or, at any rate, the starting point of the enquiry. For Kahn-Freund (like Rabel) was in many ways shaped by the Germany of Weimar and drew heavily on the sociological writings of the time as well as the post-war German industrial and labour scene which had taken such a different (and less confrontational) path from the English. In both these two senses, the practical and the theoretical, the book and his other writings set a trend. For it started a way of looking at labour law which was German in many ways but could also work in England. To be sure, some of his ideas are now dated (though some might wonder whether parts might become fashionable again). The approach, for those who still follow it, has also been modified, fine-tuned here and there. But he left a school and left a method and left people who are still willing to swear by his name.

The worst that can be levied against his legacy was that it was not as well developed in the wider context of comparative law. And yet, again, his individual articles contain gems that show how practical and concrete his mind was. Thus, to give but one example, let me point to his 'Common Law and Civil Law: Imaginary and Real Obstacles to Assimilation.'[53] There, at one point, he refers to William Maitland's aphorism that 'taught law is tough law.' Having then reminded himself and others that 'what is taught are primarily the general doctrinal foundations to which in afterlife the lawyer will cling as he may cling to the religious beliefs he learned at his mother's knees,' he concludes with a vintage sentence, which gives away his practical and focused mind. For he adds:[54]

> Practical details are negotiable. Fortunately, for the future of Europe what matters are the practical details, and the diverse doctrinal foundations can look after themselves.

Kahn-Freund, in my view, is the only exception in the English group of comparatists who went a long way towards devising a comparative methodology and keeping it firmly linked to the problems of the society of his time. That he managed to do this while not losing the ability to write black letter law works on labour law, family law, and conflicts is a sign of his true genius. And the fact that his writings remain cited in both his countries further attests to the uniqueness of his achievement.

(d) An Epilogue to the Idea of Decline

The very gifted men I have referred to thus far undoubtedly kept the flag of comparative law flying high. Yet, apart from Rabel, Kahn-Freund and, possibly, Schlesinger and Sacco (the latter only within Italian boundaries) they did little to teach those of us who followed in their footsteps how to present foreign law to national audiences, how to put foreign learning to practical use, and how to ensure its survival. The price for this omission was clear and high.

For the subject became the property of charismatic preachers, instead of an instrument to satisfy societal needs.[55] It thus flourished while the preachers were around, but on foundations that were too insecure to survive their fall. If, therefore, comparative law is nowadays in a ghetto—and by the end of the next two chapters I will be attempting a more nuanced assessment—the causes of this decay are, in part, traceable to the golden era. If a ghetto did emerge after the death or retirement of the generation of scholars I have referred to, it was a self-generated ghetto and not one externally imposed as ghettoes historically are. Worse still, it was a ghetto that seemed to thrive on the separation of academic and practising law, even though each side of the profession had its share of gifted comparatists. By ignoring each other, at times even suspecting each other, the two groups (academics/practitioners) I have described above pushed—unconsciously, I think—comparative law down the path of Roman law, to inaccessibility and gradual decline. The subject was thus wilting for all perhaps except the most academically inclined and linguistically gifted. The revival was to come not through heroes but through a politically and economically transformed world that received further impetus from the end of the cold war and growing confidence in the European idea. And to this we shall turn in the next chapter. For the future looks as if it will be event-driven and not hero-dependent.

Notes

[1] 'On the art of conversation' in *The Complete Essays*, translated and edited with an introduction and notes by M A Screech (Penguin, 1991) 1062–63.

[2] A concrete illustration of my point can be found in the letters exchanged just over 70 years ago by Gutteridge and Lord Atkin, first published by Lewis in his excellent biography of Lord Atkin (Butterworths, 1983) and reproduced in this book as Appendix 1 below. For the themes of their letters are two: the need for enhanced academic/judicial co-operation and the fact that this is not happening because the former do not target in their writings the latter. I became conscious of this exchange as I was nearing the completion of this manuscript and thus confess with some embarrassment the coincidence of my view with theirs. And yet I can also detect two redeeming factors. First, though Lord Atkin and Gutteridge believed in greater co-operation, neither seems to have developed a plan or method which would bring it about. Secondly, the Gutteridge suggestions, which triggered the Atkin response (and which my statistics, in turn, in chapter three below seem to vindicate), were, if anything, 'ahead of their times.' Seventy years thus had to elapse before the kind of changed circumstances I describe in chapter two below could make them truly relevant for our times. I note, finally, that Gutteridge (an experienced practitioner in the commercial area), was writing when Rabel was at his peak. In that capacity and as a fellow comparatist of great distinction he was thus fully conscious of the 'propaganda' value—Gutteridge's choice of word not mine—which an adroit use of the subject can bring to a modern legal system. Lord Goff, in his 'Foreword' to the *Annual Report for the Academic Year 1999/2000*, which I submitted to the Vice Chancellor of the University of Oxford when I was running that University's Institute of European and Comparative Law, picked up the same idea when he said (at 2) 'Professor Markesinis is, I believe, fully justified in his claim that the Institute is serving not only Oxford University and the cause of education, but also, . . . the broader national interest by promoting these and other major events of a similar kind.' (Emphasis added.)

[3] 'The Academic and the Practitioner' (1998) 18 *Legal Studies* 397 at 408.

[4] Entitled 'Adjudication and Interpretation in the Common Law: A Century of Change,' reprinted in Basil S Markesinis (ed), *Bridging the Channel: The Clifford Chance Lectures* vol I (Oxford University Press, 1996) 135 ff.

[5] The idea belongs to Lord Annan (though expressed in a (slightly) different context); see 'The Victorian Intellectual Aristocracy' in J H Plumb (ed), *Studies in Social History: A Tribute to G. M. Trevelyan* (1955) ch 8.

[6] And recorded in the latter's *Gespräche mit Goethe* on 25 February 1824.

[7] 'Ich habe den großen Vorteil . . . daß ich zu einer Zeit geboren wurde, wo die größten Weltbegebenheiten an die Tagesordnung kamen und sich durch mein langes Leben fortsetzten. . . . Hierdurch bin ich zu ganz anderen Resultaten und Einsichten gekommen, als allen denen möglich sein wird, die jetzt geboren werden und die sich jene großen Begebenheiten durch Bücher aneignen müssen, die sie nicht verstehen'; (Insel Verlag, 1992) 83.

[8] *Goethes Werke* (Hamburger Ausgabe) vol IX, 283.

[9] He tells the story himself in his marvellous autobiographical book *Les Avatars d'un Comparatiste* (1982) at 144 ff.

[10] The second edition was published in two volumes in 1968 and 1971 respectively. One must not forget that Cohn's manual had started life as a longish pamphlet meant to assist the allied forces occupying defeated Germany in the post-war era. Cohn's work has one more 'peculiarity,' which few noticed at the time and next to none now know. For it contains a section on Eastern German law written by an entirely fictitious author whom Cohn made up because he did not wish (for reasons which I never discovered) to be considered the author of the said chapter.

[11] It did not become accessible to the common law world until 1977 thanks to Weir's masterly translation.

[12] Now in its sixth edition by Professors Hans Baade, Peter Herzog and Edward Wise.

[13] In my 35 years of teaching experience in Cambridge, Oxford, and London never once have I seen the book even included in the reading lists of comparative law let alone used, as it is in the USA, as the primary teaching tool.

[14] Though, lately, Schlesinger seems to have acquired a following among some contemporary Italian academics. Thus, see the hagiography of Professor Ugo Mattei, 'The Comparative Jurisprudence of Schlesinger and Sacco: A Study on Legal Influence' in Annelise Riles (ed), *Rethinking the Masters of Comparative law* (2001) 238 ff.

[15] In two volumes, published 1968.

[16] For instance Tallon, 'La formation des contrats: recherche du fonds commun des systèmes juridiques. Réflexion sur un projet de la Cornell Law School' 4 *RIDC*, 729 (1968).

[17] Lorenz, who took part in the project, told me that this decision was taken after much discussion.

[18] Hamlyn Lecture (1951).

[19] Being the Cooley Lectures entitled *A Common Lawyer Looks at the Civil Law*, first published by the University of Michigan Law School in 1955 and reprinted in 1977 by Greenwood Press, Inc.

[20] For instance in Lawson's *Negligence in the Civil Law* (1951) as well as his Cooley Lectures, above n 19.

[21] Thus of the 'British' comparatists of the second half of the twentieth century, four began their academic lives as Romanists (Lawson, Lipstein, Honoré, Barry Nicholas) and a further two (Professor Bernard Rudden, Weir) taught Roman law for much of their academic careers. A seventh (Professor J A Jolowicz) did not teach Roman law himself, but was the son of a great Romanist. Gutteridge was primarily a commercial lawyer and Professor John Bell came into the subject via philosophy. And matters did not stop there. At the British Academy 'section' meeting of 8 January 2002, during a discussion intended to explore ways of making the election process more fair and transparent, I was intrigued to hear a senior colleague say that it was not that long ago that the chances of being considered for membership were slim if one did not belong to Roman law or maintained a strong interest in legal history. The question of finding objective ways of electing the Academy's fellowship is currently one of the thorniest issues reviewed by Britain's most senior society for arts and humanities.

[22] Such, in my view, is Birks' John Maurice Kelly Memorial Lecture, delivered at University College Dublin in 1995 and entitled 'Harassment and Hubris: The Right to an Equality of Respect'. Birks' lecture embodies his interest and learning in Roman law and the common law. So hubris and harassment appear both in the title; and an account of Roman law takes up just under one-third of the entire (adapted) written version of his speech. But where is the link between the two? Roman law did not influence the recent English Protection from Harassment Act 1997 nor was Roman law cited in any of the common law cases discussed by Birks. Though Birks indicates in isolated passages the alleged superiority of Roman law, he himself makes no point in his conclusion about the one system being able to shape the other. If anything, I was left with the impression that the central theme is the opposite: that the common law managed to reach the same position on its own. So, in the light of the above and the fact that this is not a rough transcript of a lecture but a 51 page article, one might ask what is the purpose of the long account on Roman law? For I am not sure how much it really furthers the understanding of the development of our own law; nor does it seem to me likely that Roman law will be used as a model for its improvement. The Roman law section might thus best be seen as an historiographical account, which honours the great jurist who was a Romanist (among other things) and keeps the study of Roman law in the front of our minds, albeit ignoring the critical reality that the interest in Roman law has waned and that John Kelly's Chair of Roman Law no longer exists in Dublin. I get the same impression from Lord Rodger of Earlsferry's references to Roman law in his judgment in *Fairchild v Glenhaven Funeral Services Ltd* [2002] 3 WLR 89 though those who, like me, see merits in

attracting the attention of our courts might well rejoice with the spread of the idea I have championed for over 20 years.

[23] See, eg, the bitter comments made by Lord Rodger of Earlsferry in 'Savigny in the Strand,' The John Maurice Kelly Memorial Lecture, published by University College Dublin in 1995, especially at 23 and 24. The same attitude can be found in Italy, an understandable bastion of Roman law. On this see Monateri, 'Critique et Différence: Le Droit Comparé en Italie' *Rev intern dr comp* 1999, 989 at 996. Interestingly enough, Rudolf von Jhering, one of the greatest Romanists of the nineteenth century, thought that the loss of Roman law was a blessing in disguise, as it opened up a new way towards universality via the medium of comparative law; see his classic *Geist des römischen Rechts auf den verschiedenen Stufen seiner Entwicklung I* (7th edn, 1924) 15.

[24] Oxford University Press, 1999.

[25] Italy, understandably still a stronghold of Roman law, even has a journal, *Il diritto romano attuale*, which boldly repeats in the front page of every issue that Roman law is still modern law. In fact, it typifies a long battle between two schools of Romanists, the one lead by the great Romanist Riccardo Orestano, which seems to have lost the battle for the Italian soul, and which argued in favour of seeing Roman law in its own historical context, and the currently more popular school of Romanists who, like Zimmermann, wish to show the continuing relevance of Roman law to contemporary Italian law. Orestano (1907–88), in the best tradition of continental European professors, pursued a peripatetic career teaching first at Cagliari and then, successively, Siena and Genova, finally settling down in Rome (la Sapienza) in 1958. His main work, embodying his beliefs about Roman law, was his *Introduzione allo studio del diritto romano* (1957).

[26] Oxford University Press, 2001.

[27] Sufficient time has passed since the second edition of this book saw the light of day in 1982 to tell its story. For the Lawson book, originally published by Oxford University Press, was submitted to the same publisher for its second edition under the title *Tortious Liability for Unintentional Harm in the Common Law and the Civil Law*. The publisher's reaction was, however, negative and recommended, instead, a new edition, omitting all references to Roman law and focusing on modern European law. I opposed the idea strongly, not least because of a great sense of personal loyalty to Harry, to whom (and his late wife) I have always owed a great debt of gratitude for his constant friendship and support. The book was thus re-submitted to Cambridge University Press where it very nearly met the same fate and for the same reasons. But it was 'saved' by Robbie (now Sir Robert Jennings) who was, at the time, the chief editor of the series in which the book appeared, and who, as he wrote to me at the time, 'was anxious to repay Lawson for the kindness he had showed him earlier in his (own) career.'

[28] 'In der Schule von Ludwig Mitteis' (1954) 7–8 *Juristic Papyrology* 157 at 159.

[29] With Rheinstein employed as assistant librarian!

[30] *Geist des römischen Rechts auf den verschiedenen Stufen seiner Entwicklung I* (3rd edn, 1873) 14.

[31] 'Deutsches und Amerikanisches Recht' (1951) 16 *RabelsZ* 340.

[32] Pringsheim, who had fought bravely for Germany on both the Eastern and Western fronts during the First World War, also found himself an exile in Oxford because of his Jewish background. Thanks to the exertions of his former pupil Lawson, Merton gave him some meagre assistance; but otherwise he was essentially ignored (indeed even interned after an amusing incident), and thus was eager to return to a destroyed Freiburg the moment the war was over. In his own words: 'Nobody made use of my learning for education in Oxford'; quoted by Honoré, 'Fritz Pringsheim (1882–1967)' (to be found, pending publication, in tony.honore@all-souls.ox.ac.uk). Albert Ehrenzweig was another of the émigrés who fared badly in England and found no recognition until he moved to the USA. Fleming's services to the common law were not properly rewarded by this country until the British Academy made him a Corresponding Fellow and this only towards the very end of his life. And Trinity, where he spent a year in the 1980s as Arthur Goodhart Professor, for over-technical reasons (given his age and the College statutes, it was thought that if he was given a Fellowship during the year of his visit he might be able to claim it for life), could not even bring itself to give him a Visiting Fellowship and simply described him as a Visiting Fellow Commoner. Anyone who knew Fleming, of course, would vouch that he would have never claimed such a title; indeed he was a man who cared little for titles and preferred, instead, to enjoy the good things of life.

[33] Stiefel is little known in England and probably now forgotten in the USA, where he lived for about half of his long, quite remarkable, but little-known life. Its beginnings were inauspicious, even sad, for his Jewish origins forced him to flee Germany in the mid-1930s and begin a peregrinating life (subsisting on the support of his German friends at 'Munich Re,' who greatly admired his mind, and picking up legal qualifications in France and England before settling in the USA). But after the war he became a member of various commissions charged by the US State Department with the economic reconstruction of Germany and was able to give many valuable services to the country that had earlier forced him to flee its borders and to those members of German industry who had helped him during his days of hardship. This enhanced further his standing with important representatives of German industry, and laid the foundations of a successful practice in New York and Germany. My former pupil Dr Bernhard Scheifele, now also working for Munich Re, introduced me to Stiefel in the early 1990s; and Stiefel, in turn, introduced

me to Professor Marcus Lutter and the then German Foreign Minister Dr Klaus Kinkel. These meetings, one in Düsseldorf and two in Bonn, resulted in a most generous gift by the Brost family in favour of the Oxford Institute of European and Comparative Law, which I was busy setting up at the time. Early in 1997, and after a long correspondence with Stiefel, I again visited him in his New York apartment to discuss his intention to donate his German library to my Oxford Institute and his personal papers to me. His ensuing (unexpected) death brought our friendship to an end and the proposed transaction was never completed. But the Brost family, again prompted by Stiefel and Lutter, provided a further generous gift to help me enhance by about one-third the German holdings of the Bodleian Law Library. Stiefel's writings were largely in the area of comparative procedure. Like Pringsheim, Stiefel remained loyal to Germany despite his sufferings at the hands of the Nazis; and a year before his death, while receiving an honorary doctorate at the University of Konstanz, was awarded by a grateful nation the *Großes Verdienstkreuz mit Stern*—a very high decoration, which, interestingly enough, was also given to Pringsheim near the end of his life.

[34] Émigrés who pandered to English tastes and illusions have, invariably, done better in their new country than those who remained faithful to their cultural heritage. In her celebrated *Britons Forging the Nation 1707–1837* (1992), Professor Lynda Colley offers the examples of Handel and Canaletto who, as a result, became 'national institutions.' Mann neither pandered; nor did he become a 'national institution.' But his oft-proclaimed preference of English over German law strengthened further his appeal to certain sections of the English legal establishment.

[35] Though both Mann and Schmitthoff produced some excellent books and many articles, which also appeared in collections of essays. Mann's *The Legal Aspect of Money* (4th edn, 1982) is, in particular, the work that clinched his fame as a practitioner with impeccable academic credentials.

[36] Sacco's ability to multiply the chairs of comparative law in Italy and help place on them able protégés such as Professors Mauro Bussani, Antonio Gambaro, Mattei, and Giuseppe Monateri, is a matter of both admiration (mainly) abroad and criticism in his own country.

[37] His followers included, at one time or another, talented colleagues such as Professors Anna de Vita, Nicolò Trocker, Vicenzo Varano, Vicenzo Vigoritti and, in the USA, John Merryman. Professor Alessandro Pizzorusso, originally a scholar within the gravitational force of the late Constantino Mortati (who later served as a distinguished judge), was also for a time with the Cappelletti team.

[38] Rheinstein largely influenced the work and careers of such learned colleagues as Professors Mary Ann Glendon and John Langbein. David's method of perpetuating his approach was more ingenious. For early in his career, he persuaded the French Ministry of Education to make the teaching of comparative law compulsory and then set about writing

what, in effect, has remained the main textbook since. See his own account in the most readable *Les Avatars d'un Comparatiste* (1982) 1944.

[39] For an interesting account of the history of the German institutes for comparative law see E Wadle, *Einhundert Jahre Rechtsvergleichende Gesellschaften in Deutschland* (Baden-Baden, Nomos, 1994).

[40] Lord Annan regards this theme as being of central significance to British university life for he devotes two chapters (out of 27) to it in his earlier book *Our Age: Portrait of a Generation* (1990). By means of scattered sentences and the mentioning of a few historic names, Lord Annan also tries to imply that the phenomenon was as prevalent in other countries. For Germany, for instance, he mentions the scandal of Prinz von und zu Eulenburg which forced him out of public life. But the incident, described in its proper setting by the distinguished historian Professor John C G Röhl in *The Kaiser and His Court* (1994) is far too complex to support Lord Annan's undeveloped thesis; and, in any event, in no way supports the view that what Lord Annan refers to as the 'homosexuality cult' acquired a foothold in the German school and university worlds in anything remotely similar to what afflicted the English public school system. It need hardly be stressed that the entire issue is raised here only because of its potential to include (or exclude) individuals in the university networking.

[41] In *Our Age: Portrait of a Generation* (1990) 377, he places this between 1945–75.

[42] Which, of course, is not to say that academic careers on the Continent are not subject to their own hazards and are not influenced by different, local, but often equally capricious, factors. But that, of course, is a subject of another book.

[43] It is thus difficult to imagine a German sharing, even as a joke, Cecily's view of Dr Chasuble as 'a most learned man. He has never written a single book, so you can imagine how much he knows' (Act II, *The Importance of Being Earnest*). In reality, Wilde's bons môts have been seriously espoused by many an English academic. Lord Annan's *Our Age: Portrait of a Generation* (1990) is peppered with such statements (see, eg, ch 24). The Thatcher revolution of the mid-1980s, with the multiple types of 'assessments' that it set in motion, has effectively put an end to such philosophy.

[44] 'The world will not record their having been there . . . Let's not discuss them; look and pass them by.': Dante Alighieri, *La Commedia Divina, Inferno*, III, 49–51 (English translation by Mark Musa, Penguin Classic edn).

[45] Taken from his obituary in *The Times*, 7 February 2002.

[46] The subject of a number of books and, most recently, a sad essay by Lord Annan in his book *The Dons* (1999).

[47] Indeed, I agonise over this issue in one of the essays included in this volume.

[48] I tried to attempt this—always within specific contours—in two papers, the most recent one entitled 'Tutorial and Repetitorium: Parallel and Different Techniques of Teaching Law in England and Germany' in *The British Contribution to the Europe of the Twenty-First Century: The Clifford Chance Lectures* vol VI (2002) 63 ff.

[49] For a glimpse into the very different, but not necessarily worse, Italian world see: Grossi, *Scienza giuridica italiana, un profilo storico 1860–1959* (2000). Also, Alpa, *La cultura delle regole: Storia del diritto civile italiano* (2000).

[50] 'How to do Comparative Law' (1998) 46 *Amer J Comp L* 617–18. The view seems to be shared by Mattei and Reimann, 'Symposium on New Directions in Comparative Law: Introduction' (1998) 46 *Amer J Comp L* 597, a somewhat odd but, perhaps, not surprising statement given that the second co-author has actually come up with the view that comparative law lacks any serious purpose. See his 'The End of Comparative Law as an Autonomous Subject' (1996) 11 *Tul Eur & Civil L Forum* 49 at 54.

[51] *Che cos'e'il diritto comparato* (Milano, 1992) 285, cited and translated by Mattei in 'The Comparative Jurisprudence of Schlesinger and Sacco: A Study in Legal Influence' in Riles, above n 14, 238 at 250.

[52] Developed in many Italian works and available to English speakers as 'Legal Formants: A Dynamic Approach to Comparative Law' (1991) 39 *Amer J Comp L* 1 ff. and 343 ff.

[53] In Mauro Cappelletti (ed), *New Perspectives for a Common Law of Europe* (1978) 137 ff.

[54] *Ibid* at 147.

[55] The latest book, in the form of a collection of essays by comparatists with a link to the USA, confirms this. Thus see Riles, above n 14.

2

Reflections on the State of Comparative Law II: The Death of Heroes and the Era of Societal Needs

Andrea: 'Unglücklich das Land, das keine Helden hat'
Galileo: 'Unglücklich das Land, das Helden nötig hat'

(Pity the Nation that lacks heroes
Pity the Nation that needs heroes)

Bertold Brecht, *Leben des Galilei* (Scene 13)

1. THE EMERGENCE OF A STRATEGY

My own efforts to 'combat' what I saw as shortcomings of the older school of writers, especially of the David variety, are well known. Specific examples, covering private and public law, can be found in chapters four and five below. In most respects they are influenced by the Rabel philosophy and nothing more need be added at this stage. But the need for practicalities or, as I have come to call them, 'functional practicalities' has given my work a special bent which I have not found in that of others. For my efforts have focused on making the foreign material first and foremost attractive to judges. In that context, I treated academics as secondary players. But since English judges rely heavily on information and argument coming from practitioners, a second aim has been to encourage as far as possible the co-operation of these two sides of the legal profession which could help the judges. Ultimately, I thus saw the relationship in triangular terms; and the remaining side of the triangle was occupied by the academics, playing a supporting but useful role by making the material, which they could best assemble, user-friendly and clear for the ultimate consumer: the judge. In chapter three below I have called this 'packaging.' This may sound rather pejorative. Yet who can deny the fact that the package often sells the product?[1]

The *Greatorex* decision, discussed in chapter four below, offers a perfect if incomplete example of the approach; but I had to wait a long time for it. This had to be so. For my approach marked a conscious effort, with effects that go way beyond comparative law but are based on continental European experience, to weaken the prevalent position, so eloquently expressed by Sir Robert Megarry,[2] that judges and academics were performing *entirely* different tasks. However right Megarry may have been when he made the pronouncement I am citing, with the passage of time it seemed to me to be less attractive, calling for fine-tuning. Lord Goff's Maccabean and Denning Lectures of the 1980s encouraged me further down this path of thought even though his text did not steer too far away from the crucial part of the Megarry message. But his subsequent judicial and extra-judicial forays into foreign law convinced me that if judges like him could be helped with suitably packaged foreign material, the study of foreign law could become a more acceptable method of interpreting and making law. Interestingly enough this wider issue has also been confronted in Germany and I will return to it again towards the end of chapter three below. But I raise it here merely in order to stress that often some of the most 'basic issues' pop up in all systems and are not excluded by the different histories or other peculiarities of each of them, making mutual borrowing possible. The way two out of three law lords treated foreign, especially European material, in *Fairchild v Glenhaven and others*[3] would suggest the truth of this premise and the promise it holds for comparative lawyers.

The theory I began to develop was also being made more palatable to the courts by being linked to the ever-growing shift of emphasis away from Roman to modern European law. The strategy was complex; it clearly required (and requires) more time to work; but I think that in the end it can and will, given that it has emerged from the environment within which

I have been working and is designed to serve our current needs. The fact that by the end of the 1990s Lord Goff was no longer the only senior judge willing to cite judicially modern civil law, gave further impetus to those who, like me, had turned their efforts to this kind of comparative law. For by now Lord Goff had been joined by Lords Woolf, Bingham, Steyn, Hope, Clyde, Rodger of Earlsferry, Lord Justice Sedley and Lord Justice Schiemann. Even the current Lord Chancellor was, extra-judicially, displaying a keen interest in developments on the European front. The judicial references to modern civil law were growing at a reasonable rate and were exceeded only by the number of extra-judicial pronouncements made by our top judges stressing that the similarities between common law and civil law were not as great as they had been thought to be.

My agenda and methodology have both been explained through many inter-linked articles in my previous two volumes of *Essays on Foreign Law and Comparative Methodology* by the same publisher.[4] I do not intend to return to them again for they are known to those I wish to influence. And, even if their message is repeated, it will not persuade those *who do not wish* to be persuaded or those who see it, wrongly I think, as a very 'English approach.'[5] Instead, I would like to focus on two issues. The first is concerned with the alleged shortcoming of the Rabel method which, for me as indeed for so many others, has proved the starting point of our work. The second is to look at the kind of problems I encountered in chapter four below, which epitomises the method and the strategy just described and which must be read in conjunction with the material in Appendix 1 below. I use all this as an example of the rigours of my method—linguistic, conceptual, and methodological—but also as an illustration of how something that can begin as a detailed study of a narrow topic can *organically* grow into a wider enquiry about another legal system. Finally, I use this example as an illustration of how focused and practical my method is compared to the more sociological and even trendy theories which have emerged in recent times in the USA and which I criticise at the end of this chapter. For a cosmopolitan approach to law need not, as Professor William Twinning once remarked, 'lack in depth.'[6]

2. THE RABEL METHOD OVER TIME

So how has the Rabel approach fared over time?

First, we must note that though many comparatists (beyond Rabel's immediate pupils) have followed it, their indebtedness to it is not always recorded. The answer, of course, is that such acknowledgements are not called for on a routine basis. Still, the 'omission' if not the indebtedness, cannot be allowed to pass unnoticed, for, if nothing else, it contrasts with what could be seen as a 'cliquish' cross-referencing in which certain Italian comparatists (belonging to the same 'school') seem to over-indulge. Indeed, in chapter three below I hope to show that a fair percentage of the references to the comparative literature of the Italian scholars is due to their technique (conscious or almost spontaneous, I am not sure which) of auto-citation and cross-citation. This does not, of course, detract from the intrinsic value of some of the contemporary Italian writings; on the contrary, I am on record as being an admirer of the Italian legal culture and regret that it is so little known in England. Nonetheless, this practice does mean that one must read the literature with caution. Additionally, one must recall Judge Richard Posner's[7] warning that 'reputation is conferred by the people doing the reputing rather than produced by the reputed one—and it is conferred for their purposes, not his.'

Secondly, Rabel's method has not escaped criticism. Here, I shall look briefly at four aspects, mainly in order to show how I tried to address them in my own work. They are: (i) 'particularism,' (ii) 'statics,' (iii) 'process,' and (iv) 'neglect of public law.' Unless otherwise stated, all (but the last) of these headings and the summary form of the criticisms that follow, come from Professor David Gerber's essay on Rabel; and this is cited once only in order to avoid the unnecessary multiplication of notes, not to belittle its importance.[8] Where others have shared these doubts, I give references in the notes.

(a) Particularism

Gerber first argues that the knowledge derived from the Rabel-type of approach is 'particularist . . . largely independ-

ent of and unrelated to other knowledge.' If that means, as he
suggests himself, that Rabel is not interested in 'theorising'
and 'generalisations,' then Gerber is broadly right. But I see
no reason why a researcher or an author cannot set out his
own parameters and then work within them. Gerber's accusation, however, could be more serious if the statement that
the Rabel product was 'unrelated to other knowledge' is
meant to suggest that his approach was legalistic and his
results unrelated to the socio-economic and historical circumstances that dictated them.

Though Rabel may not have refined the way one was to set
about understanding the 'problem' that was being investigated, he was fully conscious of the need to see it in its proper
and wider context. Gerber may on this point thus be somewhat
unfair to Rabel whose comparison of legal institutions seems to
me to proceed by seeing their growth (and their parallels)
squarely within their social context. English readers of this
book need not concern themselves with reviewing Rabel's
entire work, reprinted in the four-volume series edited by
Professor Hans G Leser,[9] to reach their own conclusion on this
point. But a glance at Rabel's article in the 1947 volume of the
Law Quarterly Review on 'The Statute of Frauds and
Comparative Legal History'[10] will, I think, confirm my view
about the value and interest of his wider method. This meant—
and means—investigating all the factors that played a part in
the production of the problem being studied and the solution
it received. Indeed, anyone reading Rabel's seminal 'Aufgabe
und Notwendigkeit der Rechtsvergleichung'[11] can pick up
immediately the importance of this point which his disciples
developed further in their own work. Rheinstein, for instance,
did this elegantly and I think effectively—especially considering the time when this work was being produced—in such
areas as family law. Glendon, a Rheinstein disciple, applied
these teachings to her powerful (but controversial) *Abortion and
Divorce in Western Law: American Failures, European Challenges*
(published in 1987) where philosophy and law were inter-
twined in a masterly but also specific manner. And Langbein—
another Rheinstein disciple—did the same with the help of
either history or civil procedure in his own prolific work. These
works, and others, suggest that the Rabel emphasis on looking

at rules 'in their context' encourages a multi-dimensional approach to law even if Rabel, himself, did not *always*[12] do it.

Professor Hein Kötz, a famous disciple of the Rabel school, has equally shown great sensitivity to the wider setting of the rules and done so both in his masterly treatise with Konrad Zweigert and in his many articles written both in German and English.[13] But this study of the law in its context can also be seen in the excellent recent edition of his *German* (not comparative) tort textbook.[14] For not only does the book have the courage to ascribe a radically different emphasis to the parts of the law of torts that it regards as important in practice and relegate others to a few lines or paragraphs. It also presents its German material constantly supported by cross-references to insurance, social security, and statistics. For a book, which is meant to teach German students the rudiments of their tort law, it thus breaks new ground (though I add, for the sake of completeness, that I know that not all of my German colleagues share my admiration for his work to the same degree). And, in my view, its uniqueness owes much to the fact that both its current authors are comparatists with long exposure to the Anglo-American legal culture.

So, while not denying the fact that the Rabel teachings are capable of improvement and refinement, I do not see them as having acted as brakes upon those who have used their main tenets some 60 years after they were designed.

(b) Statics

But what about the second critique—that the 'knowledge [derived from a Rabel study] is largely static.' 'The Method' says Gerber, no doubt echoing the views of others as well, 'creates a careful still photograph, a snapshot . . . change is not its concern.' Even if the conclusion is correct that analysing a detailed problem does, indeed, create a 'snapshot,' this can be an extraordinary useful product in the light of the reasons that prompted this analysis: law reform; judicial inspiration, or whatever. But the snapshot accusation seems, again, unfair if not inaccurate if one puts together the individual pictures collected by such a method. *Einführung in die Rechtsvergleichung* by Zweigert and Kötz, again, gives the illustration I need. For if a pictorial image is required, panorama rather than snapshot is the word that springs to mind, a panorama, moreover, which though wide in its coverage also remains extraordinarily detailed and usable. The comparison with David's treatise brings this point out most clearly. The commercial and academic success of Zweigert and Kötz' book must surely reduce the appeal of the criticism. Moreover, Rabel's work is invaluable mainly not for its particular solutions—even though in his lifetime he hit quite a few nails on the head—but for the methodology he suggested and to a large extent developed in the course of his own life.

(c) Process

Gerber also regrets that Rabel paid little attention to 'the processes that created the artefacts of the law.' Certainly those who like me have approved in general of the Rabel approach have tried to investigate the insurance and other economic factors that led to the results. And I have done the same in other areas such as the developing law of human privacy and even disparate areas of medical law where, with the help of judicial dicta, I have tried to stress how solutions must be explained against the social background of their time. My *German Law of Torts*[15] is replete of examples which show German judges sensitive, *almost to excess*, to go down certain paths of reasoning given the way their recent experience under the National Socialist regime weighs on their own and their nation's psyche. And I stress 'almost to excess' for, at times, in our (laudable) eagerness to condemn the experimentation on humans conducted by the Nazis we may have forgotten another school of thought: a school of thought that goes back over two thousand years and which refused to adopt the view that life was always preferable to death or that impaired life should always be seen as a gift.[16] This underlying philosophy may be extraordinarily important when discussing such legal issues as abortion, or claims for failed sterilisations, or wrongful birth, and life. And if that is not law emerging from a particular social context, what is? And many more examples can be given in the context of women's or worker's rights. Again, the Rabel method in no way stops us from giving credit to these 'extra legal' factors if and when they help shape the content of legal rules. In my view, it is the Rabel method that alerts us to the need to enquire whether it is good enough for the child if the system only compensates the mother for its needs and costs. And it does so by helping us link narrowly and concretely rules found in different parts of a legal system. No fluffy jargon here but law in context in the best possible sense of these words.

Gerber's discussion of the importance of the 'process,' as he puts it in his 1998 article, 'of how legal actors think, talk, process information, interpret conduct and make decisions,' appears to ignore two works which I, for one, found extraordinarily useful. Chronologically the first is Atiyah's and Professor Robert Summers' *Form and Substance in Anglo-American Law*, published in 1987. A year later came Fleming's *The American Tort Process*. Between them, these books reveal an enormous amount of information about how 'back-drop' factors—such as the presence or absence of social security, the method of financing litigation, the wider constitutional framework, the structure and mentality of the judiciary—can account for substantial differences in outcome to emerge in the solutions of systems that belong to the same legal family. Both these books deal with English and American law. But, as stated, I have drawn on the methodology (and ideology) myself—both in my writings and my international practice. The long piece included in the Baade Festschrift[17] on the potential liability of public authorities for the failure to provide adequate educational training to their inhabitants along with chapter five below confirms, I hope, my view that one can combine the Rabel method of 'snapshots'—to use Gerber's terms—with the lessons taught by the Atiyah, Summers, and Fleming approaches to living law. For in my view, the comparison of Anglo-American law revealed, surprisingly some would say, English law as more 'frank' and more 'complete' in its judicial reasoning than American law. Fleming in particular, with whom I had endless discussions in the 1980s on the subject of judicial styles, was invariably critical of the long and 'uninformative' English judgments (as he often described them). Yet here, as stated, we have an example that supports—I believe—the opposite conclusion. But we also have an illustration where the wider factors which Fleming in particular explored in his book might prevent the transplantation of the English result, assuming it was deemed to be superior. It would be a shame if this were to prove the last word on the matter, for I still believe that Lord Nicholls' opinion in *Phelps v Hillingdon London Borough Council*[18] is as full of wider ideas about the notion of duty of care as it is stylistically attractive.

If I have laboured this point more than others it is not only because I feel that studies such as these go some way towards showing that Gerber's concerns can be addressed by neo-Rabelists such as myself, but also because I feel that they show how traditional comparative law can, with suitable adaptations, be of use to the contemporary American scene. And, conversely, studies of 'American law in action' should provide useful warnings to those who are sometimes too eager to bring it to Europe. In a sense, these thoughts also provide a limited reply to Professor Mathias Reimann's assessment that 'legislators and judges [in the USA pay] . . . scant attention to foreign ideas.'[19] But though the assertion is correct, the reason (blame?) for such contemporary insularity must lie with the so-called full-time comparatists. For it is up to them to show American judges why the fruits of their efforts are worthy of some consideration. To this tack the answer, of course, will be 'I still bet it won't happen in the States.' But if the approach I am favouring fails to move an American court, I doubt that any of the alternatives on offer (such as 'post-modernism') will hold out any more appeal. So, if no one is singing our tune, it may be because we have failed to come up with something catchy. More about this, later.

(d) Neglect of public law

Rabel's 'methods' have also 'tended to exclude issues of public law.' This is the last of Gerber's positions with which I feel uncomfortable. The point is, likewise, adopted by Reimann[20] who cites Zweigert and Kötz as an illustration of this sinful tendency of comparatists. But Reimann, for whose meticulous work I have much time, unforgivably (it seems to me) forgets the superb work done in his (adopted) country in the area of public comparative law by Professors David Currie (Chicago), Donald Kommers (Notre Dame), Inga Markovitz (Texas), and Peter Quint (Maryland), in his own fatherland (indeed, his former university) the learned work of Professor Jürgen Schwarze and in Italy the work of Professor Giovanni Grottanelli de' Santi. To be sure, Rabel focused largely on contract and trade issues *because they were so relevant to him and his country during the Weimar period*. But this is not the same as saying that his pragmatic and particularist *method* does not work in the area of public law. I have, myself, tried to use it in a number of areas of public law proper, or public law that lies on the borderline with tort law, and I feel it has worked well; and others, far more important than I, have done it likewise. The rich extra-judicial work of (former) Judge Tim Koopmans of the Netherlands is probably the best example of concrete comparative constitutional law in practice. I say nothing of Chief Justice Barak of the Supreme Court of Israel, who has not only written on comparative constitutional law; he has also made it in his court.

Take for instance the discussion on *Drittwirkung*, which is now receiving much attention in England but was first brought to the attention of the English public by a thesis of a human rights lawyer[21] and my own third edition of *The German Law of Torts*. I think the collective work done on this subject shows how right Rabel was to suspect language and try, instead, to reach the core of the problem by means of a factual and contextual analysis. My own attempt to compare[22] a leading decision of the German Federal Labour Court[23] with *Novosel v Nationwide Insurance Co*[24] shows, I think, how approaching the problem in a Rabel kind of way can reveal similarities seriously hidden by language. Such an approach can further give the writer the opportunity to try to explain the differences by reference to the wider context (see the previous point) and also suggest to him and his students ways of comparing issues which, at first glance, appear to be incapable of proper comparison. I think the same could be said about the work done in the context of privacy where, though starting with factual equivalents in a very narrow context, one has been able to address wider issues and fears that underlie the privacy debate. If Reimann familiarised himself more with the current English literature on human rights and public law, I think he would find a shining example of comparative law that brings together American, continental European, and Commonwealth ideas. A glance at the case law of the South African Constitutional Court would also show him that the method I favour is working in the court-room as well. Israel, as I said, offers another example. A brief allusion to this phenomenon will, again, be made in chapter three. In any event, I am one of those who keep saying that the distinction between private and public law is becoming increasingly tenuous.

And one concluding thought. Personally, I am not convinced that the Rabel approach has exhausted its utility. But this does not mean that its scope should not be widened or, more crucially, its targets not redefined. Method, in the broad sense of thinking how to achieve one's goals, may also necessitate re-defining these goals. For Rabel, as a German mainly active in the mid-war period, internationalisation of trade was the paramount idea. His desire to improve the German practitioner's ability to operate effectively in a new and unstable socio-economic environment greatly influenced his goals and his targets. My main variation to this theme has been, as I already stated, to switch most attention to the judge in the belief that if the judge becomes interested, the practitioner will have to cite foreign law to him. And since he cannot do this on his own he will be forced to seek the assistance of the academic. But this does not mean that the legislator or the bureaucrat should be ignored; nor that they are less likely to be persuaded by detailed, pragmatic and inter-disciplinary studies rather than trendy language and theorising.

3. FUNCTIONAL SPECIFICITY: MORE OF THE SAME MEDICINE

Let me now turn to my second issue: the difficulties associated with my approach. Here I would like to point out two things.

First I wish to show in the context of a very concrete example how the co-operation of academics, practitioners, and judges can further the study of different laws and their comparison. Secondly, I am anxious to underline yet again how my emphasis on practical issues does not strip my method of intellectual or even philosophical content. My search for a method of presenting foreign law to practitioners may thus not only be useful to the real world—especially if others can be persuaded to continue with it and refine it. It may also be educationally (if not even philosophically) a stimulating, additional, way of looking at the law.[25] For like Montaigne, whose name and example I invoke out of admiration and not presumption, I feel one can start from one particular example (or individual) and end up by discovering 'the whole of human kind.'[26] In my case this meant remaining faithful to the idea of teaching foreign law from specific litigated situations and then slowly fanning out towards a bolder attempt to better understand a foreign system. I readily accept that, at best, I have only partially succeeded in this aim. But, in my view, this kind of attempt is crucial. For what I have advocated and tried to do is what separates the comparative lawyer from the expert in foreign law; and we have not done that enough in this country.

My very narrow approach can be seen at work in the *Greatorex* litigation,[27] which I describe from a comparative point of view in the fourth of the essays included in this volume. Yet even that short commentary managed to conceal the difficulties and benefits that lie in this meticulous approach to foreign law.

My piece on the *Greatorex* litigation was based on the belief that the best use of foreign law came from academics making suitable foreign material available to practitioners who could then use it in court to mould the law when, in its present state, it was either unclear, unsatisfactory or contradictory. *Greatorex* showed how the foreign material could slide into national law if properly packaged. It also showed how the problem the court had to confront was only partially solved because of the special facts of that case. The German cases, reproduced in Appendix 2 below and mentioned in my article, deal with the unsolved part of the problem. Simply put, it is this: can the primary defendant (the person I henceforth call D1) claim a contribution from the secondary defendant (henceforth D2) for any damages which he may have paid to the plaintiff (henceforth P)? Or should he carry the entire consequences himself? A third possibility would be for him, alone, to be liable *but then only to the extent that his personal fault contributed to the plaintiff's loss*. At one level the problem appears to be a straightforward problem of joint debtors or, as we would call them, joint tortfeasors. (The two terms in the two systems are not identical but, for present purposes, this need not be pursued.) In reality, however, the waters are muddied by the fact that D2 enjoys some immunity or privilege vis-à-vis P. This factor can 'distort' the normal rules about internal contribution and that is why the Germans refer to this problem as 'disturbed internal settlement between joint debtors' (*gestörter Gesamtschuldnerausgleich*).

The German approach is sketched out in chapter four below; and the crucial and most recent decision by the Federal Court (Bundesgerichtshof, BGH) is reproduced in Appendix 2 below. No doubt, readers of the original (also reprinted for the sake of linguistic comparison) and the translation, produced by Raymond Youngs, an able translator and, himself, an author of two well-known works on German law and German and French law, might wish to change his text here and there. Such changes might improve readability, perhaps by sacrificing something to complete accuracy. But apart from raising the perennial problems of what a translation—especially one of a legal text—should aim to achieve, the fact remains that the German text is heavy going. The problem of making it usable requires more than linguistic talents: it requires packaging it, linguistically, conceptually, and functionally, in a way that makes it usable. Some colleagues in the comparative law area such as Professor Pierre Legrand of the University of Paris I, cringe at these efforts to anglicise foreign law sensibly. My own view has always been that if we do not attempt them, we shall never benefit from foreign law; nor will foreign lawyers ever see their legal ideas spread further than their national boundaries. I have worked long enough in France and Germany to be able to say with complete confidence that the French and Germans would love to see their law studied abroad, especially in *les pays anglo-saxons*. And I have also worked and spoken with many a learned English judge whom I have always found eager to borrow good ideas from wherever they came if and when the need presented itself—provided it was packaged in a way they could use it. Someone must thus attempt the task and not be deterred by academic purists. My life's work has been nothing more than an attempt to provide a workable model for such enhanced contacts. Am I exaggerating its importance? Or is my method so 'British' as to be of little use to other countries and their systems? Let us stick to *Greatorex* and ask a simple question: why was German law used there instead of French or Italian? I was asked that question by colleagues who teach the subject in both Oxford and Cambridge. Now, even those who admire German legal science would be slow to suggest that it was used because it was 'better' than the others. But it was nonetheless used and the reason supports my thesis perfectly: it was used because its material and its ideas had been made available to English counsel and he, in turn, could make it work to his advantage.

Let me amplify this point by inviting the reader to consider my further thoughts and observations, alongside the text of a decision of the German Federal Court of 1 March 1988. For this decision of the BGH is, in a sense, the logical sequel to the *Greatorex* problem; and might even have undermined part of the rationale of BGHZ 56, 163 (on which *Greatorex* relied so much). English lawyers should consider it, especially its second part, however taxing the text of the case may be.[28] For *Greatrorex* decided that P could not sue D2—the primary victim of the accident in question. But because of its unusual facts, it did not have to consider the liability of D1 (in most cases the main tortfeasor), for there was no D1 in that case. Nor, as a result, were D1's rights considered for contribution and indemnity from D2. Nor, finally, was any thought given to another intriguing question namely, whether D2, if he was a 'privileged victim'—ie one enjoying vis-à-vis P protection because of a contractual clause or a legal immunity—could rely on these immunities to avoid liability, even if sued by D1. The German decision deals with all these questions, directly or indirectly (if one sees it in comparison to the case it appeared to overrule: BGHZ 35, 317). The English common law answer, I suppose, would be that if D2 were not liable to P, D1 would be unable to claim any contribution under the Civil Liability (Contribution) Act 1978. The American position, that D1 might be liable, but only to the extent of his fault, would probably be unsupportable under our Act. And the German line of argument why this is the best answer would be unknown. Those who can consult German material would not easily get much further or, at any rate, find the right answer because the Germans themselves have not agreed on one yet. The German decision is obviously written against this background of heavy juristic writing. This, in itself, is interesting for the teacher of comparative law as he can develop this theme of judicial/academic co-operation both in historical terms as well as comparative. More importantly, however, the injustice—in my view—reached by the German decision in making the local authority/defendant (D1) solely liable for the plaintiff's injuries even though his father was also careless in looking after him must make one search for the policy reasons behind such a result. One can even go further and ask if it is right that such immunity for D2 (the father in this case) should exist because of his status as a married man but denied if he was merely cohabiting with the mother. The reasoning of BGHZ 56, 163 is certainly wider in this respect than § 1359 BGB[29] and, perhaps, better for that reason. But even this case depends largely on the closeness of the relationship and would not work at all if P and D2 were strangers.

So what should a common lawyer in search of new ideas do? The easy answer, no doubt taken by most, is to abandon German law and, indeed, run away from it. But the problem that has to be addressed will not go away; and the American literature, the other huge source of material, is not very clear on this point. So the answer is to return to the three-sided partnership—the judge, practitioner, and academic—and see how the junior can help the middleman to convince the senior. If the work is done properly, the process commenced in *Greatorex* will be brought to a successful conclusion. Learning, inventiveness, and fairness will be brought into some kind of balance; and a solution may even emerge, backed by the assertion that it has been tested elsewhere and not found wanting.

4. OLD (BAD) HABITS AND NEW (SILLY) THREATS

In the first chapter I spoke of some old (bad) habits and how, in my view, they affected adversely the growth of my subject. Let me now turn to some new (silly) threats which have in common one important point with the old faults: they both ignore the realities of the world we inhabit. So what are these new trends which I, for one, deplore?

(a) Eurocentrism: is it a Vice?

The first trendy accusation is that comparative law is too Eurocentric for its own good and that it should, therefore, be re-oriented in its focus.[30] Consider the following statements from two American comparatists (joined here to give the essence of the trend):[31]

> Colonialism and Social Darwinism were the primary contributors to the ethnocentric illusion of the superiority of . . . Western law. . . . Today, the presumption seems to be that legal systems [which?] . . . jostle with one another in a market-place of possibilities.

Such generalisations strike me as dubious—not just because I find their tone somewhat ponderous, but for two practical reasons.

First, in the European world (which is also present, physically and intellectually, in the Australian, New Zealand, and Northern and Southern American worlds) one finds the most developed ideas likely to deserve careful study. Is it really suggested that this is not a fact? And if it were not, why would hugely important countries such as China, Korea, and the former Eastern block, be studying these (Western European) systems and trying to import their notions and institutions as they build their own financial markets and the legal infrastructure that goes with them? I am not aware of any of these countries making a particular effort to understand, let alone import, 'primitive' legal systems, 'native American law' or, come to that, religious systems.

Secondly, even if we were convinced that other models should be jostling for our attention, we must remind ourselves of Professor Bernard Brodie's admonition[32] that 'reading time, even for the most favored, is a sharply limited commodity.' The warning must be taken even more seriously when we digest fully the implications of what we are being asked to do. For we are not just advised to read the extra book or article in order to widen our horizons but, I take it, to try and immerse ourselves in completely different legal cultures. Is our life span so long and are our library resources so unlimited as to allow us the luxury suddenly to shift direction and start studying, say, African law, native American law, or religious law as a first priority? I fully accept that some colleagues may have an interest in these subjects; and, of course, they must be free to pursue them. But the *wider call* for comparative scholarship to become 'mostly . . . devoted to *radically different* [sic] cultures'[33] is, in my view, utopia of the most extreme kind. In any event, should we develop such tastes, through trendiness, political correctness, or (I readily accept) even genuine intellectual curiosity, would any students follow us in the classroom? I say nothing of practitioners, judges or businessmen investing in different countries. Of course, I pose the question rhetorically for, personally, I have no doubt whatsoever of the answer.

(b) The Opacity of Post-Modernism

The second trend found in American literature is linked to calls to introduce 'modernist' or 'post-modernist' literature and ideas into comparative law. This re-heated critical legal studies approach deserves to be shunned even more strongly than the native American variety, which has lost much of the shine it thought it had gained in the 1970s and early 1980s. For not only does it strike me as being linguistically unattractive to all but those who indulge in it; more importantly, I have the impression that it may be useless from a practical point of view.

Let us start first with the language. Consider, for instance, the following sentences:

> Postmodernsim constructs previous movements as an historical past from which to borrow.[34]

or:

> This Article discusses the political implications of the postmodern condition in the making of European law. It looks at contemporary movements in art and architecture to understand and gain perspective in the postmodern condition of European law.[35]

or, finally:

> Comparative legal scholarship has managed to move quite beyond legal positivism, formalism, realism, and black letters. We know how to approach both conscious and unconscious phenomena; the tacit or mute dimension of the law is never neglected.[36]

Sentences such as the above, found in some of the contemporary literature on comparative law, convey the impression that whatever the merits of such works, their authors do not appear to appreciate correctly the needs of the legal world they live in. Worse still, linguistic opacity, which can never qualify as a sign of 'learning', can only lead to a loss of students in the classroom, or potential users in the courtroom, or any legislative chamber or transnational organisation contemplating law reform. Indeed, I do not merely 'suspect' such consequences but predict them, having myself shown some of these texts to some judges and practitioners (not to mention a number of respected academic colleagues) from different countries and asked them what they thought of them. To put it moderately: the responses were not encouraging for those who propagate such views; and the statistical information assembled in chapter three below, fully supports this reaction. But I accept these are my views; and however honestly held, they may not be shared by others. Indeed, we find 'echoes' of this approach in some continental European universities (such as Frankfurt for instance) where some scholars seem to delight in the creation of a 'language' that is opaque to all but the initiated.

Now I would not be deterred by the accusation that civilian colleagues could levy against me—that my targeting of courts and practitioners is un-intellectual or, even, skewed by the fact that I live in a country which gives a premium to courts of law.[37] For I repeat my earlier conviction that all other agents of law creation that I know of, be they national legislators or Brussels or GATT technocrats, are just as repulsed by texts vague in their formulations and devoid of practical, prescriptive value. Indeed, our own Law Commission's recent interesting forays into foreign (including continental European) law show clearly what kind of works are consulted and, needless to say, they are works giving detailed and reliable evidence of the solutions of a foreign legal system to a given problem. When

Lord Woolf was drafting his monumental proposals to reform our law of procedure he, likewise, sought information about foreign law; and that, too, was of the kind I am talking about.

This impression is confirmed by foreign experience. More detailed research about the recent practices of the German legislator, reported in the next chapter, confirm the same picture and suggest that this is a fertile topic for further detailed research. But what has been unearthed thus far strengthens my view that the method of 'functional specificity' which I am advocating is just as appropriate for courts as it is for legislators and other agencies of law reform. In a long letter commenting on an early draft of this book Professor Wulf-Henning Roth, Director of the Institute of International and Comparative Law of the University of Bonn, confirms emphatically the views advocated here (and elsewhere in this book). Indeed, one of his main criticisms of my text was that I gave inadequate illustration of how what I am advocating is *de rigeur* in the entire area of commercial, economic and European Union law as it is currently taught in Germany. Lack of space (and expertise) account for my omissions. And the same, admittedly lame reasons are my primary excuse for not conducting a specific study on the use of comparative law in the valuable work done by the Advocates General of the Court of the European Communities.[38] But I mention the comments of my learned colleague for they, essentially, criticise me for not exposing fully how much material nowadays exists to support my own belief that only focused, specific, primarily (but not exclusively) legal examination of foreign rules is likely to attract the attention of a court or a modern legislator. The fruits of the research contained in chapter three below reinforces the belief shared, in principle, by all who saw early drafts of my text. In law, ideas and notions that cannot be put to practical use, are likely to satisfy only those who spend their time devising them and then quoting each other with self-satisfaction.[39] For the rest of society, such ideas will come and go, end up submerged by the sands of time, and only help give the academic world the nefarious image that ordinary people so commonly have about it. It takes academic principles to unattractive extremes to argue that in law (at least) the search for knowledge can, *alone*, justify such exercises, especially if they depend—as they do these days—on public money. And it also contributes to the wider problems of the academic world to get its work properly funded if it comes up with these kinds of arguments alone.

(c) A Suffocating Embrace

The above thought brings me to the third trend: to make the subject captive to the theorising of a certain type of philosophers. Here is how Professor George Fletcher, Cardozo Professor of Jurisprudence at Columbia University Law School, put it:

> The great challenge for comparative lawyers is to probe our legal culture for its sources of resistance, for its implicit judgments about the normal way of doing things, for the way in which our identity is bound up with our practices.

In the same article Fletcher gives examples of things that could be done, questions that could be asked, to help rehabilitate the subject which he, too, regards as marginalised. Yet nowhere in his enticement to be 'subversive'—and he admits he is using the term in a 'playful' way—do we find a single word about making the subject more appealing to practitioners and the courts. His own position is quite clear; he is targeting 'the inner circles of the academe.' For courts he seems to have no time. 'One can understand' he writes, as if it was the most natural thing to say, 'why lawyers [sic] and judges pay little attention to foreign law. They have a job to do.'[40] How about *us* showing *them* that *our* discipline is linked to the job *they* have to do? If the notion ever crossed the learned Professor's mind, there are no signs of this in his article. No wonder then that our subject is suffering (or is seen to be suffering) when colleagues tell us that we should be writing for those in the cloisters and not those in the boardroom or the courtroom. Writing from Columbia (locked in fierce competition with NYU), Fletcher should have been able to appreciate the force of globalisation, the power of fund-raising, the challenge from competition, the importance of reaching the constituency of practitioners of all kinds.

So let philosophers use the information comparatists unearth and the insights they produce and weave them into their theories; but do not allow them the chance to shape either the agenda or the methodology of comparatists. For if they do, they can (like the historians) help separate the subject from the world of practice and thus not further its wider use.

(d) The Shared Error of the Old and New Schools

The above indifference to the real world is, in my view, the main reason why legal history in general and Roman law in particular have lost and, more importantly, deserve to lose their decisive grip over comparative law and their protected status in the law curriculum in general. Let me back this assertion with a specific example since I was once involved in teaching Roman and Byzantine law. Consider, thus, the instance of the lex Aquilia—a topic that once took up much of my time.

Today, the average English lawyer cannot be asked even to reflect on the wording and scope of its third chapter (even in translation) for he has almost certainly never heard of it. And if he happens to be one of those who read law during my Cambridge days and took Roman Law II (as it was then called) as a third-year option, he will, almost certainly, have forgotten everything. My hypothetical—for how many are there these days?—contemporary reader of the lex Aquilia may be even more surprised to be told that the preoccupation with the chapter's 31 words has been a particularly British hobby-horse, having attracted the attention of such great jurists as David Daube and Felix Jolowicz, not to mention Lawson and Honoré.

But Roman law, even though it once had at its service some of the finest legal minds in the land, could not bring itself to address the needs of our times. Like Goethe's frustrated student, their scholars reside in halls of learning, devoid of hearing, sight or sense of the real world.[41] Unlike him, however, they seem to be unaware of their isolation. On the 'live and let live' principle, I would not have cared a great deal about so much effort being expended on such subjects, were it not for the fact that in my time it affected adversely, or at the very least slowed down, the growth of comparative law. For in England (maybe elsewhere as well) this cohabitation of Roman law with comparative law harmed the latter by preventing it from turning its attention to contemporary, practical issues rather than cultivating assiduously an air of excessive intellectuality and separateness and boxing itself into a corner. For Roman law, the consequence had to be gradual atrophy. I regret this because it was a fine creation of fine minds. But, more important still for me is that the same fate does not fall on comparative law.

But my argument goes beyond this thought. If Roman law, one of the finest creations of human endeavour, did not avoid this decay, surely the same will happen to the ephemeral contemporary material, which appears with excessive regularity in some American law journals and is desperately trying to dominate the comparative law agenda. These killing habits must not affect contemporary foreign law and the science of comparative methodology. The statistics provided in chapter three support the view/complaint that Roman law:

(a)   took up a disproportionate amount of the time and effort of British comparatists, diverting them from comparative law;

(b)   affected (for what it is worth) adversely the citation rates of these authors; and, arguably,

(c)   diminished, as a result, the impact they could have had on others and reduced the legacy they could have left to posterity.[42]

The above arguments and, more importantly, the lessons that must be drawn from the statistical survey attempted in the next chapter, are not to be dismissed lightly. In purely intellectual terms, however, there is no doubt that the practical slant that I chose to give to my work may strike many—such as Sacco[43] and like-minded purists—as a sad negation of what true scholarship should stand for. For these colleagues believe that the accumulation and systematisation of knowledge is more important than finding a way of putting this knowledge, even eventually, to wide use. I note in passing that to many of Sacco's (Roman) ancestors,[44] the academic pursuit of knowledge for its own sake was often treated as a form of dilettantism. But be that as it may, this conflict between the 'elegant'

and the 'utilitarian' represents, of course, a clash of philosophies as regrettable as it is old.[45] I once thought that in law
ways could be found to breach the chasm. In striving for reconciliation I experienced in a very real sense the Faustian
agony (which can, I think, be read in a non-theological way)
that follows when 'two souls dwell within one breast.' That
beautiful passage can show how being pulled in opposite
directions can tear a soul apart.[46] But 35 years of teaching service in some of the world's leading law faculties make me less
hopeful now than in my earlier days that a complete reconciliation can be achieved. And since I am, *above all*, anxious to
serve my students and play my part in keeping my subject
alive, I am trying to find ways to ensure its survival, jettisoning
if need be anything that weighs it down. The orientation I have
tried to give to my subject is thus a compromise born of my
life's experience in teaching on both sides of the Atlantic and
both sides of the Channel, not in all of its aspects one of first
choice.

This personal agonising runs deeper than most readers
might think on reading my text and reflecting on my substitute
solutions. But the sadness it generates can only be measured
against a lifetime of experience. I recall vividly, for instance,
how, less than 20 years ago, I joined the famous Leiden Law
Faculty as one of its few, tenured, part-time members. And I
found there a second Professor of comparative law, a Professor
(and a flourishing Institute) of Eastern European law, two and
a half chairs of Roman law, a chair in ecclesiastical law, and two
posts in papyrology, ancient and modern, not to mention a
fully fledged Department in European Community law! By the
time I resigned my chair in the late 1990s, the Professor
of Roman law was doing some teaching in English law, the
university could not fill my chair even on a part-time basis,[47]
and the other posts had disappeared—all except the European
Community law section. The same is true of other chairs of
Roman law as far apart as Scotland and South Africa.
Increasingly they stand empty or filled by colleagues who
claim Roman law as a secondary string to their bow.
Understandably, Italy and Germany, probably, still provide the
main exceptions to this trend (though in the latter Roman law
is a non-examinable subject and thus attracts ever-decreasing

numbers of students).[48] In administrative terms, the trend also seems to me to be for such chairs to be treated as forming a sub-division of the (larger) legal history Departments.

In the light of the above one is inclined to feel amused with the title of a recent Dutch collection of essays under the title *Viva Vox Iuris Romani*. How such ebullience can be voiced in a country where, for nearly 20 years, I experienced at first hand the stranglehold that public finances have placed on Dutch law faculties is a mystery. For this economy drive has affected first and foremost chairs of legal history and Roman law. In such gatherings and Festschriften I thus see most clearly what Professor Michael Grant, formerly Fellow of Trinity College, Cambridge and Professor of Humanity at Edinburgh University meant when he wrote about Cicero in the following lines:[49]

> what he [Cicero] wanted was unrealizable. His central interest (in very Roman fashion) being the state, he resembled his contemporaries in having no constructive ideas for its much-needed reform. Instead he looked back longingly and conservatively to a stable and balanced republic . . . submitting voluntarily to the guidance of a small élite of enlightened leaders. But the old order which Cicero saw in so rosy a light never truly existed in this ideal from. More importantly, it certainly could not be brought into existence now.

All one has to do is change the word 'Cicero' for the words 'romanists and legal historians'and, I feel, one gets a pretty good picture of the contemporary scholars who yearn for the past, are unable to live happily with the present, and seem unwilling to accept the future.

Though legal history is not my immediate concern it, too, has followed this pattern. When, as far back as 1888, the great Maitland gave his inaugural lecture at the University of Cambridge under the title 'Why the History of English Law Has Not Been Written,' he pinned his hopes of completing the necessary research for writing it on 10 'failed barristers.' In return for a modest stipend, he thought, they would be willing to edit a goodly number of yearbooks. Professor John Baker, the current holder of the Maitland Chair, pointed out[51] that the problems of recruitment remain unsolved. Editorship offers neither monetary reward nor enhanced career prospects. Funds, or lack of funds, played a key part in ensuring the failure of Maitland's own appeal. Can we—must we?—avoid asking the question whether they are, nowadays, likely to be more forthcoming? The inevitable contrast must thus be drawn with the attractive offers made to students who are high achievers, willing to work in multinational law firms, banks, and the industry. One may regret the decline in interest in the topics that interest Professor Baker just as much as one regrets (this author more than many) the dying of languages in which the founding values of our civilisation were once expressed with great economy of words. Greek was, after all, the language of his father; Latin the language of his Venetian ancestors, so he feels the loss keenly. But no amount of nostalgia can revive a dead language. As university leaders we must come to realise that our agendas, unlike our dreams, must be shaped in the light of the current financial condition of European law faculties. If this means adjusting the optic of our subjects, to save what we can in the interests of a broader legal education, we should do it. Emulating Julian the Apostate is as successful a strategy as is the ostrich's burying of its head in the sand and wishing the danger away.

To sum up, the environment we live in has little time left for flirting with legal history and Roman law except as optional subjects;[51] and it has even less need of politically correct orientations. Likewise, it will not tolerate comparative law falling into the hands of philosophers, anthropologists, and incomprehensible (to me at least) 'post-modernists'—assuming these disciplines can offer anything to the subject.[52] For the reasons I just sketched out, these trendy ideas have little chance of becoming the orthodoxy of tomorrow, though in a country such as the USA, the super-abundance of law journals will always offer such ideas the chance to break out in print. In Pirandellian terms, however, their authors are producing a subject doomed to spend its life in search of an audience.

Yet even those who sympathise with my views might look at the number of American-based authors agitating for such changes and come to the conclusion that I am the *vox clamantis in deserto*. But when one reflects deeply on the above-mentioned politically trendy literature in the area of comparative law, one is spurred on by Montaigne's remark that in times such as these 'we can only improve ourselves by walking backwards, by discord not by harmony, by being different not by being like.'[53] Academics, on the whole, have always struck me as a cowardly lot, despite the security given to them by 'tenure.' For my part I share the view expressed by one of Mikhail Bulgakov's characters who denounces 'cowardice [as] one of the most terrible *sins*.'[54] It would be cowardice not to make a stand and denounce past practices and emerging trends, which one honestly believes to be bad.

But if, in this instance, I wish to 'walk backwards,' could I not only be different but also wrong? Could my emphasis on practice and the real world be entirely misconceived? It has been said, for instance, that the American scene is showing us how the emphasis in law is shifting from the judge to the scholar.[55] I have been teaching in the USA for over 20 years and I honestly doubt that this represents an accurate reading of the current scene in the USA. My view remains unchanged even if one makes allowance for the fact that American academics have been more actively involved than their English counterparts in the shaping of the policy of the law. For as long as American legal education retains its professional features, aims to train lawyers—and not just civil servants and bankers—and not merely provide a general degree, the concrete, the pragmatic, the utilitarian method I have advocated will find a fertile soil to germinate. And the American approach, aided by the spreading dominance of the English language and the fact that the financial world (in all its forms) remains largely Anglo-Saxon in mentality, provides the background which *needs* my method. Not, it must be stressed again, that this ignores either the principles or the interests of the jurist. On the contrary, it is an approach that believes that by engaging the attention of the judge, it will force greater and fruitful collaboration between the practitioner and the academic and thus secure the survival of the subject. How right I am can, I think, be seen by looking at the figures assembled in the next chapter. Bluntly, they paint a simple picture: most of the comparatists included in my survey have left courts and practitioners unmoved. In this sense, and maybe this sense alone, Birks may be right when he implies that comparative law, in its actual state, is irrelevant to the real world. But if it is, it is largely the fault of its high priests. That is my verdict; and that is my *j'accuse*.

5. FROM HEROES TO MOVEMENTS OF CONTEMPORARY GLOBALISATION

So let me return to the starting point of the first chapter: is comparative law in a ghetto, or doomed to stay in a ghetto or, as many American scholars prefer to put it, performing a 'marginal role'?[56] Clearly there are signs of restlessness; and with some a disappointment which has been voiced in even gloomier imagery. Merryman, for instance, has written that[57] 'comparative law languishes in a narrow dungeon of its own construction, deprived of light and air by a perversely constricted academic vision.' Yet others have expressed their hopes in millenarian terms, claiming that comparative law 'desperately' needs the intervention of 'towering figures.'[58]

To deal with such views one must ask: to what do such cries of despair refer? Are their proponents, for instance, claiming that fewer universities are offering courses on foreign and comparative law? The answer here is easy: no. Are they, alternatively, saying that few students take such classes? Again, I think, the answer is probably no, especially if one looks at the picture within the time frame I have chosen for my study. Is, then, the (quantity of) writing on the subject in decline? A negative answer can here be entered with even greater assurance than in the previous ones. Are the citations that comparatists are getting for their work—as a measure of their wider reputation—substantially lower than those made of writers of mainstream subjects? The information provided in the next chapter suggests that this may be the case in the USA but is not the case for English authors where the non-comparatists do not score better than the comparatists. Finally, are the personal and intellectual exchanges between lawyers of different countries weakening instead of strengthening? This question, in my view, cannot even be posed, for the last 10 or 15 years have witnessed a veritable explosion of intellectual co-operation and exchange,[59] which even my heroes of yesterday could not have anticipated coming about so rapidly. And these changes have created a real need for applied comparative law.

Yet, despite the above undoubted progress, which gives the lie to the ghetto theory, it would be difficult to deny that there is something 'marginal' about the subject. Marginal, first, in the sense that those who devote their energy to it attract fewer citations and, more importantly, even less attention from the general educated public compared to those who devote their minds to core or trendy subjects. Marginal, secondly, because their work has failed to attract the attention of practitioners and the courts in the way that the great treatise writers have. Marginal, finally, because the greater understanding of foreign law has yet to be exploited by the globalisation of trade, finance, and social intercourse. I will attempt to back these opinions with the help of statistics in the next chapter.

The marginalisation that I have described above, however, seems to me to be radically different from the one the critics of the subject have in mind; and it is a marginalisation that is very different in kind from that experienced by Roman law and for very different reasons. Just as importantly, the marginalisation that I detect is a self-inflicted one. Self-inflicted, as explained in chapter one above and repeated here, by the past generation, which allowed its subject to be hijacked by legal history and Roman law and spent too much of its time and effort serving the latter instead of promoting the former. And likely to be self-inflicted again by some of our contemporary comparatists who threaten to marginalise the subject further by placing it at the service of trendy causes. If there is thus a cloud on the horizon, it is generated by those who identify a crisis in the American academic scene and propose remedies which, in reality, would enhance it not solve it. For these American 'complainers' cannot see what world-shrinking is bringing in its wake, just as many of their English counterparts do not understand that universities are increasingly driven by the needs of the real world and cannot be dominated by dead disciplines. But before I elaborate my views on these rebel dogmas, let me return briefly to my earlier image of a golden era, inhabited by fallible heroes. Greek mythology shows us how the heroes often brought about their own demise. The light of contemporary scrutiny can be even more destructive.

Each age, I think, has the tendency to idolise the one that preceded it; to see it in terms of a *belle époque*. I have slipped into such elegiacal moods myself, so I try to guard against them. But in our case one must do more than guard against them; one must try to understand their causes. Primary among them, I think, is some kind of psychological need to inflate the past in order to bolster greater confidence in the present. My own attitude has been to admire (and learn) from past masters but not to idolise them or treat their beliefs as immutable or untouchable. Post-1960s scepticism towards all canonical figures and phenomena could not leave comparative law or its heroes untouched; and in the preceding and succeeding chapters I have done some demystifying and even criticising of my own. But demystifying or deconstructing is not all that happens with the passage of time. Even those who are not 'un-pegged' simply get forgotten.

In one sense, this is much worse than being criticised. I am, for instance, constantly surprised to realise how few contemporary comparatists have read Lord Macmillan's 'Two Ways of Reasoning' even though it is as relevant today as it was 60 years ago when it was delivered as a lecture at the University of Cambridge.[60] And I shall never forget the case of a German student of mine who had never heard of Rudolf von Jhering and mistook his (Austrian) title of nobility[61] as a being a *versus*, not a *von*, and treated him as a case: the case of Rudolf against Jhering! If this can happen to Jhering—the man who studied Roman law not as an end in itself but as a means to a new legal order—what does the future hold for most of us ordinary mortals? It is salutary (and not painful) to contemplate the answer: nothing![62]

So the images of ghettoes and good neighbourhoods, towering figures and mortal descendants, should not be over-used. For though, as individuals, we may fade into the background, and our work becomes blurred and even extinguished with time, we still exist as parts of movements. This sobering thought fits in well with the current anti-heroic academic culture of our times, a culture in which committees have replaced leaders, political correctness robust and clear language, trendiness sound judgement, and research assessment exercises the slow but inevitable accolade of peer recognition that time invariably (but not always) brought to those who deserved it but did not seek it. I make no secret of the fact that I regret some of these shifts. I also see in them dangers for my subject (and, worse still, for academia as a whole). For those criticising the state of comparative law in the USA are, it seems to me, consciously rebelling against the philosophy of the heroes of the golden era which, with all its faults,[63] had some attractions.

And yet in this 'de-personalisation' of academic life, which I see ahead of us if not with us already, I also see the chance for a real breakthrough for comparative law. It is this new environment which will make law faculties discover the true utility of studying foreign law and comparative methodology. And it is again this environment which will defeat the calls to give the subject the trendy apparel which the American-based reformers wish for it but which I find most unattractive.

So it is the political and economic realities that prevail at the turn of the twenty-first century—European integration, world trade, globalisation of human rights, multinational law firms—that have changed the background and created the right conditions for the survival of my subject. It is these conditions that largely account for the revival that started slowly in the 1990s and brought the subject out of the ghetto to which it was being consigned. It is these changes which enabled the study of foreign law to replace Roman law as the only medium of becoming aware of another legal system in the course of a short legal study. For they embedded European law into the modern syllabus in England and, progressively, even in the USA brought comparative law indirectly into the syllabus of many specialist subjects. It is political developments and changes in the social environment, which have brought about the changes that are making the study of foreign law necessary. In short, whether one shares the sentiments that Bertold Brecht puts into the mouth of Galileo in the passages cited at the beginning of this chapter, it is events and not heroic figures that are nowadays determining my subject and shaping its future. Among these causes or developments or events I include 'Europe' as one of the most significant. And that is another reason why the 'eurocentric' approach of comparative law has not yet gasped its last breath.

Europe, first, in the form of the output of the courts in Luxembourg and Strasbourg, bringing new ideas, new concepts, and new doctrines into subjects which 30 years ago had a distinctly parochial if not stale look about them. Ideas, incidentally, which should make English lawyers appreciate that on all the major legal issues of our times—human rights, patterns of federalism, individualism versus socialisation of risks—there exist plausible European alternatives, and that the USA and the Commonwealth are not the only source of attractive ideas.

Europe, secondly, as an idea that has already captured the imagination of English judges more so than the country's politicians. For since the pioneering Hamlyn Lectures of Lord Scarman[64] some 25 years ago, numerous articles have been written by some of our leading judges which bear deep marks of European legal thinking. I have in mind, for instance, judges such as Goff,[65] Lord Mustill,[66] Bingham,[67] Lord Hoffmann,[68] Woolf,[69] Steyn,[70] Sedley,[71] Lord Justice Laws[72] and, indeed, the Lord Chancellor[73] making my country (proportionately with its population) the one with the most academically-oriented judges in the Western world. Though in their judgments as well as their extra-judicial pronouncements one finds the whole gamut of emotions from the most pro-European to the most sceptical, all are infinitely more open-minded in accepting the impact of European law than many of my academic colleagues. Through their example they have also created a trend—the trend of the writing judge which, in its own way, will also contribute to breaking down the old barriers that separated bench and academic cloister as well as the barrier which the Channel used to present. For all of the above, and I could give more names and illustrations, have dwelled in their work on comparative law, or foreign law, or both, and used it intelligently to shape, inspire, and even change national law.

And Europe, thirdly, because it is increasingly (not decreasingly) going to occupy American business and its legal advisers as they realise the size of the new emerging market and wish to stake a claim in it. And this market, from the Atlantic to the Urals, will need practitioners to draw their contracts, shape the language of their transactions, sort out the mess when things go wrong as they are bound to do. These lawyers will not be shaped by sociological or anthropological theories but by an environment which will require pragmatic and focused thinking, training in languages, a talent not to be chauvinistic, the need to be mentally agile. And when, perhaps, comparative law ceases one (distant) day to be a separate subject and becomes an integral part of employment law, enterprise law, corporations law, defamation law, immigration law, and so on, it may, finally, also have achieved its double intellectual aims of teaching foreign law and making us think about our own. I see these paramount aims as being interlinked; and for someone like me, resolutely unwilling to commit myself to one culture and ignore others, I see also in these qualities another great merit of my subject: that it only works if it is seen as a two-way street.

Europe, the end of the cold war, and trade globalisation, have thus been some of the 'causes,' the 'catalysts,' the 'needs that have to be addressed.' Indeed, they were first recognised by the multinational law firms—not the universities—as issues that need to be tackled. It was thus major city firms which in divers ways helped leading law schools to expand their ambitions in the direction of Europe and indirectly encouraged the ever-growing number of joint courses by eagerly employing those who took them as part of their university studies or offering scholarships to students spending time abroad. It is events such as the above which are in the process of rejuvenating a subject, which once existed only because a bunch of talented émigrés and a handful of local geniuses saw its intellectual appeal. The 'de-personification' of the subject is its salvation not its nemesis. Necessity, *practical commercial necessity*, is what will make the study of foreign law grow further and deeper, not dreamers of the past nor trendy preachers of the present (such as one finds in the USA—the country which will always find followers for even the most eccentric of prophets). And we have it on the good authority of one of the seven sages of antiquity that 'even the Gods do not fight against necessity'.[74]

Notes

[1] This was one way—my way—of rectifying what Gutteridge described to Lord Atkin as 'the almost complete lack of contact between the practitioner and the academic lawyer.' See Appendix 1 below.

[2] 'The process of authorship is entirely different from that of a judicial decision. The author, no doubt, has the benefit of a *broad and comprehensive survey of his chosen subject as a whole*, together with a lengthy period of gestation and intermittent opportunities for reconsideration. *But he is exposed to the peril of yielding to preconceptions,* and he lacks the advantage of that impact and sharpening of focus which the detailed facts of a

particular case bring to the judge. Above all, he has to form his ideas without the aid of the purifying ordeal of skilled argument on the specific facts of a contested case. Argued law is tough law.' *Cordell v Second Clanfield Properties* [1969] 2 Ch D 9, at 16 ff. I have italicised two sentences, which I would be inclined to discuss (with illustrations) in a classroom and state why they may militate for a less rigid separation of the two tasks.

3 [2002] 3 WLR 89.

4 Published by Hart Publishing in 1997 and 2001.

5 See, eg, the very generous review which my good friend Professor Denis Tallon did of my collection of essays entitled *Always on the Same Path: Essays on Foreign Law and Comparative Methodology* in (2001) 4 *RTDC* 1027–28. But 'my method,' with its strong emphasis on detail and practical need, is, I submit, just as applicable to law reformers or law harmonisers of the legislative or administrative variety. For they are no more enamoured of theorising, anthropology or post-modernism than I think judges are. But more about this later.

6 'A Cosmopolitan Discipline? Some Implications of "Globalisation" for Legal Education,' (2001) 8/1 *International Journal of the Legal Profession* 23 at 24.

7 Richard A Posner, *Cardozo. A Study in Reputation* (1990) 59.

8 Gerber, 'Sculpting the Agenda of Comparative Law: Ernst Rabel and the Facade of Language' in Annelise Riles (ed), *Rethinking the Masters of Comparative Law* (2001) 190 ff, esp at 204 ff. Gerber's piece attracts by its condensed learning as much as its moderate tones. An earlier piece of his, 'Towards a Language of Comparative Law' (1998) 46 *Amer J Comp L* 719 foreshadows some of these ideas but also pursues different paths which deserve attention.

9 Entitled *Gesammelte Aufsätze*, published by J C B Mohr between 1965 and 1971.

10 (1947) 47 *Law Quarterly Review* 174–237.

11 Written in 1925 and reprinted 1967 in his *Gesammelte Aufsätze* vol III (edited by H G Leser).

12 *Always* is the operative word; for Rabel made brilliant use of multiple factors when explaining the difference between German and common law of contact in general and sales in particular in his *Das Recht des Warenkaufs* vol. I (1936, reprinted in 1957) and vol. II (1958). Rheinstein did the same in his *Die Struktur des vertraglichen Schuldverhältnisses im anglo-amerikanischen Recht* (1932), a work written under the guidance of Rabel and full of magnificent insights into both common and civil law.

13 Of his numerous writings I pick here his address to the Trento Circle where he points out succinctly how 'the doctrinal development of a country's contract law typically depends on the types of contracts litigated before the country's higher courts.' His point is made with the aid of statistics, which in turn support knowledge that emerges from history and the knowledge of different societies; and it is presented devoid of neologisms

or opaque jargon. See 'The Common Core of European Private Law: Presented at the Third General Meeting of the Trento Project' (1998) 21 *Hastings Int'l & Comp L Rev* 803, esp at 805–6.

[14] Hein Kötz and Gerhard Wagner, *Deliktsrecht* (9th edn, 2001).

[15] *The German Law of Torts: A Comparative Treatise*, co-authored with Dr Hannes Unberath (4th edn, 2002).

[16] I touch upon this issue in my article 'Réflexions d'un comparatiste anglais sur et à partir de l'arrêt Perruche' (2001) *RTD civ* (1)(Jan–Mar) 77 ff.

[17] See 'Tortious Liability for Negligent Misdiagnosis of Learning Disabilities: A Comparative Study of English and American Law' (2001) *Texas Int'l LJ* (April), which contains the full text of the Baade Festschrift.

[18] [2000] 3 WLR 776.

[19] 'Stepping out of the European Shadow: Why Comparative Law in the United States Must Develop its own Agenda' (1998) 46 *American Journal of Comparative Law* 637 at 644.

[20] Above, n 19, at 639 ff.

[21] A Clapham, *Human Rights in the Private Sphere* (Oxford, OUP, 1993).

[22] 'Our Debt to Europe: Past, Present and Future' in *The Clifford Chance Millenium Lectures: The Coming Together of the Common Law and the Civil Law* (2000) 37 at 57 ff.

[23] BArbGE 1, 185 of 1954.

[24] 721 2d 894 (1983).

[25] One must again stress that Rabel and his school, though not enamoured of the kind of work that philosophers tend to do to comparative law, were quick to stress—even to novices—that their preoccupation with the 'practical utility' of their method did not deprive it of 'intellectual challenge.' See, eg, Rheinstein's observations in 'Comparative Law: Its Functions, Methods and Usages' (1968) 22 *Arkansas Law Review and Bar Association Journal* 415, at 424.

[26] On which see M A Screech, *Montaigne & Melancholy: The Wisdom of the Essays* (1999) esp at 162–63—an incomparable example of condensed and yet lucid English academic writing at its best. In law, Lawson wrote in the same manner, making subsequent editing of his work almost impossible. My generation cannot write like that; and I often get the impression, especially in the USA, that my younger colleagues are not even conscious of the appeal of such pithy language. The contrast with those who have resorted to what they call 'post-modernist' language and ideas and tried to bring them into law is, aesthetically at least, most unattractive. For an illustration, see Mattei and di Robilant, 'The Art and Science of Critical Scholarship: Postmodernism and International Style in the Legal Architecture of Europe' (2001) 75 *Tulane L Rev* 1054.

[27] The facts of the case (and the decision itself) are discussed more fully in chapter four below. But it might help the reader here to be told that in that case the court had to grapple with the question whether a victim of

self-inflicted injuries owes a duty of care to a third party not to cause him psychiatric injury. In *Greatorex*, a young man was injured in an accident caused by his own grossly negligent driving. The plaintiff, his father, a professional fire officer stationed nearby, suffered serious post-traumatic stress disorder as a result of attending his (unconscious) son at the scene of the accident. He claimed damages from the Motor Insurance Board (since the driver/ son was uninsured).

[28] And should consider it with the following abbreviations in mind which attempt to bring together the English and German terminology. Thus, P stands for plaintiff (or creditor in German law since this system looks at substance rather than procedure). He is also the secondary victim of the accident that has provoked the litigation, his damage in a sense flowing from that suffered by the primary victim, referred to as D2. D1 is the tortfeasor and primary defendant in the action. Finally, D2 is the primary victim of the tortfeasor. But because he may have contributed through his own negligence to the accident leading to P's loss, he may also be sued by the tortfeasor. He is thus called D2. German lawyers may also refer to D2 as the 'privileged defendant' because he may enjoy some protection vis-à-vis the plaintiff, should he choose to sue him. This may stem from a contractual exemption clause or it may be an immunity of sorts conferred *ex lege*. The details are discussed more fully in chapter four below.

[29] § 1359 states that one spouse is liable to the other only if he (or she) failed to attain 'the degree of care which they are accustomed to exercise in their own affairs.' So the spouse sued can avoid liability if he can show that in his own affairs he would have displayed a lower standard of care than that required by ordinary negligence. (A similar rule can be found in § 1664 1 BGB dealing with the parent/child relations). The rationale of both provisions is to avoid legal disputes between persons who are in such close family relationships and in many respects draws on policy reasons.

[30] Reimann, 'Stepping out of the European Shadow: Why Comparative Law in the United States Must Develop its own Agenda' (1998) 46 *Amer J Comp L* 637. See, also, Monateri, 'Black Gaius: A Quest for the Multicultural Origins of the "Western Legal Tradition" ' (2000) 51 *Hastings L J* 479–555 and Hondius, 'The Supremacy of Western Law' in *Viva Vox Iuris Romani, Essays in Honour of Johannes Emil Spruit* (2002) 337 ff.

[31] N Demleituer, 'Challenge, Opportunity and Risk: An Era of Change in Comparative Law' (1998) 46 *The American Journal of Comparative Law* 647, 653.

[32] In his excellent edition (with Sir Michael Howard) of *Carl von Clausewitz On War* (Princeton paperback, 1989) 49.

[33] Mattei, 'An Opportunity Not to be Missed: The Future of Comparative Law in the United States' (1998) 46 *Amer J Comp L* 709 at 711, note 7.

³⁴ Mattei, 'The Comparative Jurisprudence of Schlesinger and Sacco' in Riles, above n 8, at 253.

³⁵ Mattei and di Robilant, 'The Art and Science of Critical Scholarship: Postmodernism and International Style in the Legal Architecture of Europe' (2001) 75 *Tulane L Rev* 1053 at 1055.

³⁶ Mattei, above n 34, at 715.

³⁷ A criticism made by Tallon in *Rev intern dr comp* 2000, 1027 at 1028 where he wrote: 'ces textes [a collection of my essays] s'adressent essentiellement aux juges. Ils négligent les autres acteurs de la réforme du droit qui eux aussi doivent s'appuyer sur le droit comparé: législateur, commissions de réforme, ministères de la justice. L' évolution du droit, même en Angleterre, ne passe pas nécessairement par le juge.'

³⁸ Comparative law and methodology in the context of Community law is discussed by Professor Walter van Gerven in 'Comparative Law in a Texture of Communitarization of National Law and Europeanization of Community Law' in Heins-Dieter Assmann, Gert Brüggemeier, Rolf Sethe (eds), *Unterschiedliche Rechtskulturen—Konvergenz des Rechtsdenkens* (2001) 49 ff.

³⁹ Cf Lord Atkin's strong views in Appendix 1 below.

⁴⁰ 'Comparative Law as a Subversive Discipline' (1998) 46 *Amer J Comp L* 683 at 690.

⁴¹ 'Und in den Sälen auf den Bänken, Vergeht mir Hören, Sehn und Denken': Faust, Part I (Insel Verlag edn) vol iii, 57.

⁴² Though as I explained in my John Maurice Kelly Memorial Lecture, published by the Faculty of Law of University College Dublin (2003), scholarship, reputation of scholarship, and legacy and not made up by the same ingredients.

⁴³ 'Legal Formants: A Dynamic Approach to Comparative Law' (1991) 39 *Amer J Comp L* 1 at 4.

⁴⁴ Lucius Annaeus Seneca in his *Epistulae Morales ad Lucilium*, Letter LXXV, thought 'what we say should be of use, not just entertaining' and in Letter XX he argues that even 'philosophy is there to teach us to act not just talk.' Purists all-too-often condemn the search of knowledge with a practical aim in mind as more fit to polytechnics, vocational training schools, but not universities.

⁴⁵ The resolution of potential conflicts between 'honourable' and 'useful' conduct has thus occupied philosophers at least from the time of Aristotle; and Cicero, for instance, in the third book of *De officiis*, drawing on earlier Greek stoics, tried a compromise on the grounds that that intrinsically useful is identical with the honourable.

⁴⁶ Zwei Seelen wohnen, ach! in meiner Brust,
Die eine will sich von der andern trennen;
Die eine hält in derber Liebeslust
Sich an die Welt mit klammernden Organen;

Die andre hebt gewaltsam sich vom Dust
Zu den Gefilden hoher Ahnen.
(Two souls there dwell, alas, within my breast,
and one would cut itself away from the other;
one of them clutches with lustful senses
at the world it loves,
the other rises powerfully from the dust
to reach the fields of lofty ancestors.)
Faust, Part I (Insel Verlag edn) vol iii, 37.

[47] And this despite the fact that in my time I had created for it an Institute of Anglo-American Law and left it with a substantial endowment on my departure in 2000.

[48] The decline in Germany will, in my view, be accelerated by the recent amendment of the Deutsches Richtergesetz, which has re-distributed the roles of the state and the universities in the grading of the First State Exam. For, henceforth, 70 per cent of the marks will be gained on the basis of the State-examination component (which is largely vocational in nature) while the remaining 30 per cent of the mark will be earned by points given in a university-controlled examination in 'special subjects' (*Schwerpunktfächer*). Professor Dr. Hans-Joachim Cremer of the University of Mannheim, with whom I have been in contact discussing the 'common' problems facing contemporary universities and who knows much about the modern economic pressures applied to universities, thus informs me that they are under strong pressure to design these 'special courses' around subjects such as tax law, labour law, corporate law, mergers and acquisitions etc and downplay Roman law, legal history and even legal philosophy. In Cremer's view—which I have double-checked with other German colleagues—this will lead to a decrease of students taking these subjects and (worse still) fewer students in the long run writing dissertations in these subjects, thus leading to their gradual decline. In his view, comparative law is under no such pressure, not least because it is increasingly linked with conflicts of law, a subject growing in popularity because of its intellectual fascination and practical importance. Finally, he and other colleagues believe that the pressure on German law faculties to attract private funds (*Drittmittel*)—a task for which thus far they seem to be singularly unprepared—is also going to lead to the further diminution of law chairs which are not related to branches of the law which present a strong practical significance. At the risk of being boringly repetitive one must stress that making a diagnosis is not tantamount to approving the predicted consequence. But forward academic planning cannot ignore such potent signs.

[49] *Cicero, Selected Political Speeches* (Penguin Classics), Introduction, 10.

[50] 'Why the History of English Law Has Not Been Finished' (2000) 59 *CLJ* 62 at 73.

[51] The fact that many of our best faculties make the subject a compulsory one shows how little faith they have in the subject's ability to draw in the crowds.

[52] See, eg, Mattei and di Robilant, above n 35.

[53] *On the Art of Conversation, The Complete Essays,* translated and edited with an introduction and notes by M A Screech (Penguin, 1991) 1045.

[54] *The Master and Margarita* (Fontana, 1969) 336 (my emphasis). In an earlier section of the book (at 322) the thought is more openly attributed to Jesus.

[55] Mattei, 'Why the Wind Changes: Intellectual Leadership in Western Law' (1994) 42 *Amer J Comp L* 195 at 207 ff.

[56] Reimann, above n 30; Curran, 'Dealing in Difference: Comparative Law's Potential for Broadening Legal Perspectives' (1998) 46 *Amer J Comp L* 657 at 665; Mattei, above n 34.

[57] 'Comparative Law Scholarship' (1998) 21 *Hastings Int'l & Comp L Rev* 771 at 784.

[58] Mattei, above n 33, at 711.

[59] How far we have come in this field of endeavour can be seen by reading von Bar, Lando and Swann, 'Communication on European Contract Law: Joint Responses of the Commission on European Contract Law and the Study Group on a European Civil Code' (2002) 2 *European Rev of Private Law* 183–248.

[60] And published in his collection of essays entitled *Law and Other Things* (1935).

[61] When he left his Vienna Chair in the early 1870s, he was given the Knight's Cross in the Order of Leopold, which carried with it the title of *von*, which he proudly used ever since. One sees the change even in the way he signed his private letters to his friend Windscheid: *Jherings Briefe an Windscheid* 1970–1891, edited by Karl Kroeschell (1988).

[62] An even more dramatic example must surely be that which emerged from a recent 'survey of students of German literature at Cologne University [sic] [who] believed Schiller to be a play by Goethe'; see Lesley Sharpe, *The Cambridge Companion to Goethe* (2002) 4.

[63] A 'fault' that Merryman has pointed out is the neglect of Italian law. But leaving aside the fact that Italian is the fourth foreign language in order of priority of study in English schools—I would have thought it is even lower in the USA—the conclusion is still too pessimistic. For first, Merryman and others have, in recent years, supplied casebooks and textbooks about Italian law. Secondly, also in the last 10 years or so, at least two major law faculties in the United Kingdom—Oxford and UCL—have started offering courses in Italian law (given in Italian). Thirdly, a new wave of travelling Italian scholars has done much to give us a new picture of Italian scholarship both in the area of comparative and public international law. Finally, the other missing major system is that of the Hispanic world (old and new). To some (small) extent, however, this

ignorance is made up by some knowledge of the underlying French legal ideas. One wonders, therefore, whether allusions to prisons lacking light or air are not over-dramatisations!

[64] His seminal Hamlyn Lectures, *English Law the New Dimension* (1974) could be credited for having started this whole debate in its contemporary form.

[65] For instance, his classic 'The Search for Principle' (1983) 69 *Proceedings of the British Academy* 169; 'Judge, Jurist and Legislature' (1987) 2 *Denning L J* 79; 'Coming Together—The Future' in *The Clifford Chance Millennium Lectures, The Coming Together of the Common Law and the Civil Law* (2000) 239 ff.

[66] 'Negligence in the World of Finance' (1992) 5 *The Supreme Court [Malaysia] Journal* 1; 'What do Judges Do?' (1995–96) 3 *Särtryck ur Juridisk Tidskrift* 611.

[67] *The Business of Judging* (2000).

[68] 'A Sense of Proportion' in F Jacobs and M Andenas (eds), *Community Law in English Courts* (1998).

[69] *Protection of the Public: A New Challenge* (1990), Hamlyn Lectures. See, also, his F A Mann Lecture entitled 'Droit Public—English Style' [1995] *Public Law* 57 ff.

[70] For instance, 'Perspectives of Corrective and Distributive Justice in Tort Law', John Maurice Kelly Memorial Lecture, University College Dublin (2002).

[71] 'The Sound of Silence: Constitutional Law Without a Constitution' (1994) 110 *LQR* 270 ff; 'Human Rights: A Twenty-First Century Agenda' [1995] *Public Law* 386 ff.

[72] 'The Ghost in the Machine: Principle in Public Law' [1989] *Public Law* 27 ff; 'Is the High Court the Guardian of Fundamental Constitutional Rights?' [1993] *Public Law* 59 ff; 'Law and Democracy' [1995] *Public Law* 72 ff.

[73] 'Judges and Decision-Makers: The Theory and Practice of *Wednesbury* Review' [1996] *Public Law* 59 ff.

[74] 'Pittacus of Mitylene' in Diogenes Laertius, *Lives of Eminent Philosophers* (edited by R D Hicks, 1925) vol I, 79, cited also by Plato in *Protagoras*.

3

Spreading the Gospel (and the Name of the Evangelist)

1. AIMS TO BE PURSUED

Judge Richard Posner was not the first to use statistical information to measure reputation by reference to the number of citations an author receives to his works.[1] Yet his biography of Benjamin Cardozo[2] gave an impetus to lawyers to develop what one of them has since called the science of 'reputology.'[3] The word science may, in fact, be exaggerating the status of this new branch of learning since, we shall soon note, the conclusions one can draw are hedged by numerous (yet necessary) qualifications that must be made to the raw material and the way it is assembled and interpreted. At times, these qualifications make the resulting lessons vague and tenuous; and the language in which some of these pieces are written is not one which will either be familiar or attractive to most lawyers, at any rate those operating in the European area. Yet, as ways of measuring 'a "quality" that is socially defined, reflecting the utility of the writing in question to other scholars, rather than gauging its intrinsic merit'[4] these guides may by useful exercises. Moreover, despite the limitations in the methodology, the new topic is undoubtedly gaining in popularity and sophistication in the USA,[5] so it may be safe to assume that it will not be long before we begin to see its European counterparts. For American ideas and tastes, ingenious or crude, on average tend to reach Europe with a jetlag of about 10 years.

In this chapter we shall be putting this method to a narrow and less ambitious use than that attempted by those who have written before us in the USA. To that extent our use of this material may prove more acceptable. On the other hand, we have broadened the scope to include more than one system and in this sense the exercise is the first of its kind. Yet, for reasons which we explain below, this attempt is riddled with difficulties. At the very least, therefore, our efforts may prompt further investigations along the lines we are suggesting, which remain insufficiently explored by our predecessors, with a view to refining or refuting our arguments. Thus, in the context of comparative law, three points, in our view, need to be explored further with the aid of this method; and this chapter must be read in conjunction with some of the points made in chapters one and two, above, which in one sense it is meant to complement.

(a) The Importance of Language

First, reputation of scholarship in foreign and comparative law is greatly enhanced if the writer makes some of his work available in the English language. Sacco offers an excellent illustration since the bulk of the citations he receives in the American literature come from the one (of two) articles of his which has been translated into English by Professor James Gordley.[6] Whether this is sufficient to support the statement that he has thus had some tangible impact on the American (academic) scene is open to doubt. My own view is that he has not; and his impact in England is even smaller. Something of the same lesson emerges from the American citations to David's chief work—*Les grands systèmes de droit contemporain*—which receives in the American legal literature 153 references in its English version and 26 in the original (French).[7] If a third supporting illustration is needed for this point, it can come from contemporary South Africa, a country well suited, because of its past and because of its present, to serve as a testing ground for comparative law in practice. Thus, Mathew Chaskalson (co-author of a leading commentary on the South African Constitution), commenting on a study involving the constitutional protection of property, has observed:

> The selection of countries is based on my inability to read any other international languages other than English, but we should bear in mind that most South African lawyers share my limitations in this regard. Thus we can expect the case law of English speaking jurisdic-

tions to exercise a dominant influence over the development of South African constitutional law.[8]

The above would suggest that a non-English speaking scholar runs a very real risk of remaining out of reach of a substantial part of the legal readership of the world if he does not write in English. In a shrinking world this is a serious drawback, especially for comparatists. Foreign scholars who rightly feel proud of their respective languages and rich cultural heritage may regret this growing domination of the English language. But it is also a reflection of the fact that English is increasingly the *lingua franca* of the business, financial, and by extension, legal worlds. However, it also underlines another point namely, that reputation and scholarly merit are not co-terminus, the former depending on such fortuitous factors as language and also being in many ways more easy to manipulate than the latter for reasons which Posner himself explores with his usual clarity.[9] Moreover, scholarly merit may be great but undiscovered, precisely because the language element has hindered its spread and thus its recognition beyond its natural and national frontiers. Scholars who have 'suffered' from not being accessible for linguistic reasons to Anglo-Saxon audiences include such eminent jurists as von Caemmerer, Professor Claus-Wilhelm Canaris, and to some extent Stoll (all from Germany), Gorla, Sacco, and Professor Benedetto Conforti (all from Italy), and Professors Jacques Ghestin, Philippe Jestaz, Christian Atias, and Geneviève Viney (all from France) to mention but a few whom I have met in my lifetime and had occasion much to admire. Others, of course, could be added to this list. But overall and in national terms, the greatest losers are, arguably, the Italians, which is a great loss to international legal science given the originality of the Italian mind and the often very elegant way in which it expresses itself.

(b) Where One is Cited

Secondly, in this piece my co-authors and I have, inter alia, been anxious to explore, from a different angle, the validity of the thesis developed in chapters one and two above. There, my quest was for the *kind* of comparative law that has the best chance of attracting the attention of the courts and strengthening the position of the subject in the law curriculum. Though I think what follows supports this thesis, the figures reproduced must, again, be read with caution. The same is true of the propositions they are meant to support. This is partly because the figures collected are (relatively) modest. More importantly, however, in some countries (France, Italy) the collection of statistical data is seriously impeded by the fact that their courts (unlike the German and, nowadays, the English) do not cite academic literature in their opinions. It is, therefore, difficult to demonstrate an overt link between academic ideas and judicial results.[10] A final reason why it is difficult to assert with confidence whether the method I have championed (of 'targeting' judges and not, simply, fellow academics) is working in practice is due to the fact that the approach is relatively new. So it has not yet had sufficient time to produce any statistically significant evidence as to whether it is leading to the desired co-operation between the two parts of the legal profession. The most that one can say is thus that the overall picture is evolving and incomplete. Besides, many scholars would dispute my claim that targeting the judge and the legislator is the best way of ensuring the success of my subject. My own doubts about the validity of this objection were given in the previous chapters and all I can repeat here is my conviction that my subject will only take root when it has proved its worth to practitioners.

But let me return to the disappointment produced by the French and Italian practices not to reveal their sources of inspiration. This disappointment can, in fact, be minimised somewhat if one consults the conclusions of the *avocats généraux*, the *conseillers rapporteurs* and the *commissaires du gouvernement* of the French courts. For these major trial figures do cite literature. Their writings thus show that academic literature is brought to attention of the judges even though it is concealed in the judgment itself. Incidentally, they also reveal the close and constructive co-operation that exists between the *arrêtiste* (who in the French legal world fleshes out the opaque decisions of the highest courts) and the court, itself. A random selection of leading French cases confirms the accuracy of the above. Even more importantly, recent examples show that even the Cour de cassation seems to have acquired a taste for references to foreign literature and judicial practice.[11] I am also informed that, as a result of the close co-operation that exists between France and Germany, both countries have a 'national judge' attached to the equivalent foreign court. On at least one occasion I have been shown the kind of summary reports these French judges send back 'home' and confess some considerable admiration for the way the German material was reported back. But the ways of depicting the above in a statistically interesting manner are non-existent, since carrying out electronically the kind of checks we did with the American material is simply not possible. To attempt to do this work 'manually,' by looking at each reported case, would, on the other hand, require an enormous investment of time which none of us could make. So here suffice it to say that this second structural deficiency again disadvantages European scholars compared to those who operate in the USA and publish in English, especially in American journals.

(c) Inflating Reputation

My *third* and last point is based on a hunch. Though developed from long personal experience, I was, nonetheless, intrigued to see that it also finds its place in Posner's work where, in a more general context, he rightly observes that:

> reputation is conferred by the people doing the reputing rather than produced by the reputed one—*and it is conferred for their purposes, not his.*[12]

The italicised section of the quotation is immensely important, especially given the way Posner amplifies this point further on in his treatment of the subject by giving it a cynical and almost sinister twist. He thus observes that:

> the reputers may be promoting their own selfish interests by hitching their wagon to a star . . .[13]

Unfortunately, this interesting observation is not pursued further by Posner so his ideas remain to be explored further in the future.

2. WARNINGS AND CAVEATS

So let us start by mentioning some of the caveats that have to be borne in mind when reading the figures that we have managed to assemble as part of a first attempt to address the above points. This was made possible thanks to the invaluable assistance of my two co-authors, two younger colleagues,[14] and the Tarlton Law Library staff.[15] Though the piece is co-authored, the oldest of the three authors has coloured it with his ideas, so the blame for their novelty and the overall content of this chapter must fall mainly on him.

First, in this chapter we have tried to apply the citation method mainly to a number of lawyers who held chairs of comparative law or professed a strong interest in the subject and, finally, were active during the last quarter of the last century. Though the total number of scholars looked at with the aid of Lexis, Westlaw and Beck searches (supplemented by manual searches) is not insignificant—48 to be precise—and come from five countries—England, France, Germany, Italy and the USA—it is by no means complete. The omission of worthy colleagues, especially from the USA where the numbers are greater than they are in Europe, was dictated by considerations of time and space *as well as* our estimation, based on preliminary searches, of how widely cited they were outside the USA. Regrettable though these omissions are, on personal grounds as well, we stuck to the original decision in the belief that the overall conclusions would not be affected if, instead of looking at 50 names we had looked at 60 or even 70. The restriction of this preliminary survey to a small, albeit important, number of legal systems, is also immediately obvious and regrettable to none more than ourselves. Here, however, though the time factor also played a part, it was not the main reason for the omission. Inability to gain electronic access to material was the prime obstacle, in some cases nothing short of manual searches being possible. We particularly regret the omission of countries such as Canada, Japan and South Africa (which we have only looked at from one angle), and hope that one day we may expand our survey to include them in our research.

Secondly, it will be noticed that some authors appear with ratings, which are significantly higher than others. Since we operated on the basis that one citation per work would suffice (and thus ignored multiple citations to one author contained in the same piece), it soon became clear that we had to dwell deeper and to explain this marked deviation from what appeared to be normal. Our preliminary conclusions are mentioned later on in this chapter; but the exercise clearly showed that the counting of citations must be sophisticated and adjusted (downwards) to take into account some factors indicated below. Doing this is not easy; but it must at least be attempted if this enquiry is to be of any use to comparative law. Once this adjustment has been made, the surprising conclusion is that the contribution which most of our comparative lawyers have made *to their subject and the real world of practice* is smaller than most—certainly we—would have expected.

Thirdly, the time of commencement and 'cut off' of this statistical survey is 1980 to the end of 2000 respectively. The choice of the dates is not entirely arbitrary for it was meant to coincide with the period of active work done by the principal author's generation of comparatists as contrasted with that of the 'greats' of the golden era.[16] It is thus consistent with the time scale used in chapters one and two above. Yet we have included in our search list some of the 'greats' of the previous generation. This was done because their work lives on; and their omission would raise more questions than their inclusion, implying among other things that it has lost all appeal. And yet, clearly, the figures given above do injustice to the older generation for they do not include citations made while these people were at their peak. Some allowance has to be made for this fact though we are not sure how this can be done in figures. The interested reader can find more guidance about how the age factor can skew results (in both directions) in the Landes and Posner article in the *Journal of Legal Studies* cited above. Additionally, modern surveys suggest that, in most cases, the citation rate of works declines sharply after a period of time, indeed citations, apparently, peak four years after publication.[17]

A *fourth* and important proviso is related to electronically available data—a point already mentioned earlier on. This is excellent in the USA, moderate in Canada, limited in England (to courts but not legal journals), even more limited in Australia (to some courts) and almost totally unobtainable as one moves across the Channel onto the Continent of Europe.[18] This, effectively, does great injustice to the Continental comparatists, especially those who have written in less popular languages (such as Scandinavian, Greek, Portuguese etc). But we have tried to indicate these limitations by stating, where appropriate, where these figures come from or, alternatively, to which courts or journals they are limited. A glance at the information contained in Appendix 3 below may thus be advisable to anyone who wishes to become fully conscious of the difficulties we encountered in assembling our data as well as its limitations. As far as courts are concerned, however, we repeat once again the general practice of the highest French and Italian[19] courts not to cite academic authors. The position is different in Germany so, in this context, some information has been provided mainly derived from court citations. But, again, it is (largely) limited to court citations since there is no way one can access electronically (with few exceptions) the periodical literature—a great loss given that the Germans are prolific citators. These limitations accentuate the point made above about the importance of writing in English; they also underscore the limitations of our data. But we also note that a serious effort was made to neutralise some of these difficulties by laborious manual countings.

Fifthly and relatedly, the figures given in these charts have been collected from court reports and legal journals but have not included searches of the Web or newspapers. Such citations are evidence of notoriety rather than reputation and, even less so, scholarly achievement. As Landes and Posner have shown,[20] these citations are, effectively, limited to a small number of academics; and their showing is minuscule in comparison with politicians and members of the sports and arts world. It would thus be futile to extend such research to include a small branch of the legal profession such as the comparatists.

Sixthly, we regard the citation ratings in court decisions as more important than the citations by fellow academics. But then, again, this is only an acceptable argument to those who, like the principal author, believe that attracting the attention of the judge and the practitioner is the best way of keeping the subject alive and well. But we fully accept that this is certainly not likely to be the view taken in modern civil law systems. For there research and writing are often justified on the principle of *ars gratia artis* and, in any event, attracting the attention of the legislator or the academic community would, it seems, be seen as a more worthwhile activity than influencing the courts.[21] Nonetheless, we remind the reader of our belief that a method that is focused and detailed, and not platitudinous, sociological, or anthropological in nature, is likely to appeal to legislators and law reformers as well, even though we do not at present have ways of showing this in a statistically meaningful manner. Some statistical support for this comes from our section on contemporary practices of the German legislator. Though the data we have collected in this section is indicative of a number of trends and attitudes discussed in this and the previous chapters, the figures, on the whole, remain too slender to support anything more than suggestions as to how they could be interpreted.

But let us return to citations by courts. These are difficult to evaluate for another reason. The full value of such citations can only be assessed by finding out how the foreign reference was used: as secondary supporting evidence of a solution reached by other means, or by playing a more important part in the production of the final decision. The quick answer is likely to veer towards the first suggestion rather than the second; but our feeling is that even this modest use is a novelty, characteristic of roughly the period of time covered by this study and thus likely to be still in its infancy. But decisions are also beginning to appear in the common law world where the use of the comparative method played a crucial and not just supportive role. The commercially important decision of the United States Court of Appeals for the Sixth Circuit *In re Dow Corning Corp (Debtors)*[22] provides an excellent illustration for comparative law in practice in the context of a very important, worldwide legal dispute worth literally billions of dollars. The *Greatorex* case[23] of the English High Court is another example of how the skilful presentation of foreign law can tempt a national court to have recourse to it. Though in practical terms the *Greatorex* decision is nowhere near as significant as the *Dow Corning* litigation, the interest it presents from a methodological point of view is great, as the principal author has tried to show in chapter two, above. The House of Lords' most recent decision in *Fairchild v Glenhaven*[24] provides a kind of high water mark of the use of comparative law by the highest court of the land. In many ways, its significance for comparative law is likely to be more long-lived and fundamental than the earlier exercise in *White v Jones*.[25]

Court citation may call for another adjustment mentioned earlier on, namely that some high courts (Italian, French) never cite authors whereas others, such as the German courts, have traditionally resorted to academic citation at a much higher rate than their English and American counterparts. We could think of no way of making any allowance in our tables for these different practices. However, we do refer the reader to some specialist literature that discusses this phenomenon.[26]

Seventhly, a further refinement of these statistics is important if one is to derive some concrete lessons from them. One such aspect that still remains to be investigated is who is citing whom. Auto-citation, for instance, in our view seems to be more frequent in the civilian traditions than it is in the common law systems. This is because in the latter—at any rate the English world—authors tend to restrain themselves in the number of notes they insert in their texts, especially to their own work. Whether this is due to the real or assumed attitudes of modesty of the English we cannot say. But the fact remains that (most of) the English, unlike the Germans and, we feel, more so the Italians, are less likely to inflate the number of cita-tions to their own work. But we repeat, in our view this is an English and not a common law habit and Australian authors, for instance, do not appear to share this English self-control. At the other end of the spectrum one finds American authors who seem to have a taste for long (and sometimes even useless) footnotes.

While the above points must be treated as being open to further discussion, another is still more important for the purposes of the ideas found in this essay (and the previous chapters). By this we do not mean that the reputer is seeking self-aggrandisement through an association with a great man. More interesting for the thesis about 'schools of thought' discussed in greater detail in chapters one and two above, is another point. It would thus be interesting to be able to corroborate what at present seems to us to be indicated by the literature, namely that disciples of a grand master tend to cite their master more than others and even inflate his importance. Likewise, adherents of one school tend to cite more those who share the same broad philosophical attitude towards the subject that they subscribe to and even exaggerate the value of the movement. We suspect there may be some truth in the first observation, judging at least from the number of references that Sacco gets from his protégés. In one sense this could be seen as evidence of the 'school theory' suggested earlier on; but it could also be countered by the argument that few comparatists are proficient in Italian with the result that interesting Italian ideas rarely figure in their writings. This is a phenomenon that must be regretted not only in countries such as Italy, Spain and Scandinavia, which figure less prominently in works on comparative law, but also by any scholar who is interested in good ideas irrespective of their system of origin. But there is, potentially, a less attractive side to this phenomenon; and it comes closer to Posner's pejorative reference to self-interested reputing. Quite simply it could be said that repeated cross-citation by members of a group or a circle can foster (to the unwary) an impression of importance which is not quite reflected by other indicators.

Finally, one technical warning about the way we searched for the names of those on whom we chose to focus. Invariably, the search was made primarily on the basis of how the author uses his own name. John G Fleming is how the late Fleming signed his books. But courts have sometimes cited him as J G Fleming; and in academic literature, references also appear in the form of 'according to Fleming so and so is right whereas . . . .' Searches using surnames, alone, have not been conducted for they would obviously produce false positives. Other difficulties with electronic searches, associated with 'local' ways of citing authors, are described in greater detail in Appendix 3 below.

3. SOME RAW DATA

Table 1: Citations of comparatists in academic literature

Americans

Author \ Country	England	Germany	Italy	USA
Hans W Baade	6	6	1	418
George A Bermann	4	0	1	478
John P Dawson	28	2	4	601[27]
John G Fleming	84[28]	7	13	316
Mary Ann Glendon	24	4	18	1872
James Gordley	9	0	16	313
John Henry Merryman	15	9	14	836
Mathias Reimann	5	2	1	148
Rudolf B Schlesinger	5[29]	9[30]	15	398
Arthur T von Mehren	21	3	3	614
Alan Watson	24[31]	9[32]	9	456[33]

British

Author \ Country	England	Germany	Italy	USA
John Bell	51	6[34]	5	109[35]
Tony Honoré	89[36]	0[37]	1	403[38]
J A Jolowicz	88[39]	1	18	86[40]
Otto Kahn-Freund	96[41]	7[42]	10	223[43]
F H Lawson	53[44]	0	9	129[45]
Kurt Lipstein	21	8[46]	2	58
F A Mann	83	11[47]	4	231[48]
Basil S Markesinis	114[49]	6[50]	12	168[51]
Barry Nicholas	26[52]	4[53]	10	215[54]
Bernard Rudden	41[55]	1[56]	1	96[57]
Tony Weir	78[58]	8[59]	6	233[60]

German

Country / Author	England	Germany	Italy	USA
Ulrich Drobnig	6	58[61]	9	102
Eric Jayme	7	—[62]	24	69
Hein Kötz	65	73[63]	54	271[64]
Werner Lorenz	14	—[65]	2	34
Marcus Lutter	0	—[66]	12	72
Peter-Christian Müller-Graf	2	11[67]	8	26
Peter Schlechtriem	9	—[68]	16	86
Christian von Bar	6	—[69]	3	25
Reinhard Zimmermann	33	—[70]	17	126[71]
Konrad Zweigert	57	—[72]	31	268

French

Country / Author	England	Germany	Italy	USA
Xavier Blanc-Jouvain	3	0	4	18
René David	31	0[73]	48	269
Mireille Delmas-Marty	6	20[74]	10	41
Pierre Legrand	17	3	18	71
Horatia Muir Watt	0	6	8	8
Denis Tallon	14	5	27	60
André Tunc	29	3	31	134

Italian

Country / Author	England	Germany	Italy	USA
Guido Alpa	0	8	189	22
Michael Joachim Bonell	3	25[75]	25	127
Mauro Bussani	0	0	28	21
Mauro Cappelletti	38	11	59	423
Antonio Gambaro	0	0	54	22
Gino Gorla	2	0	100	35
Maurizio Lupoi	2	0	10	10
Ugo Mattei	4	0	53	144
Rodolfo Sacco	4	3[76]	230	89

Table 2: Citations of comparatists by courts

American

Author \ Country	Australia	Canada	England	Germany	USA
Hans W Baade	0	0	0	0	11
George A Bermann	0	1	0	0	19[77]
John P Dawson	1	0	1	0	21[78]
John G Fleming	81[79]	678[80]	32[81]	1	12[82]
Mary-Ann Glendon	0	9	1	0	12[83]
James Gordley	0	1	0	0	9
John Henry Merryman	0	1	1	0	16
Mathias Reimann	0	0	1	0	0
Rudolf B Schlesinger	0	0	0	0	8[84]
Arthur T von Mehren	0	1	0	0	30[85]
Alan Watson	0	0	0	0	1

British

Author \ Country	Australia	Canada	England	Germany	USA
John Bell	0	5[86]	1	0	0
Tony Honoré	23	1	16[87]	0	13[88]
J A Jolowicz	20	58	38[89]	0	7
Otto Kahn-Freund	10	5	2	0	4
F H Lawson	0	—	4	0	4
Kurt Lipstein	0	0	2	0	4
F A Mann	12	7	24[90]	0	1
Basil S Markesinis	11	6	26[91]	0	12[92]
Barry Nicholas	0	0	0[93]	1	26[94]
Bernard Rudden	2	0	0	0	0
Tony Weir	1	2	6[95]	0	2[96]

German

Country Author	Australia	Canada	England	Germany	USA
Ulrich Drobnig	1	0	0	0	1
Eric Jayme	0	0	0	3	1
Hein Kötz	0	2	7	0	3
Werner Lorenz	0	0	2	0	0
Marcus Lutter	0	0	0	0	0
Peter-Christian Müller-Graf	0	0	0	0	0
Peter Schlechtriem	0	0	0	4	5
Christian von Bar	1	0	5	1	0
Reinhard Zimmermann	0	0	3	0	0
Konrad Zweigert	0	2	4	2	5

French

Country Author	Australia	Canada	England	Germany	USA
Xavier Blanc-Jouvain	0	0	0	0	0
René David	0	3	4	0	3
Mireille Delmas-Marty	0	0	0	0	0
Pierre Legrand	0	11	0	0	0
Horatia Muir Watt	0	0	0	0	1
Denis Tallon	0	1	1	1	0
André Tunc	0	3	0	1	2

Italian

Country Author	Australia	Canada	England	Germany	USA
Guido Alpa	0	0	0	0	0
Michael Joachim Bonell	0	0	0	0	0
Mauro Bussani	0	0	0	0	0
Mauro Cappelletti	0	1	0	0	1
Antonio Gambaro	0	0	0	0	0
Gino Gorla	0	0	0	0	0
Maurizio Lupoi	0	0	0	0	0
Ugo Mattei	0	0	0	0	1
Rodolfo Sacco	0	0	0	0	0

4. DRAWING THE FIRST LESSONS

(a) Lesson 1: Citations Need to be Adjusted Downwards; Each Author to be Given Individual Attention

The first thing that became evident to us as the figures contained in the tables began to settle down in their final form was that, as far as British comparatists were concerned, their citation records were no less impressive than those of leading scholars who wrote on mainstream subjects.[97] This is a significant assertion since it could be seen as undermining the 'ghetto theory' discussed in chapters one and two, above. American comparatists, on the other hand, who had thus far not been measured in this way, revealed a much less substantial citation record than their fellow core-subject writers whose figures are given in the Shapiro and Landes/Posner articles. Nonetheless, in the USA a handful of comparatists have received a significantly larger number of citations than others, approaching the high levels of other jurists. Two tentative explanations can be advanced for this discrepancy; and they seem to be supported by the material provided in the notes to this chapter.

The first is that British comparatists seem to have spread their writing efforts over a wider range of topics than their American counterparts, hence the greater overall parity in citation figures. Seen in this way, the higher citation records were, on the whole, earned by their wider work and not by their comparative law endeavours. This explanation, however, brings the British scene more into line with the American, for once the British figures are discounted for the non-comparative citations, the difference between comparatists and non-comparatists becomes, once again, very significant.

The second is that the American comparatists have not yet been studied systematically as a group or individually (on the basis of a breakdown of their figures) since they never made it to Shapiro's list of the top one hundred.[98] Looking at them more closely, however, they reveal significant variations, some like Glendon and, less so, Langbein, Merryman, and Dawson still attaining very high totals. Here, for lack of space, we shall look at the one with the highest score (Glendon); and on the basis of her breakdown figures, we suggest that the other high scorers also deserve individual attention since what they have written on is important to comparatists.

First, results such as the above made us dwell more on these figures and the works that had attracted attention. In other words we felt that for the purposes of our study it was not enough to record total numbers of citations; a breakdown also had to be attempted to weed out the comparative from the non-comparative. This was an extremely time-consuming exercise. But the enquiry suggested that a fair number of citations (in some cases the majority) made to some of these authors should not be counted as citations to foreign law and comparative methodology. A downward adjustment of the overall number of citations was (and is) thus called for if we are trying to assess the impact these scholars have had *in their capacity as comparatists*. For reasons explained more fully below, we do not feel able to recommend a scientifically correct way to attempt such downward adjustment that would work across the board and suit the richly varied work of some of our authors. Classifying a piece as comparative or not, thus often presented problems of a particular kind. Instead, we have, therefore, attempted to slot our scholars into four sub-categories, each of which may call for a different appreciation. We also supplement these observations with footnote references, especially to Tables 1 and 3, which show the works which attracted judicial attention. These copious notes make for boring reading, yet they are essential for those (few) of our readers who might wish to see what exactly has been cited and make up their own minds as to whether these works can be classified as contributions to the study of foreign law and the development of a comparative methodology or whether, on the contrary, they represent a contribution to some other branch of the law (typically legal history, Roman law, jurisprudence, torts etc). The aim, however, has been the same again: to test the 'ghetto theory' as well as the veracity of the thesis advanced in this book, namely that the comparatists themselves have brought about their own neglect by those who shape law on a daily basis. We believe that though there may be differences in classification, our overall thesis remains a valid one.

The sub-categories into which our authors seem to fall are (at least) as follows.

First, we find some authors with an exceptionally high number of citations. As stated, Glendon comes under this category with citations in a phenomenally high figure of 1,854 documents. Closer scrutiny shows that her prolific activities as a writer of books have earned her this distinction. Thus, her *Rights Talk: The Impoverishment of Political Discourse* (1991) earns her citations in 544 documents; her *Abortion and Divorce in Western Law* (1987) 336; *A Nation Under Lawyers* (1994) 298; *The New Family and the New Property* (1981) 175, while her co-authored casebook on *Comparative Legal Traditions* (2nd edn, 1994) 48. In the light of her total number of citations we question her non-inclusion in Shapiro's list and must assume that she had not attained such levels at the time when he collected his data for his well-known article 'The Most Cited Legal Scholars.'[99]

Glendon's work calls for another caveat already indicated. Though the spirit of comparative law runs through her veins, not all of her works can be easily classed as works on comparative law. Her large citation score may thus reveal more about her overall impact on American academic literature than, say, her individual input in the creation of either a school of comparatists or a particular comparative methodology. A cognate reason may be the fact that most of her books could be brought under the more cited headings of jurisprudence, constitutional law, and family law rather than pure comparative law. These, however, we readily admit may be more debatable propositions. Thus, though Glendon's work needs some downward adjustment, there is no denying the fact that she remains a very highly cited author.

The problem raised by the overall classification of Glendon's work becomes more acute in the second category, which, likewise, includes some eminent figures. For here the bulk of citations comes from works, which are *obviously* linked to other branches of the law but, tenuously, also present a link with comparative law. I include here Fleming's textbook on *The Law of Torts*[100] which, in the American legal literature, earns him citations in 122 documents out of a total of 316. His more recent *The American Tort Process* is cited in 42 documents, but is less easily described as a work on comparative law. For though this is an inspiring book, especially for foreign (non-American) lawyers, it is, essentially, a sociological and statistical survey of American tort law in practice and thus cannot be counted as a pure or traditional work of comparative law. Nonetheless, in the way it looks at American law and brings out important differences with English law, it contains many useful insights for the art and science of comparing legal systems. The remainder of Fleming's citations go to a variety of articles, many dealing with particular problems of tort law, and only very few of his truly comparative law pieces receive (passing) attention, academic or judicial. In the light of the above, it is again necessary to adjust downwards (probably substantially) Fleming's overall figures given in Table 1 to reflect the fact that much of his cited work was of national, not comparative interest. Yet many of his colleagues regarded Fleming, especially during the last quarter of his life, as one of the USA's most knowledgeable comparatists. The statistics, however, do not reflect this view.

A variant of the above category—the third group—includes jurists who held chairs of comparative law but wrote books indisputably connected to one national legal system. Such output clearly has nothing whatever to do with the title of the chair of the author.[101] The connection here with comparative law is non-existent. In this third sub-category, Jolowicz, formerly Professor of Comparative Law at the University of Cambridge, furnishes an excellent illustration. For, in American legal journals, Jolowicz is cited in 86 documents: 10 are for articles on purely English law, a further 45 citations are to Winfield and Jolowicz *on Tort*, which Jolowicz successfully transformed (and not merely updated) while he acted as its editor between its seventh and ninth editions. Unlike Fleming's tort textbook, however, which can lay *some* claims to being a comparative work (since it looks at tort law simultaneously from the optics of English, Australian, New Zealand, and American law), Jolowicz' textbook is a straightforward textbook on English law. These two figures (45+10) thus suggest that 63.95 per cent of his total citations are dedicated to non-comparative law work. So a downward adjustment of his original figure of 86 to 31 seems more necessary than in Fleming's case. Interestingly enough, the overall pattern (in this as in so many of our other examples) does not change if one looks at Jolowicz' citations in English journals. For here one finds 57 citations out of 88 (ie 64.77 per cent of the total) are to writings on English law. So where does all this leave Jolowicz as a *comparative* lawyer? Here, as stated, we are not aiming to evaluate an author's scholarship but to measure its reputation. And if one is to go by statistics, alone, the impact of Jolowicz' work on other comparative lawyers and their literature seems small, though curiously enough it is slightly greater in the USA than in his own country. Smaller still, as Table 3 demonstrates, is the impact of his comparative writings on the courts. Why this is so, given his focus on comparative procedure, can only be a matter of speculation that could be resolved only when the nature of his ideas and proposals has been carefully analysed.

The same observations could be made of the work of Professor Guido Alpa, Professor of Civil Law at the University of Rome, who, like Glendon, has written extensively on most aspects of private and commercial law and whose teaching duties in Genoa (but not in Rome) include the teaching of English law. Though the bulk of his voluminous and scholarly output is, again, of a dogmatic nature and deals with a particular legal system (the Italian) it has, in the latter years of his life, been supplemented by articles with a comparative orientation, as well as a high profile activity in transnational law projects. This, however, has not yet surfaced in the form of citations, especially in the Anglo-American legal literature. So comparisons with 'full time' comparatists such as Bonell, Cappelletti, and, above all, Sacco, are difficult. Once again, therefore, assessments and evaluations of Alpa's *work as a comparatist* must be made with caution, his overall impressive figures in the charts calling for a substantial downward adjustment if one is looking at his work purely from the angle of comparative law. In this sense, Sacco (in our times) and Gorla (in the past) stand in a category of their own.

A different (downward) adjustment must be made for another holder of a chair of comparative law, Nicholas. Here, the reason is closely linked to the English 'practice' of entrusting comparative law to Romanists discussed in chapter one. This adjustment is necessitated by the fact that over half of all of Nicholas' citations in legal literature go to his work on Roman law. Thus, in the American legal literature, his edition of (Felix) Jolowicz' *Historical Introduction to Roman Law*[102] receives citations in 31 documents whilst his own elegant (but smaller) *Introduction to Roman Law* accounts for citations in 94 documents. By contrast, his very readable student textbook on *French Law of Contract*[103] earns him citations in 46 documents, indicating once again that when the dust settles, Nicholas' main contribution to law will be seen to be more in the area of Roman rather than comparative law. This (preliminary) assessment receives some support from the citations he has received (or, more accurately, not received) for one of his most scholarly articles on foreign law,[104] which boldly predicted a great future for the French Conseil constitutionnel at a time when established wisdom thought otherwise. This remarkable piece, full of comparative insights, has been met with an even more remarkable lack of appreciation, on both sides of the Channel.

Fourthly and finally, a group of comparatists seem to have earned the vast majority of their citations on the strength of one work which contains elements of comparative law but cannot be described as a straightforward example of comparative literature. Honoré pre-eminently falls into this category, with a large number of citations (267 out of a total of 371) coming from his widely (and rightly) admired book on *Causation in the Law* (co-authored with HLA Hart). Other works of his which receive attention include *Morality of Tort Law: Questions and Answers* (1995), *Responsibility and Fault* (1999), 'Responsibility and Luck: the Moral Basis of Strict Liability' (1988),[105] *Making Law Bind* (1987), *Emperors and Lawyers* (2nd edn, 1994), *Law in the Crisis of Empire* (1998), and *Tribonian* (1978).[106] But a cursory look over these titles again suggests that his scholarly legacy is to be found mainly in the areas of jurisprudence, tort law, and Roman law. Honoré's main contribution to the literature of comparative law—the comparative variation of his causation monograph published in the *Encyclopedia of Comparative Law* and his elegantly and tightly argued Hamlyn Lectures, which made constant use of French and German material—have been almost entirely ignored by authors and courts alike. Like Nicholas' work on the Conseil consitutionnel or Weir's elegant essay on 'Friendships in the Law,' these works confirm the trend: a scholarly piece without potential practical utility bites the dust. The really surprising thing about this statement is that such pieces not only leave the courts and practitioners unmoved; they also seem to have a minuscule impact on other academic writings if one is to judge from the number of times they have been cited in subsequent pieces. We readily confess our own astonishment; and even find the emerging picture quite disturbing.

In the world of Anglo-American legal literature, the great German comparatists Zweigert and Kötz fall into the same sub-category in the sense that over 66 per cent (203 out of 270) of the citations they receive come from their jointly written *An Introduction to Comparative Law*.[107] Unlike the other authors in this category, however, the Zweigert and Kötz book is clearly a comparative law masterpiece, which, moreover, reflects in practice the efficacy of the Rabel approach. So here the picture is the reverse of that given above; for authors such as Zweigert and Kötz have, in the Anglo-American law, made their reputation on the strength of their one masterpiece. Nonetheless, this book also presents us with a peculiarity. For popular though it has proved in the USA (and England), the citation rates by courts are markedly lower than those found in legal literature. This 'neglect' extends to the German courts, though, as we explain later on, this may be due to other, particularly German, factors. By contrast, Kötz's German law-oriented works have fared much better with the courts of his own country, something which may, again, be linked to the interpretation techniques prevalent among German courts and discussed later on. So here, we simply note the paradox, namely that an author mainly known as a comparative lawyer abroad is in his own country cited largely as a national lawyer.

At this point it is also necessary to say something about the Weir phenomenon. In the American legal literature, Weir receives citations in an impressive 233 documents. 204 of these, however, refer to him as the translator of the Zweigert/Kötz and four other German books which he has rendered into English. That leaves 29 documents citing him for his own works and of these only a handful are to comparative law works and not works on the English law of torts. This figure is so minute if compared with that of his translations' figure that it calls for a comment.

On the positive side, it shows the importance that a translator has in making important works of foreign authors known and cited in the Anglo-Saxon world. For Weir's efforts are undoubtedly the single most important factor in making *Introduction to Comparative Law* known outside its country of origin. Without it, Zweigert and Kötz, two of Germany's finest comparatists, would be substantially less influential in the common law than they are at present. Fleming was thus right in referring to Weir as the Boswell of the German comparatists.[108] This is no mean service to the science of comparative law; and the detailed analysis of his figures should not be seen as attempting to belittle his learning or his sui generis service to comparative law.

On the negative side, the citations to Weir's personal work demonstrate that some of his most truly stimulating works have remained substantially unnoticed. The Catala and Weir pieces in the *Tulane Law Review* have already been cited as a paradigm of comparative methodology and pithy formulation. It is thus greatly to be regretted that not only have they not found scholarly imitators, as the authors of this great series of articles had wished, but also failed to impress the literature in the USA[109] or England.[110] The fate (in citation terms, 4 only) of Weir's 'Friendships in the Law'[111] supports, if anything, even more strongly the (sad but, it seems, unassailable) argument that pure research has no impact on the visibility of the subject or its utility in the courtroom. We stress the fate of Weir's learning in this last piece for it is as impressive in its breadth of reading as it is for the beauty of some of its sentences.

The Weir phenomenon thus reveals in stark terms the perpetual clash between the 'elegant' and 'utilitarian' approach to comparative law and, indeed, to academic legal education as a whole. It also reconfirms the picture that has been revealed by the earlier statistics. One is thus inescapably forced either to re-appraise the lessons that a statistical survey of an author's work tells us about its value to other authors (and courts) or, alternatively, draw the lessons that emerge from such neglect of their orientation and message. The next generation of academic lawyers will have to reach their own conclusions.

The above observations, taken together and in conjunction with the use made by courts of the academic output of these scholars, can help draw two main conclusions. Both are put forward in a tentative manner.

The first is that the raw data thus far assembled suggests that the scholars included in our sample have had a very modest impact on courts and practitioners. The citation exercise lends some considerable support to the thesis advanced in chapters one and two above, for the majority of what these indisputably eminent scholars chose to write about has left the courts and practitioners almost totally unmoved. Where, by contrast, they chose to use their learning in a way that could provide guidance and inspiration to the courts, the latter immediately responded. Nicholas' early piece on unjust enrichment in the civil law and Louisiana law was immediately snatched up by the courts of that State accounting for over half of the judicial citations he has received in the USA. And the same happened with another 'practical' piece of his which was used by the German Federal Court.

The second is that citation studies are not, it has already been said, a measure of scholarship but only of reputation of scholarship. Yet even that must be treated with caution. For citation references are not, by themselves, convincing evidence of reputation. Some figures given in the Landes and Posner article cited earlier on support this scepticism.[112] For it is debatable (to say the least) to claim that Rawls' reputation is greater than Bentham's because the first receives 618 citations compared to the second's 499; or that Dworkin with 1,031 citations dwarfs Aristotle with 356.[113] Such figures and comparisons must lead one to scrutinise the method of collection of the data (are we limiting our searches to references in legal journals?), the impact of topicality and how it may wane with time, and other factors. Likewise, the extraordinarily high number of citations of highly accurate and usable treatises such as those written by Professor Laurence Tribe or Dean Prosser[114] can hardly suggest that the reputation of these scholars is higher than the less widely cited but intellectually more thoughtful works of such jurists as Ackerman, Calabresi or Glendon. Judge Posner makes a similar point when he writes: 'Citations are thus an imperfect proxy for reputation, and reputation itself an imperfect proxy for quality.'

(b) Lesson 2: Reputation and Legacy in Comparative Law

What we have said about scholarship and reputation does not complete our study. We have to complement the questions asked thus far with one more: have the above scholars, otherwise than through their work and the citation it has received, left a quantifiable impact on their subject?

A thought which emerges clearly from careful reflection of the figures given above is that the frequency of citation of an author's work gives a fairly good picture of the impact that his work has on others. But this may be only part of the wider picture that deals with his contribution to the successful establishment of his subject. At this level we are thus dealing with 'legacy,' not scholarship, nor reputation of scholarship. In one sense it is a variation on the previous theme; but it is one which cannot be explored solely with the aid of statistics. And it links with the contents of the previous and following chapters.

Like reputation of scholarship, legacy, too, may not necessarily be linked to an author's scholarly merits. For a jurist may contribute to the well-being of his subject in ways other than writing scholarly pieces in his chosen area or being cited in what he has to say about it. This point deserves its own reflections. To put it differently, an author may have played a determinant role in establishing comparative law in his country even though this is not reflected, or inadequately reflected, by the citation studies or an enhanced personal profile. The ways this can come about are many. For instance—and we offer these only as illustrations—a scholar may (a) leave successors; (b) create a methodology which others follow; (c) create institutes or centres, which then act as research and teaching hubs;[115] or (d) otherwise help the subject to acquire roots in the law curriculum of his country by creating novel networks with others. I discussed (b) in chapter one above; and said as much as I wish to say at this stage about (c). Under (d) I would include such projects as the Tunc/Chloros creation of the *double maîtrise* programme between Paris I and King's College, London, in my view the most successful double qualification programme in the United Kingdom today. So let us say a few words about the first form a legacy can take.

For this we must return to Sacco, for he offers an excellent example for discussion under this heading. As stated in the first chapter of this book, he was the moving force behind the establishment of most modern chairs of comparative law in Italy and thus played a key role in strengthening its roots.[116] Citation studies do not demonstrate this directly. But it is a fact and, actually, so important that indirectly it also affects citology. For Sacco strongly supported many (of his very able) former pupils to get these chairs and they now, understandably I think, are handsomely repaying the influence he had on the formation of their legal minds by using his method and citing his works. In the long term, Sacco's virtual colonisation of the Italian law schools thus proved more successful than a similar attempt made by Cappelletti in the 1970s and 1980s. Perhaps this is due in part to the fact that the former (unlike the latter) managed to maintain the loyalty of his disciples—to him, personally, as well as to his method.[117] But those who know something of the Italian scene must also complement this picture with a postscript. This is a note on the opposition and even resentment—to be expected some would say—which the forceful pursuit of Sacco's empire building has also, it seems to me, brought in its wake. Thus, if the final verdict on the value of his scholarship remains, for some at least, open to final evaluation, his success in dominating for most of the post-war period the internal Italian scene cannot be in doubt. In citation terms, however, Cappelletti beats Sacco (in the American literature at any rate) by a ratio of 5 to 1, though this may be partly due to the fact that the former wrote most of his later work in English.

The above observations about legacy, and the different ways it is conferred, are, in some respects, self-evident. What is interesting is finding the illustrations that support them in different countries. The Sacco example of 'chair-building' for instance— good or bad, that is not the point here—for structural reasons could not have occurred in England or, even, in Germany where the federalist fragmentation in matters of education makes the pursuit of such a national policy impossible. In each country, in other words, the ways of leaving a legacy are to some extent shaped by the conditions of university life appropriate to that country. But it is also important to make, indeed stress, these points here in order to help dispel the impression that we may have overemphasised the citation criterion for the purposes of determining the contribution a particular comparative law scholar has made to his subject. This sub-section, along with earlier remarks, demonstrates that we have tried to adopt a multifaceted approach to the problem we set ourselves to examine. But what, then, is the conclusion that emerges from such effort?

For the reasons suggested earlier on, British comparatists have not been particularly adept in pursuing targets such as the above in order to secure a strong position for the subject in the law curriculum. The world they worked in, it must be stressed, did not favour such strategies. But the statistical evidence we managed to assemble also suggests that by splitting their efforts among many subjects and failing to write pieces that would make an impact on the courts they failed to use the full potential of their formidable talents for the good of their subject. The consequences of such neglect were not insignificant, for, first, they can be seen from the fact that some extremely interesting and learned works remain (or are fast becoming) unnoticed. Second, because now that the globalisation of markets demands the knowledge and dissemination of foreign law, we have not the means to facilitate it. It is thus becoming imperative for British comparatists to draw conclusions from the evidence presented here and to re-think a survival strategy for the subject. For the lack of judicial attention accorded to their work, combined with a minuscule number of references in legal literature, should make them wonder whether the targeting of a different audience would not make their knowledge more widespread and their subject more central to university studies. My own efforts to interest the courts may, of course, not be attractive to all—maybe most—of my professional colleagues. But the evidence that we have collected above suggests that it may have a better chance of reviving interest in the subject than the kind of output we have had thus far which, clearly, has not worked. If the figures supplied to support this are seen as slender (and, on balance, they could be seen as such despite some notable recent examples such as the *Fairchild*[118] decision of the House of Lords) I would reply that the method has not been tried long enough and should thus be given a better chance before it is condemned as a failure.

(c) Lesson 3: The Power of School Citation and Promotion

Thirdly, we return to a point touched at the beginning of this essay and earlier on in this concluding part. This is the power of auto-citation, of 'school citation' or even, one could say, plain propaganda. The best evidence for this phenomenon comes largely from the activities of a new generation of Italian comparatists currently working within the USA on a part-time or full-time basis. This group has overcome the 'drawback of language' and is making up for lost time by constantly citing like-minded scholars, again of Italian origin. Thus, of Sacco's 89 citations in American journals, one quarter come from his closest pupils. More precisely: 13 come from Mattei, 3 from Bussani and 3 from Monateri. A handful of authors (Professors Gordley, Gerber, Kasirer) cite him in two documents each. The remainder are single citations in different documents. This interesting 'Italian habit' seems to be reflected in Italy, itself, and the Italian literature on an even larger scale. For there, too, a substantial number of citations to the Sacco group (some these days like to be known as the Trento circle) come from each other but not, or less so, from other Italian colleagues. Finally, Table 5, below, suggests a slightly different aspect of the same phenomenon namely, that scholars also tend to receive most of their citations from colleagues from their own country. For Table 5 shows that, for instance, Cappelletti receives 59.4 per cent (35 out of 59) of his citations from his fellow countrymen, Sacco receives a hefty 64 per cent of his from Italians (39 out 61), whilst Alpa a staggering 71.4 per cent (25 of his 35). The sample is, once again, too small to justify safe conclusions about how well-known these authors are outside their own country. On the other hand one must note that, first, these figures come from a truly comparative law journal and, secondly, that they do not deviate markedly from the pattern of citations that these same authors received in the samples collected from individual countries. Moreover, one must note the pattern of other scholars who seem to receive equal attention from the writers in most major legal systems, eg, Kötz and Zimmermann seem to fall into this category, as well as the late David (and the editor of the latest editions of his grand oeuvre, Professor Jauffret Spinosi).

Such patterns and, especially, the cross-referencing between 'friends and members of the same school' could prove misleading to those who only have a faint acquaintance of the comparative law scene in countries other than their own. They can even exaggerate the importance of particular pieces by investing them with an aura of importance that is not really deserved. An example of this can, perhaps, be found in Mattei's assertion[119] that 'Schlesinger's work in Europe has been extensively cited and I believe that the volume on Formation of Contracts has received more book reviews in the old continent than any other book published in the US.' If the statement is taken literally to refer to book reviews it may well be true. The second part of it is so open-ended, we were unable to check its accuracy. But the first part strikes me as being proved erroneous by the statistics we have managed to assemble. For the figures in Table 5, composed from France's leading comparative law journal (*Revue Internationale de Droit Comparé* of the years 1980–2001) do not suggest any particular prominence of Schlesinger's work—indeed quite the opposite: a comparative neglect. And the same picture emerges from Table 1, giving citation figures in the legal literature of four countries. This, likewise, places Schlesinger third (from the bottom) of a list of 11 American scholars. Schlesinger's two-volume work *Formation of Contracts: A Study of the Common Core of Legal Systems* (1968), which particularly attracts Mattei's attention, receives a mere 23 citations in the entire American legal literature of the last 20 years. According to the same table, the picture in England and Germany is hardly different. Table 3 completes the picture by measuring the impact which a scholar's work has had on courts of law and, again, Schlesinger figures poorly. But one must again point out that this need not be a uniquely Italian phenomenon; one could easily find even in England scholars with a tendency to overpraise the work of some of their colleagues and underplay that of others. But if the practice is spreading, it does not mean that it should be condoned.

The above comments on the work of one author reinforce in our view the feeling that the scholarly evaluation of his work cannot be assessed solely by looking at his citation rates. The point was made in chapter two above, and is repeated here for greater emphasis. But statistics can help question hyperbolic statements about a work when (allegedly) based on quantitative assessments. More generally, though they cannot 'make' scholarly reputations, they can help cut down to size claims made by others about them, giving a sense of dry reality to hagiographic treatment of certain authors. The particular example we looked at—and others could be added—may also offer a concrete illustration of Posner's theory that some citations do little more than promote the citator's own intellectual agenda. But the statistics are also an indicator, albeit only one, of the impact a scholar's work has had on others. This then, as stated earlier on, is a facet of the science of reputology that needs more research.

This somewhat cynical attitude towards such multiplication of citations can be tested if we compare the citation rates of some of the above-mentioned Italian scholars with that of another—some would say the greatest—of Italian comparatists: Gorla. For Gorla suffers not only because he did not write in English but also from the fact that none of his disciples chose to pursue a career in the USA and make his name known there[120] or create an international Gorla school. Gorla's work is thus hardly known in the Anglo-Saxon world, which is a great loss to knowledge since many in the know would probably regard him as a scholar and a methodologist of the first order, especially in the way he combined the task of contemporary comparison and historical research.

Table 3: Citations of comparatists in *Revue International de Droit Comparé* 1980–2001 (by country of citator)

American

Cited Author	Canada	England	France	Germany	Italy	USA
Hans W Baade	0	0	1	0	0	0
George A Bermann	0	0	1	0	2	0
John P Dawson	0	0	2	0	0	0
John G Fleming	2	0	6	0	2	0
Mary Ann Glendon	0	0	8	4	4	0

American (*cont.*)

Cited Author	Canada	England	France	Germany	Italy	USA
James Gordley	2	0	8	2	8	1
John Henry Merryman	0	0	8	3	6	0
Mathias Reimann	0	0	1	0	0	0
Rudolf B Schlesinger	0	0	2	0	0	0
Arthur T von Mehren	0	0	4	1	1	0
Alan Watson	3	0	5	3	2	4

British

Cited Author	Canada	England	France	Germany	Italy	USA
John Bell	0	1	6	0	0	0
Tony Honoré	0	0	1	0	0	0
J A Jolowicz	0	7	8	7	0	0
Otto Kahn-Freund	0	0	5	4	1	0
F H Lawson	0	1	4	3	0	2
Kurt Lipstein	0	0	2	1	0	0
F A Mann	0	0	3	1	4	0
Basil S Markesinis	0	6	14	1	6	0
Barry Nicholas	0	1	3	0	2	0
Bernard Rudden	0	0	1	0	0	0
Tony Weir	0	0	2	0	0	1

German

Cited Author	Canada	England	France	Germany	Italy	USA
Ulrich Drobnig	2	0	3	3	2	1
Eric Jayme	0	0	2	3	1	0
Hein Kötz	0	0	19	12	18	0
Werner Lorenz	0	0	1	0	0	0
Marcus Lutter	0	0	1	1	0	0
Peter-Christian Müller-Graf	0	0	3	5	2	0
Peter Schlechtriem	0	0	3	2	6	0
Christian von Bar	0	0	3	2	0	0
Reinhard Zimmermann	0	0	7	6	10	0
Konrad Zweigert	0	1	9	6	2	0

French

Cited Author	Canada	England	France	Germany	Italy	USA
Xavier Blanc-Jouvain	0	0	13	1	4	0
René David	1	23	31	6	12	2
Mireille Delmas-Marty	0	0	13	1	4	2
Pierre Legrand	2	6	16	2	5	0
Horatia Muir Watt	0	0	12	1	0	0
Jauffret Spinosi	0	2	11	5	8	2
Denis Tallon	0	0	24	9	7	1
André Tunc	3	7	42	3	6	4

Italian

Cited Author	Canada	England	France	Germany	Italy	USA
Guido Alpa	0	0	9	1	25	0
Michael Joachim Bonell	0	0	6	4	9	0
Mauro Bussani	0	0	1	0	4	0
Mauro Cappelletti	0	1	13	10	35	0
Antonio Gambaro	0	0	0	0	4	0
Gino Gorla	0	0	7	0	18	0
Maurizio Lupoi	0	0	2	0	12	0
Ugo Mattei	0	4	13	0	16	0
Rodolfo Sacco	0	2	16	2	39	2
Anna De Vita	0	0	2	0	11	0

of inspiration and to comparative law as an accepted interpretative tool. In the field of private law, Zweigert argued 50 years ago in favour of comparative law as a universal method of interpretation (*universale Interpretationsmethode*);[137] and Professor Peter Häberle is perhaps the most prominent contemporary constitutional expert to promote comparative law as a fifth interpretative method (*fünfte Auslegungsmethode*).[138] But as Drobnig pointed out in 1986, the conservative attitude of mainstream academic opinion (so-called *herrschende Lehre*) has influenced generations of lawyers in Germany and is clearly reflected by the approach generally taken by the courts in the interpretation of the law.[139]

More than half a century after Zweigert's much cited inaugural lecture in Tübingen, Kötz, one of Germany's most respected comparatists, continues to recommend the use of comparative law by judges. But his recent analysis of *Bundesgerichtshof* decisions has shown little more use of foreign reasoning than did a count conducted by Drobnig some 14 years earlier.[140] Comparing figures from different courts is, of course, a dangerous exercise; and at the very least it must take into account the far larger number of judgments handed down annually by the higher German courts compared to their English counterparts. Nonetheless, on this score, it is tempting to give the lead to the recent generation of British judges, for they have proved to be more broad-minded than their German counterparts. The above assertion must, nonetheless, be further qualified by proposing some distinctions.

Taking a closer look at the use of comparative law by Germany's highest civil court, both Drobnig and Kötz identify two basic categories of decisions. Areas in which the court has shown itself willing to turn to comparative law include transportation and maritime issues, the international sale of goods based on CISG, and cases dealing with international private law (eg, family law disputes). A further area expected to join this category includes a wide array of rules which were introduced in the wake of European legislation and explicitly aim at harmonisation (though the BGH thus far does not appear to have used comparative material in this context).[141] In dealing with German provisions which have their origin in international treaties,[142] in special topics such as maritime law,[143] or provisions which explicitly call for comparative considerations (Article 36 EGBGB and Article 7 CISG), the Bundesgerichtshof seems fairly willing to take into account foreign material. The common denominator of these decisions—their subject proximity to internationally harmonised rules or the conflict of laws—clearly forces judges to look out of the window, otherwise obscured by the curtains of legal tradition. It could be argued that in this type of legal dispute, comparative law has established itself as an essential requirement in the evaluation of many cases. The analysis of Drobnig thus shows that approximately 50 per cent of the decisions of the Bundesgerichtshof and the German Courts of Appeal (Oberlandesgerichte) dealing with the major international treaties (eg, the Warsaw Convention) make use of foreign material. Interestingly, the percentage of cases dealing with such material is significantly lower (approximately 3 per cent) with the two Conventions on cheques and bills of exchange signed in Geneva in 1930/1931. This can be explained by the fact that these two Conventions were fully incorporated into German law, whereas the other treaties were merely ratified by Germany and thus remain distinctly international in character.[144] As the next part of this section will show, German law (or provisions which are at least regarded as genuinely German) will attract much less comparative attention from practitioners.

The second category involves cases which lack the inherent link to foreign law shared by the first group. It is this field of 'genuine' German law that most comparatists regard as the true test (*'Kürprogramm'*)[145] for the willingness of courts to look beyond the boundaries of their own legal system.[146] In this category of cases, the results are meagre. Drobnig indentified seven decisions of the Bundesgerichtshof, one decision of the Federal Administrative Court (Bundesverwaltungsgericht) and two decisions of the Bundesverfassungsgericht resorting to foreign law. Writing a few years later, Kötz pointed to seven further decisions of the Bundesgerichtshof and concluded that the voluntary use of the comparative method is still confined to exceptional cases in Germany. These decisions referred to issues of tort law,[147] family law,[148] labour law,[149] criminal law,[150] and administrative law.[151] Interestingly enough, Bernhard Aubin, writing in 1970,[152] argued that the Reichsgericht had been more open to the use of comparative material. Thus, 17 decisions, handed down between 1909 and 1928, made use of foreign legal material, a large number of these cases dealing with issues related to limited liability companies.[153]

In a another study on the use of foreign material in cases involving only constitutional law issues, Jörg Manfred Mössner counted 24 decisions of the Bundesverfassungsgericht which had recourse to comparative law. To these he adds two further decisions from state constitutional courts, two decisions of the Bundesgerichtshof and one decision of the Landgericht Lübeck.[154] These decisions fall into the second category of cases identified by Drobnig and Kötz, and deal with the interpretation of basic concepts of the German Constitution making use of foreign material.[155]

Just as interesting is to see which (foreign) legal systems provided ideas for inspiration. In the decisions looked at by Mössner, the USA heads the list with nine examples. It is followed by Switzerland with eight, France with four, the United Kingdom with three, Austria with three, Italy with two, and the Netherlands, Norway and Sweden each having one. The International Court of Justice provides one instance; and 11 cases refer to foreign experience in general without identifying a particular country.[156]

These statistics suggest that courts seem more willing to look at systems outside Germany's own (private law) legal family when dealing with constitutional issues than they are in matters pertaining to private law (where comparative material is more often taken from Austria and Swizerland).[157] This would suggest that the language barrier may play a part in this 'reluctance' to consult foreign material but that it is by no means an insurmountable obstacle.

The studies also indicate that German courts use the comparative method with caution, in some instances even with an undesirable degree of uncertainty. Many comparative observations are thus left undocumented, with decisions often refering vaguely 'to the situation in other legal systems' without further qualification,[158] or making use of unspecified quotations.[159] Given the German punctiliousness this is a somewhat surprising practice and may suggest lack of confidence on the part of the citing judge. Equally understandable but perhaps also surprising, is a certain degree of 'mistrust' of material, which comes from a different legal family. This is obvious in one of the early leading wrongful life decisions.[160] Nonetheless, it is surprising given that this was a topic that did not depend for its solution on a specific legal provision of the German Civil Code but dealt with a wider philosophical issue that transcends state borders and even religious beliefs.

By contrast the Bundesverfassungsgericht has, as already stated, shown itself more open to comparative law *in general*,[161] though the so-called Spiegel-decision[162] reflects some degree of uncertainty as far as comparative *methodology* is concerned. Here, four judges referred to foreign material in answering the question whether members of the press can refuse to give evidence in criminal proceedings involving treason and opted against such a right.[163] But the other four openly rejected this argument. The main reason was because it centred only on the foreign statutes and failed to take into account the respective legal systems as a whole, the legal practice pertaining to these statutes, and extra-legal factors such as the democratic convictions of societies in general.[164] One could see this as a good example of the Sacco theory of 'legal formants'; but no such citation was made.

Finally, it seems noteworthy that over 80 per cent of the decisions identified by Mössner (in 1973), Drobnig (in 1986) and Kötz (in 2000) were delivered by the Bundesgerichtshof and the Bundesverfassungsgericht between 1951 and 1974; only three decisions with comparative input were identified over the past 14 years. Subject to further analysis (especially of constitutional and labour law cases), this could be an indication that the use of comparative arguments has become less frequent in court decisions over the past three decades than was the case in earlier times. A convincing explanation for this decline has still to be advanced; perhaps the result is more due to the influence of individual judges or special historical circumstances than to any wider reason connected with the use of comparative law in courts. This interpretation is supported by the study of Aubin, who identifies three (partially overlapping) 'waves' of decisions with comparative input. The first covers the years 1910 to 1924, with a sequence of six decisions of the Reichsgericht on limited liability companies within five years alone, and two further decisions on § 7 Road Traffic Act[165] and family law[166] (all eight decisions focusing on Austrian law). The second phase is

between 1920 to 1928, with four Reichsgericht decisions on §
315 BGB,[167] trademarks,[168] insolvency law,[169] and § 138 BGB[170]
(these decisions involve French, English and Swiss law). The
third period covers 1951 to 1961 and has a total of 11 decisions
on private, criminal and public law issues.[171]

Finally, it should be noted that German judges use comparative
arguments mainly to support solutions they already seem to have
reached by traditional ways of reasoning; foreign material is thus
often mentioned only as a supportive addition.[172] In this sense,
the practice of the German judges seems to be comparable to their
British counterparts. We have found no German equivalent to
Greatorex (discussed in greater detail in chapter four below).

How can this reluctancy of German judges to use foreign
material—labelled as a kind of '*horror alieni juris*' by Hans
Dölle[173]—be explained? Apart from the influence exerted
by the traditional canon of interpretative methods mentioned
earlier, lack of judicial time and lack of comparative input on
the side of counsel might account for some of the difficulties.[174]
More importantly, it could (even in Germany) be the lack of up-
to-date comparative material, carefully compiled by specialists
and packaged to meet the needs of practitioners, which might
lie at the heart of the matter. Pointedly (and much in line with
the views presented in this sequence of essays), Kötz regards
the provision of such material by comparatists as a debt overdue to the science of comparative law (*Bringschuld der rechts-
vergleichenden Wissenschaft*).[175] Finally, it might also be the
caution of German judges to assume the role of the law-giver
wherever the rules of the system fail to provide answers.[176]
Their tendency to look for solutions within the framework of
positive law or acknowledged academic literature might make
it difficult for them to use comparative law where the method
is at its best. Yet the decisions of both the Bundesgerichtshof
and the Bundesverfassungsgericht on the question of recovery
of damages for non-pecuniary losses (§ 253 BGB) are clear
examples of judge-made law contra legem.

(c) Competing Sources of Comparative Material

We have already noted in the previous chapters the important
role that the various German institutes of comparative law have

played in developing both the study of foreign law and comparative methodology in Germany. Paradoxically, these institutions may also have contributed—indirectly—to the poor citation record of foreign material by German courts. This is because of the widespread practice of obtaining from these institutes written opinions (*wissenschaftliche Gutachten*) about the state of foreign law whenever such knowledge is required by the rules of private international law, and many court libraries have acquired extensive collections of such expert opinions.[177] This material can usually not be accessed by interested third parties. Many *Gutachten*, however, are now published annually in the Nomos-series *Gutachten zum Internationalen und Ausländischen Privatrecht* (edited by Drobnig and Kegel). Covering a broad range of topics and including opinions on the state of the law in countries around the world going back to 1996, this series is published on the initiative of the German *Rat für Internationales Privatrecht*. The 2001 volume includes 43 opinions from some of Germany's most prestigious insitutes,[178] covering, eg, questions of contract law, commercial and company law, family law, the law of inheritance and precedural law. Well over 20 different legal systems are thereby surveyed, each opinion giving the facts of the case, the questions put forward by the German court, a general statement on the law in the foreign jurisdiction, and the answers given by the institute.[179] Similarly, the Bundesverfassungsgericht has asked the German Foreign Office to provide reports on foreign legal systems (which do not appear in the text of the judgment itself),[180] and has even invited foreign experts to report directly to the court.[181]

(d) Comparative Law in the Field of Legislative Law Reform

Finally, we note that this 'suspicion' towards foreign law described above is not reflected in the law reform process when undertaken by the legislator.[182] Dölle has thus demonstrated that the German law-giver has made extensive use of foreign material over the past 100 years. Starting with the preparation of the Commercial Code (*Handelsgesetzbuch*) of 1897, which was influenced by an Austrian proposal as well as Dutch, Spanish and French ideas, Germany has constantly turned to other countries (including the United Kingdom, France, Spain, Norway, Sweden, Swizerland, Austria, and the USA) in order to gather new ideas for codification. This has occurred in such diverse areas as commercial law, design patents and copyright law, bankruptcy law, civil procedure, anti-trust legislation, criminal law, and nuclear energy law. The German Civil Code of 1900 and the Basic Law (*Grundgesetz*) of 1949, undoubtedly the two most prominent pieces of German legislation, were both influenced by comparative work.[183]

This obvious difference between the use of foreign material in the course of legislation as contrasted to adjudication by German courts can be explained by the freedom (and indeed the function) of the law-giver to mould society according to the prevailing political convictions of the time. Courts of law, on the other hand, must respect the notion of legal certainty and are thus less free to 'import' foreign solutions to a given problem.[184]

Notwithstanding this greater openess, one must also note that in such exercises the German legislator tends to rely on what *German* academics have said about foreign law *in German* and seems reluctant to make open use of the original material which emanates from other jurisdictions. This is confirmed by our own research, which was focused on the three pieces of legislation shown in Table 5 below: the regulation of standard contract terms in 1975 (*Gesetz zur Regelung des Rechts der Allgemeinen Geschäftsbedingungen*),[185] the reform of the German law of obligations in 2001 (*Gesetz zur Modernisierung des Schuldrechts*),[186] and the reform of German tort law in 2002 (*Entwurf eines Zweiten Gesetzes zur Änderung schadensersatzrechtlicher Vorschriften*).[187] We stress that our analysis is restricted to the explanatory sections of the respective government proposals. It can therefore only serve as a starting-point for a more detailed survey, which would have to include, inter alia, the preparatory work conducted within the ministries responsible for individual reform projects, the results of ministerial or parliamentary commissions and hearings, and any written opinions submitted by external experts and institutes.[188] This material could reveal direct access to foreign material.

On first glance, references to foreign law found in these important reform projects can be classified into three distinct categories.

116 *Comparative Law in the Courtroom and Classroom*

The first category consists of *general references* to the situation
in other legal systems. These are not attributed to any particular author and include statements on the law in specific countries or regions. Though not appearing in Table 5, it is
significant to note that the explanatory sections of many
German bills refer to the legal situation in 'other systems' or
(with regard to the European Union) in 'other Member States'
without pinpointing certain jurisdictions. These generalised
statements indicate that more comparative work has, in fact,
been done behind the scenes even though it is not apparent
from the published material itself.

The second category contains references to the situation in
other legal systems as described in *German sources*.

Finally, foreign law is also taken into account by the direct use
of *foreign authors and research projects*. Table 5 may thus be of use.

Table 5: References to comparative law in German legislation

	General references	*German sources*	*Foreign sources*
Contract terms	France Israel Italy Sweden United States Council of Europe	Hauss Neumayer Quittnat Raiser von Hippel Yardin	None
Obligations	Austria France GDR Greece Italy Netherlands Scandinavia Switzerland United Kingdom European Court of 　Justice European Union UN Sales Law	Basedow Kessler Stoll von Caemmerer Zimmermann Zweigert/Kötz	Bucher (Sw) Jud/Welser (Aus) Lando Lando/Beale Salleilles Treitel Viney Lando-Commission Unidroit
Tort law	ADR Treaty CRTD Treaty EC Directive 2407/92 EC Directive 2027/97	Braschos Diedrich von Bar	None

A closer look at these references reveals that the kind of foreign material that has been used for information and inspiration is in all cases specific, focused and informative rather than speculative, sociological or anthropological—further confirmation of the theses found in this book about the kind of comparative law which leaves a tangible impact. Comparative considerations found in the *Schuldrechtsreform*—triggered by the need to give effect to several European directives, but also to address some significant structural defects of the German Civil Code—thus focus largely on five key areas. They are: pre-contractual liability (*culpa in contrahendo*), the collapse of the basis of a contractual agreement (*Wegfall der Geschäftsgrundlage*), standard contract terms (*allgemeine Geschäftsbedingungen*), irregularities of performance (*Leistungsstörungen*) and rules on prescription (*Verjährung*). As the following three examples show, foreign law is often used to argue in favour of an overall change in structure, whereas German law is drawn upon as far as the details of a reform proposal are concerned.

Thus, the idea to codify pre-contractual liability (§ 311 BGB) is discussed with references to developments in France as described by authors (as old as) Salleilles and (as contemporary as) Viney. Other countries taken into account include the USA (as described by Kessler) and Switzerland (as described by Bucher, who also gives a reference to article 1337 of the Italian *Codice civile*). The final solution, itself, however, is exclusively based on German case law.[189]

This is also true of the references to foreign law found in the context of the new § 313 BGB, which codifies the doctrine of *Wegfall der Geschäftsgrundlage*. While drawing attention to Italian, Greek, and Dutch law as an argument for the proposed codification of the doctrine, the draft clearly attempts to develop the substance of the notion along the lines of German case law. Codification is thereby set in contrast to the situation in England, the USA, Swizerland and France as described by Zweigert and Kötz. These countries rely on case law to resolve problems resulting from a drastic change in the basis of a transaction (as Germany did until the enactment of the *Schuldrechtsreform*).[190]

Similarly, the inclusion of standard contract terms in the BGB,[191] until recently regulated by a separate statute, is justified by reference to the Dutch *Nieuw Burgerlijk Wetboek* of 1992 and similar recommendations put forward by the Lando Commission. Despite this change, the content of this new section reflects German law.[192]

In other areas, foreign sources are used as a guideline for quite substantial changes. This is true, eg, for the new system of *Leistungsstörungen* (irregularities of performance). Impossibility (*Unmöglichkeit*), late performance (*Verzug*), faulty performance (*Schlechterfüllung*) and the so-called 'positive breach of contract' (*positive Forderungsverletzung*) are now substituted by a unitary notion (*Pflichtverletzung*) codified in the new § 280 BGB. This substantial change is justified by references to international developments in general and the work of the Lando Commission as well as the approach taken by the UN Convention on the International Sale of Goods in particular.[193] Another example is the introduction of a rule dealing with the termination of long-term contracts (*Dauerschuldverhältnisse*) in § 314 BGB. The extensive reference to Articles 1559–1570 *Codice civile* and Article 73 of the UN Convention on the International Sale of Goods indicate that these two codifications have had a strong influence on the German solution.[194] Further areas where foreign sources functioned as a model in the reform of the German law of obligations include the termination of contracts (*Rücktritt*),[195] the reform of § 321 BGB (dealing with the significant deterioration of a party's financial position in mutual contracts)[196] and the rules on prescription.[197]

Finally, in some instances, comparative considerations serve to confirm the German position, and foreign solutions are openly rejected. This is true, eg, of the decision to uphold the notion of fault as a central requirement for contractual liability. The issue was discussed in the government proposal on the *Schuldrechtsreform* and contrasted to the Anglo-American approach as described by Zweigert and Kötz.[198]

As far as the reform of tort law is concerned, comparative considerations feature in two areas. The introduction of a general claim for pain and suffering (*Schmerzensgeld*) in the area of strict liability and contract is justified with references to the situation in other European countries as described by Braschos, von Bar and Diedrich.[199] It must be stressed, however, that this comparative input merely serves as an additional argument to underscore a change already initiated by German developments.[200] A second reference to international trends as described by von Bar deals with the protection of passengers in the course of non-commercial and free transportation,[201] a problem already addressed and solved by the French courts 30 years ago. In line with its solutions, the draft proposes to include this category of victims in the existing strict liability regime.

Some final observations can be made on the sources used in the process of comparative law reform. For (obvious) legal and (less apparent) political reasons,[202] the *Schuldrechtsreform* in particular draws heavily on international material. As pointed out above, solutions offered by the UN Convention on the International Sale of Goods, the Principles of European Contract Law published by UNIDROIT and the work of the Lando Commission were adopted by the government proposal in a great number of cases. Without endorsing excessive harmonisation, we think that this tendency of the German lawgiver to resort to refined concepts as found in model codes or principles of law marks the way for any comparative effort. To have impact, comparative work must be focused on clearly defined issues and produce ideas which can be easily used in the process of law reform or in the decision of cases.

A second observation concerns the language of the foreign material used in the process of German law reform. As stated, most references concern material which is presented in German. Apart from the German sources (eg, on American, English, French and Swiss law), this is true of the general references to Austria, Switzerland and the German Democratic Republic, as well as the references to Bucher (on Swiss law) and Jud/Welser (on Austrian law). The large number of unspecified references to the UN Convention on the International Sale of Goods found in the explanatory section of the *Schuldrechtsreform* can equally be counted to this category, as it seems that exclusively German authors writing on this corpus of law were used in developing the draft.[203] The close legal and cultural ties between Germany, Austria and Switzerland thereby only explain the frequent use of material from these two countries, and the fact that American, English, French or Israeli law is accessed by reference to German academics rather

than original sources calls for other explanations. Many citations probably result from practical factors, such as the accessibility of German material or limited linguistic resources (as in
the case of the reference to Israeli law as described by
Quittnat).[204] In other cases, it might be the condensed form in
which some prominent German authors have presented a
fairly wide range of foreign material. This observation is especially true for Zweigert and Kötz (*Einführung in die Rechtsvergleichung*) and von Bar (*Gemeineuropäisches Deliktsrecht*). Yet
other German comparatists are cited because they discuss
foreign law in direct context with the topic of a given reform
project; this is obvious in the case of Professor Jürgen Basedow
(*Die Reform des Deutschen Kaufrechts*), who is cited frequently in
connection with the *Schuldrechtsreform*. Though difficult to
ascertain on the basis of this limited survey, the impulse to rely
on information which has been converted into familiar terminology and concepts, and the effects of national reputation and
influence of acknowledged German academics, might be additional factors which influence the choice of comparative
sources.

To conclude this short excursion into the realm of law reform
on a cautious note, we again stress that our observations merely
serve to open the door to a fairly unexplored terrain. The influence of comparative law on legislation deserves closer analysis,
which will, hopefully, reveal more intricate patterns than was
possible on the basis of the 300 very condensed pages of legislative explanation that we were able to look into at this stage.

6. THE CASE OF SOUTH AFRICA

South Africa deserves special comment due to the innovative
approach that the country adopted towards comparative law
after the demise of apartheid. We thus offer this as our last
illustration of the thesis advanced in this and the last two chapters. We have also chosen to focus on the country's constitutional developments over the past decade because they
exemplify three of the issues highlighted above. For, first,
courts have proved willing to make use of foreign material if
suitably assisted in this task. Second, they have welcomed

comparative law as a tool for analysis when it has helped them address questions of practical importance. Finally, empirical evidence corroborates the importance of language and the earlier assertion that the work of foreign scholars suffers if it is not presented in English. The South African experience indicates, however, that even accepted foreign ideas may wither if legal material is not readily accessible in a suitably digestible form.

Let us start by providing a brief outline of South Africa's recent constitutional history. This is not only meant to set the scene but also to show how the soil was ready for legal transplants.

While restructuring the country's new legal order in the 1990s, the competing political parties agreed on a two-stage reform process, which led to the negotiation of an interim Constitution (1993/1994) and—following the first free elections in May 1994—a final Constitution (1994 to 1996). Both documents were strongly influenced by foreign constitutional ideas, the German *Grundgesetz* of 1949 proving one important source. Many prominent elements of German origin were introduced to South Africa. Among them one counts parts of the bill of fundamental rights, the concept of the constitutional state (*Rechtsstaat*), a specialised constitutional court, and a number of federal features pertaining, inter alia, to the distribution of legislative competence between the central and provincial levels as well as the concept of co-operative government. The degree of German influence is, in one sense, remarkable given that Germany was the only country outside the common law world and the English-speaking legal community which received such attention from the framers of the new South African constitutional order.

This reception of foreign ideas was mainly fostered by political parties and influential academics offering legal advice to the Multi-Party Negotiating Process at Kempton Park in 1993 and, subsequently, the Constitutional Assembly. As will be shown later, the South African judiciary was also (and remains) the third main protagonist in this development.[205] This conforms to the point made in the earlier chapters namely, that the best way to make use of foreign law is through a close co-operation between the actors who usually shape law.

The reasons why German constitutional law proved to be such a successful model are mainly two.

The first is that parts of the German Bill of Rights doctrine had already found their way into Southern Africa prior to the political changes in Pretoria, having permeated its borders via Bophuthatswana[206] and Namibia. The Supreme Court of South Africa, exercising final judicial authority in Bophuthatswana until 1982 and in Namibia for as long as 1990, found itself confronted with cases of constitutional review far ahead of the first judgments of South African courts following the enactment of the 1994 Constitution. These judgments referred to German law on more than one occasion and were discussed by academics in South Africa, fuelling the local fundamental rights debate and opening the doors for further German influence in the subsequent constitution-making process.

A second reason can be found in the fact that a number of (mostly Afrikaans-speaking) academics found opportunities for comparative studies in Germany at a time when academic institutions in other countries were hardly accessible to South African scholars due to the political isolation of the country. Thus, supported by research grants of the Alexander von Humboldt Foundation, the Max Planck Institutes, and the German Academic Exchange Service, a substantial number of scholars came into contact with German legal thinking and then brought it back to South Africa.[207]

On the constitutional level, the inclusion of the *Rechtsstaatsprinzip* in the preamble of the 1994 Constitution—inserted on the initiative of Professor François Venter—is perhaps the most remarkable direct result of this personal link between the two countries. The close linguistic relationship between Afrikaans and German must also have served as an important bridge for legal ideas. Indeed, how true this is can be seen from the fact that many key German terms (such as *'Rechtsstaat,' 'Wechselwirkung,' 'Wesensgehalt,' 'Drittwirkung'* or *'Bundestreue'*) were not even translated by South African courts and academics.

Other factors explaining the role of German law during the negotiation process seem to have included the international reputation of the *Grundgesetz* and the support rendered by the German government, political parties, politically-affiliated foundations[208] and academic institutions to the emerging new state.[209] These activities provide a shining example of how cultural initiatives can serve as vehicles for promoting political interests, something which successive English governments seem to have lost sight of, especially as they allowed the steady decline of the overseas activities of the British Council. Certainly, the senior author of this co-authored piece, having spent the last 20 years of his life working abroad and with foreign law faculties, can testify to the indifference shown towards academic relations by British Embassies abroad. Finally, to return to German/South African links, one could point out that a legal system (the German) that had, itself, been asked in the post-war period to cope with a traumatic past, must have appeared as especially relevant to a country struggling to put behind it its own tormented experience.

Yet the importation of foreign ideas and notions was neither wholesale nor always long-lasting. As far as the German side is concerned, some elements such as the *Rechtsstaatsprinzip*, the 'reading down' of statutes in the course of interpretation (*verfassungskonforme Auslegung*), the indirect or radiating effect of fundamental rights in the private sphere (*mittelbare Drittwirkung der Grundrechte*), parts of the property clause and the explicit protection of the essential content of fundamental rights (*Wesensgehaltsgaratie*) were restricted to the transitional period and later partly substituted by doctrines already developed in South Africa prior to 1993. Other elements such as the establishment of a specialised court for constitutional matters and parts of the *Bundesrat* model found their way into the 1996 Constitution, albeit in a strongly modified form. Yet again, other aspects such as the constitutional freedom of occupation, the application of certain fundamental rights to juristic persons and parts of the limitation clause, today closely resemble their German counterparts.

As indicated above, the South African judiciary played a key part in this 'reception' and still continues to play an exceptional role in this use of foreign ideas. Explicitly invited to have recourse to comparative law by both Constitutions,[210] the South African Constitutional Court in particular has repeatedly referred to foreign material in order to shape the country's new and developing body of constitutional doctrine. This demarcates a clear break with the past, when South African judges 'did not value academic writing highly,'[211] and is a change much necessitated by the absence of South African precedents in this field of law. Scrutinising Supreme Court and Constitutional Court judgments between July 1994 and August 1998, one of us[212] thus counted no less than 1,258 references to the decisions of American, Canadian, British, German, European and Indian courts alone. These little-known statistics demonstrate that Germany is the only civil law system which has had a significant input (ranking fourth with 72 citations out of the total 1,258). More importantly, it is the only major legal system in which courts do not deliver their judgments in English.

This statement calls for some explanation, and our research has shown that most of this influence is due to translations of court judgments made available through the work of a limited number of (non-German!) academics.[213] This basic comparative work is obviously one important key, which enables South African judges to take advantage of German ideas, especially in the area of human rights. A pre-condition is thereby the open-minded approach, which some judges, such as Justice Laurie Ackermann, take towards the use of foreign material. Questioned by colleagues taking a more conservative stance towards comparative law in the judicial sphere,[214] the views of these judges do not always prevail; but their dicta nonetheless infuse the South African legal system with foreign ideas. Even if unsuccessful, these ideas (such as the reference by Ackermann to article 2(1) of the German Basic Law, a provision protecting the free development of the personality, which is regarded as a residual basic right and is open to innovative interpretation in Germany) are seeds, which are then cultivated by scholars and, one day, may even bear fruit.

Notwithstanding the fact that the conditions for the reception of foreign ideas were good, we would not be surprised to witness in the years to come a decline of German constitutional influence. The main reason for this negative prognosis is the language barrier and (closely connected to it) the limited accessibility of German case law and academic work. As pointed out, our research clearly shows that much of the influence of German law depends on the translation of German court decisions. Equally, academic input will only penetrate the system if it is presented in English; even short pieces of less well-known authors will find an audience if written in the prevailing legal language.[215] One of the most interesting results of our inquiry into the South African situation is thereby the important role of non-German authors—both South African[216] and foreign—presenting German legal ideas. These findings again support the thesis that comparative law is nowadays highly dependent on English as the emerging *lingua franca* of the legal world. If this is not recognised by German comparatists, their work (and the rich ideas which the German system as a whole has to offer) will be of limited effect in the future. This of course will take time and effort. Thus, apart from turning to its own legal roots, South Africa is, in the years ahead, more likely to have recourse to readily available comparative material from Anglo-American, Canadian or neighbouring African legal systems when it comes to the interpretation of constitutional norms originating from Germany.[217] A legacy, unique in comparative law terms, may thus not last for long unless Germany harnesses to its advantage the power of the English language. If such a thing happened, it would, indeed, be a fascinating twist in the history of comparative methodology but not out of line with the themes explored in these chapters.

7. A POSTSCRIPT

Statistics can kill intuitive evaluations of facts and other phenomena. Myth, intuition, and imagination, however, also have a role to play in our lives; and this role, constructive or even destructive, is invariably more attractive than reality. The world of statistics is not only dull; it is slippery and this because of the way the data is collected. We thus spent much time—too much any true propagandist would say—setting out in section 2 of this chapter the caveats which we thought were necessary for our readers. It could be argued that in stressing them too much we may have drained our own conclusions of much of their force. Others might argue more broadly and say that the statistical method cannot be applied easily to an area such as comparative law because it is not a coherent enough field to stand up to this kind of analysis. We disagree with both views.

For first, the data we have laboriously collected, despite its limitations, is broad enough and deep enough to suggest patterns that repeat themselves in many systems and may thus be a good indication of what is actually happening out there. To put it differently, we are not convinced that if more in-depth studies were carried out concerning additional jurists and more countries, the overall picture we have presented would be significantly affected. Secondly, we feel that our data corroborates the view that comparatists have had a tiny impact on the world of practice and that this is largely for the reasons discussed in chapters one and two above. Though the picture may change in the future, more data is unlikely to disrupt what we have found thus far. Thirdly, to give but one more example why we hope we may have opened up a new path for the measuring of reputation of scholarship through statistics, are the figures we have assembled about the real and apparent citation rate of some scholars. They are statistics, which may have affected myths in the making. If they have not destroyed them, they certainly warrant a re-examination.

The figures of Schlesinger offer one example. Eminent and charismatic though he was (as repeatedly stated in chapter one above), his citations figures simply do not support the image, which his supporters have tried to build for him: that his intellectual influence has been unique and is now radiating back to Europe.[218] The figures support a range of similar or analogous propositions for other 'greats.' In one sense, these may not be earth-shattering conclusions; but they do help build up the truer picture about comparative law during the last 30 years or so. As far as England is concerned, it is thus not uninteresting to note that, overall, comparatists have done as well as other jurists working in mainstream areas of the law. In that sense they are no more in a ghetto than mainstream lawyers. In our view, however, it is equally noteworthy to mention that scholars who hold chairs in one field have made their name by writing mainly in another. The material we have collected is too voluminous to appear all in one piece; but, when it sees the light of day, it could and should make all those who decide on the proper designation of the titles of chairs re-name them or re-define their ambit and scope. Finally, we regard as not unimportant the preliminary data and interpretation we provided about the reception of foreign ideas in contemporary South Africa not least because it suggests how governments and scholars can combine in the spreading of legal ideas emanating from a particular legal culture. Though we did not discuss contemporary Dutch efforts to spread their law, mainly in Central and Eastern Europe, we mention it here as yet another example of State-supported exportation of one's legal culture. And we mention it because we wish to contrast these efforts (which our survey suggests work in practice) with the indifference shown towards this aim by successive British governments. Maybe, this is because they feel that the multinational firms or alliances generated mainly by London-based firms will perform this task for them for free. The reality, of course, is different; and what one needs in this context is a concerted effort on behalf of the public and private sector.

The significance of our statistics goes beyond what one chooses to make of the figures given above. For one, citation breeds citation, as authors who are encountered frequently will sooner or later attract the attention of readers who might not have otherwise become aware of their work. Citation, even auto-citation, if repeated over a period of time and geographical space, will add to the reputation and perhaps the kudos of the author cited. The same goes for what one could call (for lack of a better term) 'mischievous citation.'

In this last context it may be tempting to add that negative, ie critical, citation may also have this effect—somewhat along the lines of the well-known argument that even adverse publicity is good publicity. Legrand's work may provide some support for this, for undoubtedly he has had more than his fair share of criticism. Yet it has also had its beneficial side, for it has undoubtedly brought him into the forefront of the academic debate during the last 10 years or so. His ratings, especially when compared with the much more established French colleagues of his, support this view. Of course, this does not eliminate the possibility that when the dust settles, reputations thus created—and here we are emphatically *not* referring to Legrand's—may vanish into the thin air. But then given the somewhat pessimistic attitude expressed by the longevity of academic reputation in 99 per cent of all cases, this may not be so significant after all.

Yet, when all is said and done, and the various provisos have been weighed carefully and found wanting or in need of further evidence, one thing seems to be reasonably clear. The statement that comparative law is nowadays in a ghetto is not substantiated by fact. At best, the proposition must be advanced with qualifications; and the state of affairs—to the extent that it is bad—must be attributed to a large extent to self-fault. The overall negative assessment is not, in our view, warranted given that the number of scholars teaching the subject is growing and the citations that comparatists attract to their work are going up not down, at any rate if one looks solely at the academic literature. Even the stirrings against the traditional way of doing things represent a sign of life and not moribund inactivity. Thus, some of the comparatists in our lists can almost claim a place among the one hundred or so best cited authors in the USA. Others, with a smaller number of citations in any one system, more significantly, end up with a substantial intellectual presence in three or four or even five continents. Though this may still not equal the achievement of those who can claim citations in the thousands it is, nonetheless, very significant evidence of *international* reputation. The statistics also suggest that those who 'have made it' may not, necessarily, be the ones that would be upper-most in most readers minds. We thus return to the earlier point about statistics helping to correct existing impressions.

But the statistics can also be taken to support the view that the linkage of comparative law with, say, Roman law has harmed or, at the very least not benefited, the interests of the former while helping prolong the condemned life of the other. Note, for instance, the point made here and in the previous chapters, about professors of comparative law having hitherto devoted the substance of their energies to keeping their Roman law scholarship alive. Since time is a most precious commodity, this was achieved, as the statistics clearly show, at the expense of more effort being put into the study of contemporary foreign law. The danger of that happening in the future has now receded as European law, in its Community, human rights, or comparative law incarnation, has almost everywhere in Europe supplanted Roman law as the course that gives us a glimpse of another system and thus helps us understand our own better. But there was another price tag to this 'back to the past' habit which some of the new trends mentioned in chapter two above could replicate. For it produced (and if we are not careful it could again produce) works that had little or no impact on the courts and the real world. The statistics, slender though they are, support this hypothesis as well. Comparatists who get a fair number of citations in the literature are totally absent from the real world of practice. The disproportion in the figures given in Tables 1 and 2 is staggering. Here, for once, the inadequacy of raw data cannot be used as an excuse to weaken the conclusion. But this, clearly, is not because of lack of ability but because of a wrong focus. Nicholas' example shows that when his great talents were put to a contemporary and relevant purpose, the courts—even courts foreign as far as he was concerned—made use of his ideas. When they remained restricted to Roman law, they earned him respect among his peers, and a beautiful obituary by a fellow Romanist. That, however, is not legacy—not, at any rate, as we defined it above. The fact of the matter is that the Rabels of the subject can be counted on the fingers of one hand. And the successors are more likely to come from Germany, the USA, or Italy than my adopted country or France. The examination of the entrails at the time of writing gives little room for more hope.

Though much more work still remains to be done on the path we have opened up with this piece (and the remaining three chapters of the book), such work will prove even more useful if it looks at the use *legislative* bodies make of foreign and comparative law. Our hunch is that there, as well, concrete, focused, detailed, relevant studies are used and are likely to be used, and not studies which look at the past or at other areas of human knowledge, unless they can be shown to have a close bearing on the subject under scrutiny. Our suspicion also is that the legislator, as well, when using information about foreign law, derives it through the writings of his own scholars, writing in his own language. The ability to move across borders and across languages is still limited to a few jurists; and the limits are not imposed so much by language barriers or poor libraries or lack of opportunities for travel but by the most insurmountable of barriers: human mentality. In my subject it is of an inward type; arrogant in nature and stubborn in its attachment to past glories, failing to recognise new realities and yet, sometimes, apparently eager to embrace new fads. Academics who wish to break down the mentality barriers we alluded to will only do so if they can attract the support of business and the courts; and they will only succeed in this if they make their work relevant to both.

Notes

[1] See, eg, Wade, 'Citation Analysis: A New Tool for Science Administrators' (1975) 188 *Science* 429; Stigler and Friedland, 'The Pattern of Citation Practices in Economics' (1979) 11 *History of Political Economy* 1; Robey, 'Reputations vs Citations: Who Are the Top Scholars in Political Science?' (1982) 15 *PS* 199; Shapiro, 'The Most Cited Law Review Article' (1985) 73 *California L Rev* 1540.

[2] *Cardozo: A Study in Reputation* (1990).

[3] William Powers, 'Reputology' (1991) 12 *Cardozo L Rev* 1941. Two other Texas colleagues, J M Balkin and Professor Sanford Levinson, coined the acoustically equally unattractive term 'citology'; see 'How to Win Cites and Influence People' (1996) *71 Chi-Kent L Rev* 843. The corruptive effect of American linguistic inventiveness seems already to have acquired a foothold in England; see *The Guardian*, 10 May 1997, 'Glossary for the 1990s.'

[4] Shapiro, 'The Most Cited Legal Scholars' (2000) 29 *J Legal Stud* 409 at 412.

[5] Thus, see, Barrett, ' "Citology", the Study of Footnotes Sweeps the Law Schools' in *Wall Street Journal*, 22 January 1997 and, more recently, the collection of essays published in vol 29 of (2000) *Journal of Legal Studies*, especially the articles by Shapiro at 389 ff, 397 ff, and 409 ff; and by Professor William M Landes and Posner at 319 ff.

[6] 'Legal Formants: A Dynamic Approach to Comparative Law' (1991) 39 *Amer J Comp L* 1 ff; 344 ff. This article is cited 64 times in 50 documents. No other work of his approaches this level. His *Introduzione al diritto comparato* (5th edn, 1992)—possibly his magnum opus—appears 10 times in 10 documents. For a man who has written extensively in Italian (and less so in French), this is a very poor showing, though, in my view, this reflects more adversely on American legal academe, which rarely goes beyond English texts, than on Sacco. But how language has 'disadvantaged' Sacco (and other Italians) can be seen if one compares the number of his citations in the American literature (89) to those given to another Italian writing mainly in English, Cappelletti (427).

⁷ David's other major monograph written in English entitled *English Law and French Law* (1980) receives a total of 18 citations.

⁸ Chaskalson, 'The Problem with Property: Thoughts on the Constitutional Protection of Property in the United States and the Commonwealth' (1993) *SAJHR* 388, taken from Fedtke, *Die Rezeption von Verfassungsrecht. Südafrika 1993–1996* (2000), 447.

⁹ Above n 2, ch 4 in general.

¹⁰ I have, for instance, spoken to both Italian judges and academics and asked them whether prior to writing a judgment they would occasionally consult leading academics. Both replied in the affirmative; but the link cannot be proved by anything published.

¹¹ The controversial decision of the plenum of the French Court of Cassation in the *Perruche* case of 17 November 2000 demonstrates this most clearly. The documentation can be found in *JCP*, 13 December 2000, No 50, 2293 ff.

¹² Above n 2, at 59.

¹³ Above n 2, at 60.

¹⁴ Mr S C Underwood (who manually tracked down academic references in five major English law journals for the period 1980–2001) and Dr Michaella Elisabetta Marino (who undertook a similar task in Italy).

¹⁵ I particularly wish to thank its Director, Professor Roy Mersky for the constant support he gives to all those who work in his library.

¹⁶ This must be read in conjunction with the points I make in chapters one and two above.

¹⁷ Ayres and Vars, 'Determinants of Citations to Articles in Elite Law Reviews' (2000) 29 *J Legal Studies* 427 at 436.

¹⁸ The Juris system for German decisions is an exception.

¹⁹ Article 118.3 of the Rules Concerning the Application of the Code of Civil Procedure (enacted along with the Civil Code in 1942) expressly states that: '*in ogni caso deve essere omessa ogni citazione di autori giuridici.*' (In any case all citation of legal authors must be omitted.) The reasons are not that different to those once utilised in England to prohibit citing to English courts the works of living authors. But the citation of foreign judgments is not caught by the prohibition and is beginning to take hold though, admittedly, in 'supporting' manner along the lines found in the *Fairchild* decision. Professor Alessandro Somma's *L'uso giurisprudenziale della comparazione nel diritto interno e comunitario* (2001) has thus revealed 16 decisions, mainly of the Corte di Cassazione, citing foreign judgments (see, in particular, the discussion at 85, 134 and 173–74). Of these, 7 come from the highest German courts, one from the French Cour de cassation, one from the High Court of Australia, one from the Supreme Court of Canada, and two from our House of Lords namely, *Murphy v Brentwood District Council* [1991] 1 AC 398 and *White v Jones* [1995] 2 AC 207. But the trend, if trend it is, is very modest, for, as Professor Lupoi reminded me

(in private correspondence) these examples must be seen against the fact that the Court of Cassation hands down some 14,000 decisions per year. The way court results in Italy can, indirectly, be traced to the ideas of particular academics is, however, another matter; and both my colleagues Professors Grottanelli de' Santi and Alpa have assured me that this is often possible behind opaque terms which give to those in the know useful clues.

[20] 'Citations, Age, Fame, and the Web' (2000) 29 *Legal Studies* 319 at 330.

[21] We return to this point when we make some observations about the German figures.

[22] Electronic citation: 2002 FED App. 0043P (6th Cir) File Name 02a0043p.06.

[23] *Greatorex v Greatorex* [2000] 1 WLR 1970.

[24] [2002] 3 WLR 89.

[25] [1995] 2 AC 207.

[26] Eg, Kötz, 'Scholarship and the Courts: A Comparative Survey' in *Comparative and Private International Law: Essays in Honor of John Merryman on his Seventieth Birthday* (1990) 183 ff.

[27] 133 documents citing his *Oracles of the Law* and 53 his *Gifts and Promises*. Searching for Dawson was not, however, easy and the overall figure includes results for the name 'J Dawson,' which inevitably includes some false positives. However, a survey of the results indicates that the vast majority of documents in the Westlaw JLR database with a citation to 'J Dawson' refer to John P Dawson.

[28] Total citations = 84: *The Law of Torts* = 50; 'Requiem for Anns' (1990) 106 *LQR* 525 = 6; *The American Tort Process* (1988) = 5; 'Drug Injury Compensation Plans' (1982) 30 *Amer J Comp L* 297 = 4; *An Introduction to the Law of Torts* (1967) = 3; 'Comparative Law of Torts' (1984) 4 *OJLS* 235 = 3; 'Damages: Capital or Rent?' (1969) 19 *University of Toronto L J* 295 = 2; 'The Pearson Report: Its Strategy' (1979) 42 *MLR* 249 = 2; 'Probabilistic Causation in Tort Law' (1989) 68 *Canadian Bar Review* 661 = 2; 'Remoteness and Duty: The Control Devices in Liability for Negligence' (1953) 31 *Canadian Bar Review* 471 = 1; 'Products Liability' in Burns and Lyons (eds), *Donoghue v. Stevenson and the Modern Law of Negligence: The Paisley Papers* (1991) = 1; 'The Collateral Source Rule and Contract Damages' (1983) 71 *California L Rev* 56 = 1; 'Tort Law in a Contractual Matrix' (1995) 33 *Osgoode Hall L J* 661 = 1; 'The Collateral Source Rule and Loss Allocation in Tort Law' (1966) 54 *California L Rev* 1478 = 1; 'Common Mistake' (1952) 15 *MLR* 229 = 1; 'The Lost Years' (1962) *California L Rev* 598 = 1; 'The Solicitor and the Disappointed Beneficiary' (1993) 109 *LQR* 344 = 1; (1958) 32 *ALJ* 267 = 1.

[29] Total citations = 5: *Comparative Law: Cases, Text, Materials* (edited with Baade, Damaska, Herzog, 1988) = 2; 'A Recurrent Problem in Transnational Litigation: The Effect of Failure to Invoke or Prove the

Applicable Foreign Law' (1973) 59 *Cornell L Rev* 1 = 1; *Formation of Contracts: A Study of the Common Core of Legal Systems* (1968) = 1; 'The Past and Future of Comparative Law' (1995) 43 *Amer J Comp L* 477 = 1.

³⁰ *Formation of Contracts: A Study of the Common Core of Legal Systems* (1968) = 3; 'Allgemeine Rechtsgrundsätze als Sachnormen im Schiedsgerichtsverfahren' (1964) 28 *RabelsZ* 4 (with Gündisch) = 3; *Comparative Law: Cases, Text, Materials* (edited with Baade, Damaska, Herzog, 5th edn, 1990) = 1; (1926) 44 *Zentralblatt für die juristische Praxis* 44 = 2.

³¹ Total citations = 24: *Legal Transplants: An Approach to Comparative Law* (1974) = 6; *The Evolution of Law* (1985) = 3; *The Making of the Civil Law* (1981) = 2; *The Law of Obligations in the Later Roman Republic* (1965) = 2; *The Digest of Justinian: English Translation* (1985) = 2; 'Legal Transplants and Law Reform' (1976) 92 *LQR* 79 = 1; *The Lawyer in the Interviewing and Counselling Process* (1976) = 1; 'Comparative Law and Legal Change' [1978] 37 *CLJ* 313 = 1; 'Consensual Societas Between Romans and the Introduction of the Formulae' (1962) 9 *Revue Internationale des Droits de l'Antiquité* 431 = 1; 'The Structure of Blackstone's Commentaries' (1988) 97 *Yale L J* 795 = 1; 'Complex Litigation: A Comparative Perspective' (1993) 12 *ICLQ* 33 (with Lindblom) = 1; 'Constitutionalism, Judicial Review and the World Court' (1993) 34 *Harvard Int'l L J* 1 = 1; 'The Importance of "Nutshells" ' (1994) 42 *Amer J Comp L* 1 = 1; *Slave Law: History and Ideology* (1982) = 1.

³² Loman, Mortelmans, Post and Watson, *Culture and Community Law* (1992) = 4; (1979) 1 *Environmental Ethics* 99 = 1; 'Freedom of Establishment and Freedom to Provide Services: Some Recent Developments' 20 *CMLRev* 583 = 1; *Completing the World Trading System* (1999) = 1; *Legal Transplants: An Approach to Comparative Law* (1974) = 2.

³³ Because of the number of false positives it was not possible to search (electronically) for 'A Watson' alone. However, we do include occurrences of 'A Watson' that we found together with titles of works by Alan Watson.

³⁴ (2000) *ILJ* 79 = 1; *NJW* 1951, 526 = 1; Eekelaar and Bell, *Oxford Essays in Jurisprudence, Third Series* = 1; (1998) 76 *NCLRev* 566 = 1; Bell and Majestic, (1983/84) 10 *Journal of College and University Law* 63 = 2.

³⁵ Because of the number of false positives, it was not possible to search for 'J Bell.' We made an effort to control for false positive occurrences of 'John Bell.'

³⁶ Total citations = 89: *Causation in the Law* (with Hart) = 39; 'Ownership' in Guest (ed), *Oxford Essays in Jurisprudence* (1961)= 11; *Making Law Bind* (1987) = 10; 'Responsibility and Luck' (1988) 104 *LQR* 530 = 6; 'Causation and Remoteness of Damage' in Tunc (ed), *International Encyclopedia of Comparative Law* (1983) = 4; *Sex Law* (1978) = 2; *Tribonian* (1978)= 2; *South African Law of Trusts* (1992) = 2; 'Real Laws' in Hacker and Raz (eds), *Law, Morality and Society* (1979) = 2; *Responsibility and Fault*

(1999) = 1; 'Herbert Lionel Adolphus Hart 1907–1992: In Memoriam' (1993) 84 *Proceedings of the British Academy* 295 = 1; essay in Daube (ed), *Studies in the Roman Law of Sale* (1959) = 1; *The Quest for Security: Employees, Tenants and Wives* (1982) = 1; 'Hedley Byrne v Heller' (1965) 8 *JSPTL* 284 = 1; 'Reflections on Revolutions' [1967] 2 *Irish Jurist* 268 = 1; 'The Primacy of Oral Evidence' in Tapper (ed), *Crime, Proof and Punishment* (1981) = 1; 'A Theory of Coercion' (1990) 10 *OJLS* 94 = 1; 'The Morality of Tort Law' in D Owen (ed), *Philosophical Foundations of Tort Law* (1995) = 1; 'Obstacles to the Reception of the Trust? The Examples of South Africa and Scotland' in Rabello (ed), *Acquitas and Equity* (1997) = 1; (1956) 72 *LQR* 398 (with Hart) = 1.

37 We only found one book review of *Responsibility and Fault* (1999).

38 *Causation in the Law* (with Hart) = 269; 'Ownership' in Guest (ed), *Oxford Essays in Jurisprudence* (1961) = 99. The remaining articles cite a range of works in the areas of Roman law, tort law, and jurisprudence. For example: *Ulpian* (1982) = 13; *Tribonian* (1978) = 9; 'Necessary and Sufficient Conditions in Tort Law' in *Philosophical Foundations of Tort Law* (1995) = 6; 'Must We Obey? Necessity as a Ground of Obligation' (1981) 67 *Va L Rev* 39 = 14. His Hamlyn Lectures, entitled *The Quest for Security: Employees, Tenants, Wives* (1982) is cited 5 times.

39 Total citations = 88: Winfield and Jolowicz *on Tort* = 57; 'Damages in Equity: A Study of Lord Cairns' Act' [1975] 34 *CLJ* 224 = 5; 'Protection of Diffuse, Fragmented and Collective Interests in Civil Litigation: English Law' [1983] 42 *CLJ* 222 = 3; *Roman Foundations of Modern Law* (1957) = 2; 'The Forms of Action Disinterred' [1983] 42 *CLJ* 15 = 2; 'Liability for Accidents' [1968] 27 *CLJ* 50 = 2; *The Division and Classification of the Law* (1970) = 1; 'Protection of the Consumer and Purchaser of Goods Under English Law' (1969) 32 *MLR* 1 = 1; 'Court of Appeal or Court of Error?' [1991] 50 *CLJ* 54 = 1; 'Representative Actions, Class Actions and Damages: A Compromise' [1980] 39 *CLJ* 237 = 1; 'The Law of Tort and Non-Physical Loss' (1972) 12 *JSPTL* 91 = 1; 'On the Nature and Purpose of Civil Procedure Law' in I R Scott (ed), *International Perspectives on Civil Justice* (1990) = 1; 'The Judicial Protection of Fundamental Rights Under English Law', Pt II *Cambridge-Tilburg Law Lectures*, 2nd Series (1980) = 1; *Lectures on Jurisprudence* (1963) = 1; 'Some Twentieth Century Developments in Anglo-American Civil Procedure', *Studi in Onore de Enrico Tullio Liebman* (1979) = 1; 'Adversarial and Inquisitorial Approaches to Civil Litigation' in Baldwin (ed), *The Cambridge Lectures* (1983) = 1; 'Abuse of Process of the Courts: Handle With Care' [1990] *CLP* 77 = 1; 'Product Liability: The EEC and the House of Lords' [1980] 39 *CLJ* 263 = 1; 'Should Courts Answer Questions? Does Statutory Authority to Build Confer Immunity From Liability for Use?' [1981] 40 *CLJ* 226 = 1; 'Justiciable Questions are Justiciable After All' [1986] 45 *CLJ* 1 = 1; [1979] 38 *CLJ* 54 = 1; 'L'expert, le temoin et le juge en droits français et anglais' (1977) *Rev trim dr comp* 285 = 1.

[40] Various edns of Winfield and Jolowicz *on Tort* = 45; *International Enforcement of Human Rights* (co-edited with Rudolf Bernhardt 1987) = 12; *Public Interest Parties and the Active Role of the Judge in Civil Litigation* (co-authored with Mauro Cappelletti, 1975) = 6; 'Product Liability in the EEC' in *Comparative and Private International Law: Essays in Honor of John Henry Merryman* (1990) = 3; *Le Contrôle Juridictionnel des Lois* (co-edited with Louis Favoreu and Mauro Cappelletti, 1986) = 3; 'Procedural Questions' (ch 13) in *XI (Torts) International Encyclopedia of Comparative Law* = 4; 'Comparative Law and the Reform of Civil Procedure' (1988) 8 *Legal Studies* 1 = 2; 'On the Nature and Purposes of Civil Procedural Law' in *International Perspectives on Civil Justice: Essays in Honour of Sir Jack I. H. Jacob, Q.C.* (1990) = 1; the contribution of Jolowicz to the symposium 'L'Enseignement du Droit Comparé' (1988) *Rev intern dr comp* 703 = 1; *On Civil Procedure* (2000) = 2. The following writings of Jolowicz are cited in one article each: 'Abuse of the Process of the Court: Handle with Care' (1990) 43 *Current Legal Problems* 77; 'Comment, Representative Actions, Class Actions and Damages: A Compromise Solution' (1980) 39 *Cambridge LJ* 237 at 239; 'Damages in Equity: A Study of Lord Cairns' Act' (1975) 34 *Cambridge LJ* 224; 'The Immunity of the Legal Profession' (1968) 30 *Cambridge LJ* 23; 'The Judicial Protection of Fundamental Rights Under English Law' *Cambridge-Tilburg Law*, 2nd Series (1980); 'Protection of Diffuse, Fragmented and Collective Interests in Civil Litigation: English Law' (1983) 42 *Cambridge LJ* 222; 'The Woolf Report and the Adversary System' (1996) 15 *Civ Just Q* 198.

[41] Total citations = 96. 'General Problems of Private International Law' (1974 III) 143 *Recueil des Cours* 139 = 16; *A Source Book of French Law* (with Levy and Rudden) = 14; 'Introduction' to Karl Renner, *The Institutions of Private Law and their Social Functions* (1949) = 8; 'On Uses and Misuses of Comparative Law' (1974) 37 *MLR* 1 = 6; *Labour and the Law* (1972) = 4; 'Blackstone's Neglected Child = The Contract of Employment' (1977) 93 *LQR* 508 = 4; 'Common Law and Civil Law: Imaginary and Real Obstacles to Assimilation' in Cappelletti (ed), *New Perspectives for a Common Law of Europe* (1978) 158 = 4; 'A Note on Status and Contract in British Labour Law' (1967) 30 *MLR* 635 = 3; 'Industrial Democracy' (1977) 6 *ILJ* 65 = 3; 'Comparative Law as an Academic Subject' (1966) 82 *LQR* 41 = 3; *Labour Relations and the Law: A Comparative Study* (1965) = 2; 'Recent Legislation on Matrimonial Property' (1970) 33 *MLR* 241 = 2; 'Some Reflections on Company Law Reform' (1944) 7 *MLR* 54 = 2; 'Legal Framework' in Flanders and Clegg (eds), *The System of Industrial Relations in Great Britain* (1952) = 2; 'Reflections on Legal Education' (1966) 29 *MLR* 121 = 2; 'Labour Law and Social Security' in Stein and Nicholson (eds), *American Enterprise in the European Common Market: A Legal Profile* (1960) = 2; *Matrimonial Property: Where Do We Go from Here?*, Unger Memorial Lecture (1971) = 2; 'English Law and American Law: Some Comparative Reflections', *Essays in Jurisprudence in Honour of Roscoe Pound* (1962) = 1; 'Jurisdiction

Agreements = Some Reflections' (1977) 26 *ICLQ* 825 = 1; 'Lord Chorley 1895–1978' (1978) 55 *LSE* 8 = 1; 'Corporate Entity' (1940) 3 *MLR* 226 = 1; 'The Impact of Constitutions on Labour Law' (1976) 35 *CLJ* 240 = 1; 'The Tangle of the Trade Acts' (1949) 4 *ILR* 2 = 1; 'The Trade Unions, Law and Society' (1970) 33 *MLR* 241 = 1; 'Case Note' (1951) 14 *MLR* 505 = 1; 'Labour Law' in Ginsberg (ed), *Law and Opinion in England in the 20th Century* (1989) = 1; 'Reflections on Public Policy in the English Conflict of Laws' (1953) 39 *Trans Gro S* 39 = 1; *The Growth of Internationalism in English Private International Law* (1960) = 1; 'Divorce Law Reform' (1956) 19 *MLR* 573 = 1; Book Review (1980) *JSPTL* 81 = 1; (1939) 3 *MLR* 61 = 1; *Federation News*, vol 14, April 1964 = 1; (1960) 3 *Revista di diritto internationale e comparato del lavoro* 307 = 1; (1989) 22 *MLR* 413 = 1.

⁴² *General Problems of Private Law* (1976) = 1; 'Delictual Obligations in Private Law' (1969) Ann Inst Dr int 53 = 1; 'Das britische Gesetz über die Arbeitsbeziehungen von 1971' in *Festschrift für Ballerstedt* (1975), 51 = 1; 'Some Reflections on Company Law Reform' (1944) 7 *MLR* 54 = 1; *RdA* 1949, 316 (a German publication dealing with English law) = 1; (1968 II) *Recueil des Cours* 1 = 2. Some 37 additional citations refer to German publications on labour law, of which 30 refer to the various edns of *Betriebsrätegesetz* (with Flatow).

⁴³ Kahn-Freund is cited for a broad range of articles in the fields of comparative law, conflict of laws, labour law, and family law: 'On Uses and Misuses of Comparative Law' (1974) 37 *MLR* 1 = 49; 'Comparative Law as an Academic Subject' (1966) 82 *LQR* 40 = 20; *A Source Book on French Law* (various edns) = 15; *Labour and the Law* (various edns) = 29; 'Inconsistencies and Injustices in the Law of Husband and Wife' (1952) 15 *MLR* 133 = 8; 'General Problems of Private International Law' (1974 III) 143 *Recueil des Cours* 139 = 18.

⁴⁴ Total citations = 53. *The Law of Property* (with Rudden) = 11; *Tortious Liability for Unintentional Harm in the Common Law and the Civil Law* (with Markesinis, 1982) = 10; *A Common Lawyer Looks at the Civil Law* (1955) = 5; *Cases in Constitutional Law* (with Keir) = 4; *Remedies of English Law* = 4; *The Rational Strength of English Law* (1951) = 4; 'Das Subjektive Recht' in *The English Law of Torts: Selected Essays* vol 1 (1977) = 3; *The Oxford Law School 1850–1965* (1968) = 3; *Roman Law and Common Law: A Comparison in Outline* (edited by Lawson) = 1; 'The Passing of Property and Risk in Sale of Goods: A Comparative Study' (1949) 65 *LQR* 352 = 1; 'Institutes' in Graveson, Kreuzer, Tunc and Zweigert (eds), *Festschrift für Imre Zajtay* (1982) = 1; 'The Art of Drafting Statutes—English Style' in *Festschrift für Konrad Zweigert* (1981) = 1; 'Taking the Decision to Remove the Child from the Family' [1980] *JSWL* 141 = 1; 'A Common Lawyer Looks at Codification' in *Selected Essays I: Many Laws* (1977) = 1; 'Improving Arbitrator Performance' (1984) 39(4) *Arbitration Journal* 49 (with Rinaldo) = 1; Amos and Walton, *Introduction to French Law* (edited with Anton and Brown) = 1; (1981) 131 *NLJ* 933: 1.

⁴⁵ *A Common Lawyer Looks at the Civil Law* (1953) = 44; *Negligence in the Civil Law* (1950) = 19; Amos and Walton, *Introduction to French Law* (of which Lawson is co-author of the second and third edns, 1963 and 1967 respectively) = 19; *Tortious Liability for Unintentional Harm in Common Law and the Civil Law* (with Markesinis, 1982) = 18; *Law of Property* (with Rudden, two edns 1958 and 1982 respectively) = 16; Buckland and McNair, *Roman Law and Common Law: A Comparison in Outline* (of which Lawson was editor of the second edn 1965) = 11; various chapters of vol 6 of the *International Encyclopedia of Comparative Law* on property and trust (of which Lawson was chief editor) = 10; *Remedies of English Law* (two edns, 1972 and 1980 respectively) = 6. Other writings of Lawson on comparative law or Roman law are cited in a few articles each.

⁴⁶ 'Case note on Wilson, Smithett and Cope v. Terruzzi' [1976] 1 All ER 817 (CA) = 1; (1954) *Cambridge LJ* 181 = 1; 'Characteristic Performance: A New Concept in the Conflict of Laws in Matters of Contract for the EEC' (1982) 3 *Northw J Int'l L B* 402 = 2; 'Conflict of Public Laws: Visions and Realities' in *Festschrift für Imre Zajtay* (1982) 357 = 1; 'Conflict of Laws and Public Law' in: Banakas (ed), *Harmonisation of Private International Law by the EC* (1978) = 1; 'Das Haager Abkommen über die internationale Abwicklung von Nachlässen' (1975) *RabelsZ* 29 = 1; 'Öffentliches und Internationales Privatrecht' in *Internationales Privatrecht, Internationales Wirtschaftsrecht* (1985) = 1.

⁴⁷ These hits were only found in the commentaries searched: 'Bemerkungen zum Internationalen Privatrecht der Aktiengesellschaft und des Konzerns' in *Festschrift für Barz* (1974) 219 = 2; 'Die Konfiskation von Gesellschaften, Gesellschaftsrechten und Gesellschaftsvermögen im IPR' (1962/63) 27 *RabelsZ* 1 = 1; *NJW* 1974, 492 = 1; *NJW* 1977, 2160 = 1; *JZ* 1981, 327 = 1; (1963) 79 *LQR* 252 = 2; (1971 I) 132 *Recueil des Cours* 107 = 1; *Festschrift Wahl* (1973) = 1; (1984) 33 *ICLQ* 196 = 1. The number of hits in journals (above 400), by far most of which are false positives due to the ambiguous meaning of 'Mann' in German, was too large to analyse.

⁴⁸ *The Legal Aspect of Money* (various edns) = 62; 'The Doctrine of Jurisdiction in International Law' (1964) 111 *Recueil des Cours* 9 = 48; 20 articles cite the companion essay 'The Doctrine of International Jurisdiction Revisited After Twenty Years' (1984) 186 *Recueil des Cours* 9. *Studies in International Law* (1973) is cited without further specification in 32 articles. *Further Studies in International Law* (1990) is cited without further specification in 24 articles. *Foreign Affairs in English Courts* = 17; 'Lex Facit Arbitrum' in *International Arbitration: Liber Amicorum for Martin Domke* (1967) 157 = 21; 'Reflections on the Prosecution of Persons Abducted in Breach of International Law' in *International Law at a Time of Perplexity* (1989) 407 = 25. Further articles also cite a broad range of Mann's writings on international law, conflict of laws and arbitration.

⁴⁹ Total citations = 112. *Tort Law* = 17 (4 with Dias, 2nd edn, 1989, and 13 with Deakin, 3rd edn, 1994); *The Gradual Convergence* (1994) = 13;

German Law of Torts: A Comparative Introduction = 13; 'An Expanding Tort Law: The Price of a Rigid Contract Law' (1987) 103 *LQR* 354 = 10; 'Privacy, Freedom of Expression and the Horizontal Effect of the Human Rights Bill = Lessons from Germany' (1999) 115 *LQR* 47 = 8; *Tortious Liability for Unintentional Harm in the Common Law and the Civil Law* (with Lawson, 1982) = 8; *The Impact of the Human Rights Bill on English Law* (1998) = 5; 'Our Patchy Law of Privacy: Time to do Something About It' (1990) 53 *MLR* 802 = 4; 'Litigation-Mania in England, Germany and the USA = Are We So Very Different?' (1990) 102 *CLJ* 372 = 4; 'The Random Element of their Lordships Infallible Judgment' (1992) 55 *MLR* 619 = 4; 'Comparative Law: A Subject in Search of an Audience' (1990) 53 *MLR* 1 = 4; *The German Law of Obligations*, vol. 1, *The Law of Contracts and Restitution* (1997) = 4; *The Clifford Chance Millennium Lectures: The Coming Together of the Common Law and the Civil Law* = 3; *Outline of Agency* (with Munday) = 3; 'Negligence, Nuisance and Affirmative Duties of Action' (1989) 105 *LQR* 104 = 2; *The Clifford Chance Lectures: Bridging the Gap* (1996) = 2; 'The Law of Agency and Section 9(2) of the European Communities Act 1972' (1976) 35 *CLJ* 112 = 1; 'A Matter of Style' (1994) 110 *LQR* 607 = 1; 'Eternal and Troublesome Triangles' (1990) 106 *LQR* 556 = 1; *Tortious Liability of Statutory Bodies: A Comparative and Economic Analysis of Five English Cases* (with Auby, Coester-Waltjen and Deakin) = 1; 'Compensation for Negligently Inflicted Pure Economic Loss = Some Canadian Views' (1993) 109 *LQR* 5 = 1; 'The Royal Prerogative Re-Visited' (1973) 32 *CLJ* 287 = 1; 'Solicitor's Liability Towards Third Parties: Back into the Troubled Waters of the Contract/Tort Divide' (1993) 56 *MLR* 558 (with Lorenz) = 1; (1981) 131 *NLJ* 108 (with Tettenborn) = 1; (1993) 109 *LQR* 622 = 1; (1978) 37 *CLJ* 53 = 1.

    [50] *Tort Law* = 3 (1 with Dias, 2nd edn, 1989, and 2 with Deakin, 3rd edn, 1994); 'Privacy, Freedom of Expression and the Horizontal Effects of the Human Rights Bill: Lessons from Germany' (1999) 115 *LQR* 47 = 1; *The German Law of Torts* (2nd edn, 1990) = 1; *Foreign Law and Comparative Methodology: A Subject and a Thesis* (1997) = 1.

    [51] *A Comparative Introduction to the German Law of Torts* (various edns) = 20; in addition, vol 2 on the law of torts of *The German Law of Obligations* (1997) is cited in 5 articles; *The German Law of Obligations*, vol 1, *The Law of Contracts and Restitution* (1997) = 7; *Tortious Liability for Unintentional Harm in the Common Law and the Civil Law* (1982) = 18; *Tort Law* (various edns, co-authored with Dias or Deakin) = 16; 'Comparative Law: A Subject in Search of an Audience' (1990) 53 *MLR* 1 = 13; *The Gradual Convergence: Foreign Ideas, Foreign Influences, and English Law on the Eve of the 21st Century* (1994) = 18; 'Litigation-Mania in England, Germany and the USA: Are We So Very Different?' (1990) 49 *CLJ* 233 = 10; *Foreign Law and Comparative Methodology: A Subject and a Thesis* (1997) = 9; *The Coming Together of the Common Law and the Civil Law* (2000) = 6; 'Why a Code is Not the Best Way to Advance the Cause of European Legal Unity' (1997) 5

European Rev of Private Law 519 = 4; *Protecting Privacy* (1999) = 4; *Tortious Liability of Statutory Bodies: A Comparative and Economic Analysis of Five English Cases* (1999) = 3; 'Conceptualism, Pragmatism and Courage: A Common Lawyer Looks at Some Judgments of the German Federal Court' (1986) 34 *Amer J Comp L* 349 at 354 = 4; 'A Matter of Style' (1994) 110 *LQR* 607 = 2; *The English Law of Torts: A Comparative Introduction* (1976) = 3.

[52] Total Citations = 26. *The French Law of Contract* (2nd edn, 1992) = 14; *An Introduction to Roman Law* = 3; 'Fundamental Rights and Judicial Review in France' [1978] *Public Law* 82 = 2; 'Unjustified Enrichment in the Civil Law and Louisiana Law' (1961–62) 26 *Tulane L Rev* 605 = 2; 'Rules and Terms: Civil Law and Common Law' (1974) 48 *Tulane L Rev* 947 = 1; essay in Daube (ed), *Studies in the Roman Law of Sale* (1959) = 1; *Historical Introduction to Roman Law* (with Jolowicz, 1972) = 1; essay in Harris and Tallon (eds), *Contract Law Today* (1989) = 1; 'Unjust Enrichment and Subsidiarity' in Passarelli and Lupoi (eds), *Scintillae Iuris: Studi in Memoria di Gino Gorla* (1994) = 1.

[53] 'Impracticability and Impossibility in the UN Convention on Contracts for the International Sale of Goods' in Galson and Smit (eds), *International Sales* (1984) = 1; Mercuro, Nicholas, Medena and Steven, *Economics and the Law: From Posner to Post-Modernism* (1997) = 1; contribution to Bianca and Bonell (ed), *Commentary on the International Sales Law* (1987) = 2.

[54] *Introduction to Roman Law* (1962) = 94; *French Law of Contract* (both edns) = 46; *Historical Introduction to the Study of Roman Law* (3rd edn, 1972) = 31. Other articles cite a range of writings on comparative law and international sales law, eg, 'The Vienna Convention on International Sales Law' (1989) 105 *LQR* 201 = 14; 'Force Majeure and Frustration' (1979) 27 *Amer J Comp L* 231 = 12; 'Unjustified Enrichment in the Civil Law and Louisiana Law' (1962) 36 *Tulane L Rev* 605 = 11.

[55] Total citations = 40: *A Source Book on French Law* (edited with Kahn-Freund and Levy) = 16; *The Law of Property* (with Lawson) = 10; 'Things as Thing and Things as Wealth' (1994) 14 *OJLS* 81 = 2; 'Torticles' (1991–92) 6/7 *Tulane Civil Law Forum* 105 = 2; 'Corespondence' (1990) 10 *OJLS* 288 = 2; 'Le juste et l'inefficace [:] pour un non-devoir de renseignements' (1985) *Rev trim droit civil* 91 = 1; 'Soviet Tort Law' (1967) 42 *New York University L Rev* 583 = 1; 'Consequences' (1980) *Judicial Review* 194 = 1; 'The Rule in Hadley v Baxendale: Some Notes on Ancestry' (unpublished) = 1; *Basic Community Laws* (edited with Derrick Wyatt) = 1; 'Review of Markesinis, German Law of Torts' (1987) 46 *CLJ* 161 = 1; *Comparing Constitutions* (edited with Finer and Bogdanor, 1995) = 1; (1963) *Conv* (27) *(N.S.)* 51 = 1.

[56] (1999) *European Rev of Private Law* 199.

[57] *A Source Book on French Law* (edited with Kahn-Freund and Levy) = 18; *Law of Property* (2nd edn, 1982) = 11; *Basic Community Laws* (various edns) = 22; 'Courts and Codes in England, France, and Soviet Russia' (1974) 48 *Tulane L Rev* 1010 = 9; 'Economic Theory v. Property Law: The

Numerus Clausus Problem' in *Oxford Essays in Jurisprudence*, 3rd series (1987) = 11; 'Civil Law, Civil Society, and the Russian Constitution' (1994) 110 *LQR* 56 = 7; 'Torticles' (1991–92) 6/7 *Tulane Civil Law Forum* 105 = 4.

[58] Total citations = 78: translation of Zweigert and Kötz, *An Introduction to Comparative Law* (various eds)= 20; *Casebook on Tort* = 20; 'Governmental Liability' [1989] *Public Law* 40 = 5; *Economic Torts* (1997) = 3; 'The Common Law System' in *International Encyclopaedia of Comparative Law*, vol II, ch 2 = 3; 'Complex Liabilities' in Tunc (ed), *International Encyclopaedia of Comparative Law* (1986) vol XI/2, ch 12 = 2; 'Contracts in Rome and England' (1992) 66 *Tulane L Rev* 1615 = 2; 'Down Hill—All the Way?' (1999) 58 C.L.J. 4 = 2; translation of Wieacker, *A History of Private Law in Europe* (1995): 2; 'Chaos or Cosmos? Rookes, Stratford and the Economic Torts' (1964) 22 *CLJ* 225 = 2; 'Wrongful Life—Nipped in the Bud' (1982) 41 *CLJ* 227 = 1; 'Rylands v Fletcher Reconsidered' (1994) 53 *CLJ* 216 = 1; 'A Damnosa Hereditas?' (1995) 111 *LQR* 357 = 1; 'The Developer and the Clerk' (1982) 2 *OJLS* 440 = 1; 'Doing Good by Mistake: Restitution and Remedies' (1973) 32 *CLJ* 23 = 1; 'Liability for Syntax' (1963) 22 *CLJ* 216 = 1; 'A Strike Against the Law' (1986) 46 *Maryland L Rev* 133 = 1; 'Delict and Torts: A Study in Parallel' (1963) 37 *Tulane L Rev* 573 (with Catala) = 1; *Structured Settlements* (1984) = 1; 'The Staggering March of Negligence' in Cane and Stepleton (eds), *The Law of Obligations: Essays in Celebration of John Fleming* (1998) = 1; 'Errare Humanum Est' in Birks (ed), *The Frontiers of Liability* = 1; 'The Parodist's Nirvana: Droit Moral and Comparative Copyright Law' (1994) 11(4) *Copyright Rep* 1 = 1; translation of Horn, Kötz and Leser, *German Private and Commercial Law* (1982) = 1; translated case in Markesinis, *German Law of Torts* (various eds) = 1; (1972) 3 *CLJ* 238 = 1; (1990) 49 *CLJ* 212 = 1; (1969) 28 *CLJ* 189 = 1.

[59] *ZEuP* 1995, 840 (cited in connection with English law) = 1; 'Complex Liabilities' in Tunc (ed), *International Encyclopedia of Comparative Law* (1986) vol XI/2, ch 12 = 4; 'Die Sprachen des europäischen Rechts: Eine skeptische Betrachtung' *ZEuP* 1995, 368 = 1; 'The Common Law System' in *International Encyclopedia of Comparative Law* (1971) vol II, ch 2 = 1; 'The Story of Moral Rights or the Moral to the Story' (1992) 3 *AIPJ* 232 = 1.

[60] Translations of Zweigert and Kötz, *Introduction to Comparative Law* (various edns) = 130; translation of Horn, Kötz and Leser, *German Private and Commercial Law* (1982) = 35; translation of Grossfeld, *The Strength and Weakness of Comparative Law* (1990) = 17; translation of Wieacker, *A History of Private Law in Europe* (1995) = 16; translation of Kötz and Flessner, *European Contract Law* (1997) = 6; these translations account for citations in 204 documents out of a grand total of 233. Citations to Weir's own works include: 'Delict and Torts: A Study in Parallel' (1964) 38 *Tulane L Rev* 221 at 259–61 (with Pierre Catala) = 9; 'Contracts in Rome and England' (1992) 66 *Tulane L Rev* 1615 = 7; 'Complex Liabilities' in Tunc (ed), *International Encyclopedia of Comparative Law* (1986) vol XI/2, ch 12 = 5; 'The Common Law System' in *International Encyclopedia of*

Comparative Law (1971) vol II, ch 2 = 4; 'Friendships in the Law' (1991–92) 6/7 *Tulane Civil Law Forum* 61 = 4.

[61] This amounts to 56 per cent of the total number of citations in the journals. A detailed analysis of the total number of citations in the commentaries (243 hits) is, at present, not possible.

[62] A detailed analysis of the total number of citations (above 642 hits) is, at present, not possible.

[63] Zweigert and Kötz, *Einführung in die Rechtsvergleichung* (various edns) = 34; Kötz and Flessner, *Europäisches Vertragsrecht* (1997) = 5; Basedow, Hopt, Kötz and Dopffel, *Die Rechtsstellung gleichgeschlechtlicher Lebensgemeinschaften* (2000) = 6. Further comparative articles: 35, eg, 'Rechtsvereinheitlichung—Nutzen, Kosten, Methoden, Ziele' (1986) 50 *RabelsZ* 1 = 5; 'Gemeineuropäisches Zivilrecht' in *Festschrift Zweigert* (1981) = 6; 'Europäische Juristenausbildung' *ZEuP* 1993, 268 = 1; *Trust und Treuhand* (1963) = 2. Citation of publications on German law in the same commentaries/journals amount to 163 (eg, the various edns of *Deliktsrecht* = 26; Kötz's contribution to the *Münchner Kommentar zum Bürgerlichen Gesetzbuch* = 81). The citations of Kötz' comparative work in this count thus amount to just below 31 per cent of the total number of citations.

[64] Various German and English eds of *Introduction to Comparative Law* (with Zweigert) = 203; Horn, Kötz and Leser, *German Private and Commercial Law* (1982) = 27. Other articles cite a range of writings in comparative law, eg, 'Rechtsvereinheitlichung—Nutzen, Kosten, Methoden, Ziele' (1986) 50 *RabelsZ* 1 = 11; the German and English edns of *European Contract Law* (1997) = 10; 'Civil Litigation and the Public Interest' (1982) 1 *Civ Just Q* 237 = 9; 'Taking Civil Codes Less Seriously' (1987) 50 *MLR* 1 = 7; 'Gemeineuropäisches Zivilrecht' in *Festschrift Zweigert* (1981) = 7; 'Europäische Juristenausbildung' *ZEuP* 1993, 268 = 6; *Trust und Treuhand* (1963) = 6; *Deliktsrecht* (various edns) = 7.

[65] Werner Lorenz can only be searched under 'Lorenz,' producing above 800 hits. Lorenz' contribution to *Staudinger, Bürgerliches Gesetzbuch* received 218 citations. A closer analysis is, at present, not possible.

[66] Marcus Lutter can only be searched under 'Lutter,' producing above 800 hits. The analysis was restricted to the following works of Marcus Lutter: *Konzernrecht im Ausland* (1994) = 1; *Europäisches Unternehmensrecht: Grundlagen, Stand und Entwicklung nebst Texten und Materialien zur Rechtsangleichung* (1996) = 1; *Der Einfluß deutscher Emigranten auf die Rechtsentwicklung in den USA und in Deutschland* (1993) = 3; *Das Eheschließungsrecht in Frankreich, Belgien, Luxemburg und Deutschland* (1963) = 1; *Die GmbH in Belgien* (1966) = 0; 'Die Auslegung angeglichenen Rechts' *JZ* 1992, 593 = 4; 'Perspektiven eines europäischen Unternehmensrechts' *ZGR* 1992, 435 = 1; *Der Letter of Intent: zur rechtlichen Bedeutung von Absichtserklärungen* (1998) = 0; *Gestaltungsfreiheit im Gesellschaftsrecht: Deutschland, Europa und USA* (1996) = 0.

[67] The citations all deal with European private law.

68 'Schlechtriem' received above 621 hits. The analysis was restricted to the following works of Peter Schlechtriem: *Restitution und Bereicherungs-recht in Europa* (2000) = 0; Schlechtriem's contribution to the *International Encyclopedia of Comparative Law* (1984) = 0; *Ausländisches Erbrecht im deutschen Verfahren: dargestellt am Falle der Maßgeblichkeit französischen Erbrechts* (1966) = 3; *Vertragsordnung und außervertragliche Haftung: eine rechtsvergleichende Untersuchung zur Konkurrenz von Ansprüchen aus Vertrag und Delikt im französischen und deutschen Recht* (1972) = 16.

69 A detailed analysis of von Bar's citations is, at present, not possible due to the ambiguous meaning of the 'von' and 'Bar' in the German language. Citations of the following works were analysed: von Bar's contribution in *Staudinger, Bürgerliches Gesetzbuch* (together with Mankowski) = 225; *Gemeineuropäisches Deliktsrecht* (1996) = 12; 'Grundfragen des Internationalen Deliktsrechts' *JZ* 1985, 961 = 1.

70 The common name 'Zimmermann' does not, at present, allow a full search. Citations of the following works were analysed: *Roman Law, Contemporary Law, European Law: the Civilian Tradition Today* (2001) = 0; *Good Faith in European Contract Law* (2000) = 3; *The Law of Obligations: Roman Foundations of the Civilian Tradition* (1992) = 1; *Das römisch-holländische Recht in Südafrika: Einführung in die Grundlagen und usus hodiernus* (1983) = 3; 'Der europäische Charakter englischen Rechts' *ZEuP* 1993, 4 = 0.

71 *The Law of Obligations: Roman Foundations of the Civilian Tradition* (1990) is cited in 65 articles. Other articles cite a broad range of Zimmermann's writings in comparative law and legal history. Examples: 'Der europäische Charakter englischen Rechts' *ZEuP* 1993, 4 = 10; 'Civil Code and Civil Law: The "Europeanization" of Private Law within the European Community and the Re-emergence of a European Legal Science' (1994/95) 1 *Colum J Eur L* 63 = 8; 'Das römisch-kanonische Ius Commune als Grundlage europäischer Rechtseinheit' *JZ* 1992, 8 = 8; 'Roman Law and European Legal Unity' in *Towards a European Civil Code* (1994) = 7.

72 Zweigert produced a total of 354 hits. Citations of the following works were analysed: Zweigert and Kötz, *Einführung in die Rechtsvergleichung* (various edns) = 34; 'Rechtsvergleichung, System und Dogmatik' in *Festschrift Bötticher* (1969) = 1; 'Grundsatzfragen der europäischen Rechtsangleichung, ihrer Schöpfung und Sicherung' in *Festschrift Dölle* (1968) = 1; *Die materielle Gültigkeit von Kaufverträgen = ein rechtsvergleichender Bericht* (1968) = 0; Zweigert/Puttfarken, *Rechtsvergleichung* (1978) = 0; 'Zum Kollisionsrecht der Leistungsschutzrechte' *GRUR Int* 1973, 573 = 4; Möhring, Schulze, Ulmer and Zweigert, *Quellen des Urheberrechts* (1961–2002) = 31.

73 David is directly mentioned in one article by Coing. There are two book reviews: *Arbitration in International Trade* (1985) and David and Jauffret-Spinosi, *Einführung in die großen Rechtssysteme der Gegenwart* (2nd edn, 1988).

74 *Corpus Juris der strafrechtlichen Regelungen zum Schutz der finanziellen Interessen der Europäischen Union* (1998) = 12; *The European Union and Penal*

Law: What Kind of Criminal Policy in Europe? (1996) = 1; Delmas-Marty and Greve in Jareborg (ed), *Towards Universal Law, de lege* (1995) = 1; *Quelle politique criminelle pour l'Europe?* (1993) = 2; *Pour un droit commun* (1994) = 1; *Droit penal des affaires*, vol 1 (3rd edn, 1990) = 1; Delmas-Marty and Teitgen-Colly, *Punir sans juger?* (1992) = 1; (1988) *Revue International de Droit Pénal* 27 = 1. Apart from these references, Delmas-Marty is cited twice with reference to a German publication: Tiedemann (ed), *Multinationale Unternehmen und Strafrecht* (1980).

[75] *An International Restatement of Contract Law: The UNIDROIT Principles of International Commercial Contracts* (1994/1997) = 8; (1992) 56 *RabelsZ* 274–89 (dealing with CISG) = 4; 'Das autonome Recht des Welthandels. Rechtsdogmatische und rechtspolitische Aspekte' (1978) 42 *RabelsZ* 485 = 5; (1996) 37 *ZfRV* 156 = 1; (1978) 27 *ICLQ* 413 = 1; (1997) *Revue dr unif* 1 = 1; *Le regole oggettive del commercio internazionale* (1976) = 1; 'The Relevance of Courses of Dealing, Usages and Customs in the Interpretation of International Commercial Conracts', in UNIDROIT (ed) = 1; 'The UNIDROIT Principles of International Commercial Contracts and the Principles of European Contract Law, a Comparison' in *Essays in Honour of Roy Goode* (1997) = 2; Bianca and Bonell, *Commentary on the International Sales Law* (1987) = 1.

[76] *Einführung in die Rechtsvergleichung* (2001) = 1; *Introduzione al diritto comparato* (5th edn, 1992) = 1; 'Legal Formants: A Dynamic Approach to Comparative Law' 39 *Amer J Comp L* (1991) 1 = 1.

[77] Over half of Professor George Bermann's citations (11) are for his 'Integrating Governmental and Officer Tort Liability' (1977) 77 *Columbia L Rev* 1175, whereas in a further 4, courts refer to him as an expert witness (on French law of succession and insurance and the German law of notarization and promises to make a gift). In one more case he is cited as an expert on international commercial arbitration. The remaining three citations go to a work he co-edited entitled *French Law: Constitution and Selective Legislation* (1994) and an article on provisional relief in international litigation at (1997) 35 *Colum J Transnat'l L* 553.

[78] Dawson receives 9 citations for a non-comparative piece entitled 'Lawyers and Involuntary Clients: Attorney Fees from Funds' (1974) 87 *Harv L Rev* 1597 and 4 citations for a related article entitled 'Lawyers and Involuntary Clients in Public Interest Litigation (1975) 88 *Harv L Rev* 849. His remaining 8 citations are to various pieces, broadly in the area of unjust enrichment and with a strong comparative component. The pieces are 'Economic Duress and the Fair Exchange in French and German Law' (1931) 11 *Tulane L Rev* 345; 'Negotiorum Gestio: The Altruistic Intermeddler' (1961) 74 *Harv L Rev* 817; and 'The Self-Serving Intermeddler' (1974) 87 *Harv L Rev* 1409.

[79] Of which 77 refer to the *Law of Torts* (1998). The following articles also received one citation each: 'Damages Against a Helpful Tortfeasor' (1992) 66 *ALJ* 388; 'Probabilistic Causation: A Postscript' (1991) 70 *Can Bar*

Rev 136; 'The Passing of Polemis' (1961) 39 *Can Bar Rev* 489; 'The Impact of Inflation on Tort Compensation' (1978) 26 *Amer J Comp L* 51.

⁸⁰ A record 671 of these citations are to his *Law of Torts* (1998). The following articles also receive one or two citations each: 'Probabilistic Causation in Tort Law' (1989) 68 *Can Bar Rev* 661; 'Probabilistic Causation in Tort Law: A Postscript' (1991) 70 *Can Bar Rev* 136; 'Retraction and Reply' (1978) 12 *UBCL Rev* 15; 'The Negligent Auditor and Stakeholders' (1990) 106 *LQR* 349; 'The Passing of Polemis' (1961) 39 *Can Bar Rev* 489.

⁸¹ Of which 30 refer to the *Law of Torts* (1998), 1 to *The American Tort Process* (1988) and 1 to 'Libel and Constitutional Free Speech' (a truly comparative piece) published in Peter Cane and Jane Stapleton (ed), *Essays for Patrick Atiyah* (1991).

⁸² Because the forms are common and therefore generated large numbers of false positives, we did not search on either 'John Fleming' or 'J Fleming.' This means that inevitably some true positives were missed.

⁸³ *Comparative Legal Traditions* (co-authored, 2nd edn, 1994) = 3; *A Nation Under Lawyers* (1994) = 2; *Rights Talk: The Impoverishment of Political Discourse* (1991) = 1; *The New Family and the New Property* (1981) = 1; 'Marriage and the State: The Withering Away of Marriage' (1976) 62 *Va L Rev* 663 = 1; 'Modern Marriage Law and Its Underlying Assumptions: The New Marriage and the New Property' (1980) 13 *Fam L Q* 443 = 1; *The Law of Decedent's Estates* (with Rheinstein, 1971) = 1; *A World Made New: Eleanor Roosevelt and the Universal Declaration of Human Rights* (2001) = 1. In one case she is quoted without citation.

⁸⁴ All but 2 of the citations are to *Comparative Law: Cases, Text, Materials* (edited with Baade, Damaska, Herzog, 1988). The 2 are to his *Formation of Contracts: A Study of the Common Core of Legal Systems* (1968).

⁸⁵ 9 of these citations are to *The Civil Law System* (1st and 2nd edns) ; the others refer to several of his articles dealing with aspects of conflicts of laws.

⁸⁶ Due to the number of false positives it was possible to search only on the full name 'John Bell,' which returned 5 cases: 2 cite his *Policy Arguments in Judicial Decisions* (1985) and 3 cite his edition of *Cross' Statutory Interpretation* (with George Engle, 2nd ed, 1987).

⁸⁷ All but one are citations to *Causation in the Law* (with Hart, 1st and 2nd edns). The isolated citation is to 'Necessary and Sufficient Conditions in Tort Law' in Owen (ed), *Philosophical Foundations of Tort Law* (1995).

⁸⁸ Every citation is to *Causation in the Law* (above n 87).

⁸⁹ 36 out of the 38 citations are to various edns of Winfield and Jolowicz *on Tort*. Likewise, 6 out of the 7 citations by American courts are also to the same work.

⁹⁰ 4 citations are to *Legal Aspects of Money* (various edns) and the rest fall to various pieces on private international law.

⁹¹ 11 citations are to the two edns of *Tort Law* (various edns), 9 citations to the *German Law of Torts* (various edns), and the remaining 6 to various other comparative law books or articles.

⁹² 2 citations to the two edns of *Tort Law* (various edns), 3 citations to *An Outline of the Law of Agency* (various edns) and the remaining 7 to various comparative law pieces.

⁹³ An electronic search using Professor Nicholas' initials or the name 'Barry' revealed no hits. The use of the surname 'Nicholas,' alone, revealed over 2,000 documents which, because of their volume, could not be searched but which, theoretically, could contain 'true positives.' The figure given in the chart must thus be read with the above qualification in mind.

⁹⁴ Of which 13 citations to his 'Unjustified Enrichment in the Civil Law and Louisiana Law' (1962) 36 *Tulane L Rev* 605 come from Louisiana Courts and 1 from the US District Court of the District of Puerto Rico. 10 citations are to his *Introduction to Roman Law*. Specifically, the US Court of Appeals for the 2nd Circuit cites the book in 3 cases, and the Appellate Division of the New York Supreme Court cites it in 2 cases. Five courts cite the book in 1 case each: the Oklahoma Supreme Court, the Washington Supreme Court, the California Court of Appeals, the US District Court for the District of New Jersey; and the US Court of Appeals for the 5th Circuit (in a case from Louisiana). Finally, the *French Law of Contract* is cited in 2 cases, one from the US Court of Appeals for the 11th Circuit and one from the US District Court for the Northern District of Illinois.

⁹⁵ A translated decision reproduced in Markesinis, *The German Law of Torts* (various edns) = 1; *Casebook on Tort* (various edns) = 1; 'Down Hill all the Way' (1999) *CLJ* 41 = 1; a book review in (1993) *CLJ* 520 = 1; 'Complex Liabilities' in Tunc (ed), *International Encyclopedia of Comparative Law* (1986) vol XI/2, ch 12 = 2.

⁹⁶ A translated decision included in Markesinis, *The German Law of Torts* (various edns) = 1; Zweigert and Kötz, *Introduction to Comparative Law* (translation, various edns) = 1.

⁹⁷ The following mini-table makes this surprising assertion very plausible:

Author	USA literature	Engl literature	USA courts	Engl courts
Asworth, A	164	95	4	7
Atyah, P	894	207	16	31
Birks, P B H	153	144	0	14
Goode R M	143	69	0	51
Treitel, G	99	118	2	71

⁹⁸ Shapiro, above n 4, at 412.

⁹⁹ *Ibid.* Shapiro has kindly informed me (e-mail dated 22 May 2002) that Glendon 'fell just short of the 1000-citation minimum needed to make' his list when he completed his searches in January 1999. But if that is so, and our figures are right, that means that Glendon almost doubled

her citations in about two years time since our searches counted until the end of 2001. Since this seems difficult to believe, one is forced to consider another possibility, namely that Shapiro's database is less complete than ours is (see Appendix 3 below for further details).

¹⁰⁰ 9th edn, 1998 (published posthumously).

¹⁰¹ The phenomenon can be found in other branches of the law (and there it may raise different questions). Birks, for instance, who holds with much distinction the Regius Chair at the University of Oxford, has devoted most of his writing to restitution; and it is this, which (according to statistics) has had most impact on his colleagues. Roman law, traditionally the topic of his chair, features in the following figures in a much lower position. They are gleaned from the last 20 years of the following law journals: *Cambridge Law Journal, Law Quarterly Review, Modern Law Review, Oxford Journal of Legal Science* and *Legal Studies*. (The figure gives the number of times the piece has been cited.) The breakdown is as follows: *An Introduction to the Law of Restitution* (1985) = 60; 'Misdirected Funds: Restitution from the Recipient' [1989] *LMCLQ* 296 = 5; 'Civil Wrongs: A New World' *Butterworths Lectures 1990–91* = 5; *Frontiers of Liability* (1994) = 6; *The Legal Mind: Essays for Tony Honoré* (edited with MacCormick, 1994) = 5; 'In Defence of Free Acceptance' in Burrows (ed), *Essays on the Law of Restitution* (1985) = 1; *Restitution: The Future* (1992) = 2; *Restitution and Equity*, vol 1, *Resulting Trusts and Equitable Compensation* = 1; 'Mixing and Tracing: Property and Restitution' [1992] 2 *CLP* 69 = 2; *Laundering and Tracing* (1995) = 3; 'The Law of Restitution at the End of an Epoch' (1999) *UWALR* 13 = 1; *Wrongs and Remedies in the Twenty-First Century* (1995) = 3; 'The Concept of a Civil Wrong' in Owen (ed), *Philosophical Foundations of Tort Law* = 3; 'On the Nature of Undue Influence' in Beatson and Friedman (eds), *Good Faith and Fault in Contract Law* (1995) = 4; 'The English Recognition of Unjust Enrichment' (1991) *LMCLQ* 473 = 3; 'Restitution and Wrongs' (1982) 35 *CLP* 53 = 2; *Privacy and Loyalty* (1997) = 1; *What are Law Schools For?* (1994) = 4; *Reviewing Legal Education* (1995) = 2; 'Equity in the Modern Law: An Exercise in Taxonomy' (1996) 26(1) *UWALR* 1 = 2; 'The Independence of Restitutionary Causes of Action' (1990) 16 *QULJ* 1 = 1; 'Personal Restitution in Equity' [1988] *LMCLQ* 128 = 1; 'Trusts in the Recovery of Misapplied Assets' in McKendrick (ed), *Commercial Aspects of Trusts and Fiduciary Obligations* = 1; (1989) 105 *LQR* 528, noting *Agip v Jackson* = 1; *The Institutes of Justinian* (1987) = 1; 'The Implied Contract Theory of Quasi-Contract: Civilian Opinion Current in the Century Before Blackstone' (1986) 6 *OJLS* 546 = 1; 'Intermingling of Property in English Law' in *Proceedings of Anglo-Polish Legal Symposium 1989* = 1; 1 *Polytechnic Law Review* 39 = 1; 'Restitution and the Freedom of Contract' (1983) *CLP* 141 = 2; 'Restitutionary Damages for Breach of Contract: Snapp and the Fusion of Law and Equity' [1987] *LMCLQ* 421 = 2; 'Adjudication and Interpretation in the Common Law: A Century of Change' (1994) 14 *Legal*

Studies 156 = 3; 'Failure of Consideration' in Rose (ed), *Consensus ad idem* = 1; *Pressing Problems in the Law*, vol 1, *Criminal Justice and Human Rights* (1995) = 1; 'No Consideration: Restitution After Void Contracts' (1993) 23 *UWALR* 195 = 1; '*Negotiorum Gestio* and the Common Law' (1971) 24 *CLP* 110 = 2; *English Private Law* (2001) = 1; 'Trusts Raised to Reverse Unjust Enrichment' [1996] *RLR* 3 = 1; *The Classification of Obligations* (1997) = 2; 'Change of Position: The Nature of the Defence and its Relationship to Other Restitutionary Defences' in McInnes (ed), *Restitution: Developments in Unjust Enrichment* = 1; 'Konkurrierende Strategien und Interessen: Das Irrtumserfordernis im Bereicherungsrecht des Common Law' *ZEuP* 1993, 554 = 1; 'A Lifelong Obligation of Confidence' (1989) 105 *LQR* 501 = 1; 'When Money is Paid in Pursuance of a Void Authority: A Duty to Repay?' [1992] *PL* 580 = 1; 'Restitution After Ineffective Contracts: Issues for the 1990s' (1990) 2 *JCL* 227 = 1. Total = 144.

[102] 3rd edn, 1972.

[103] 1st edn, 1982; 2nd edn, 1992.

[104] 'Fundamental Rights and Judicial Review in France' [1978] *PL* 82 with only 2 citations in the English literature of the last 20 years.

[105] (1988) 104 *LQR* 530.

[106] This list is incomplete in that it does not include his monumental treatise on *The South African Law of Trusts*, once entirely his own work but now, in its 5th edn, up-dated by four colleagues, which is widely cited in South Africa.

[107] Which, incidentally, earns Weir, as its translator, the bulk of his citations.

[108] Book review in (1978) 26 *The American Journal of Comparative Law* 495.

[109] Judging from the fact that it is only cited in 9 documents.

[110] Where only one document seems to have cited these articles.

[111] (1991–92) 6/7 *Tulane Civil Law Forum* 61.

[112] (2000) 29 *Legal Studies* 319.

[113] These figures come from Posner, above n 2, at 78 and cover citations in law articles over a much shorter period (1982–89) than that covered by Shapiro's later works.

[114] According to Shapiro, above n 4, at 424 ff, Tribe *American Constitutional Law* (3rd edn, 2000) earns him 5,351 citations; Prosser's similarly popular tort book earns him 4,984. Though these figures also include citation of important articles, these authors seem to be 'primarily cited for one or two standard treatises' (*ibid*, at 414). Professor Bruce Ackerman comes in with a healthy but less impressive 2,547 while Judge Guido Calabresi overtakes him by some 300 citations with 2,887 to his credit.

[115] To a traditional English reader, unaccustomed to the idea of institutes or centres as hubs of learning, networking and research, this may even appear as an odd criterion. Yet, not only are they beginning to grow

in number; in one or two instances we can see how beneficial they are to the entire academic community. The institution I have in mind is the Centre for Commercial Law Studies of Queen Mary and Westfield College, London created by Sir Roy Goode. In my view, it is one of the greatest examples of a legacy-making event in the English legal world of the last 50 years. For Sir Roy beat the odds that were stacked against him from a disadvantaged location; he overcame—helping from afar an able team of successors—the almost inevitable decline that could have followed his move to a chair in Oxford; and he ensured, through the careful cultivation of two donors, that eventually his creation would end up being properly, indeed generously, endowed from private funds as no other centre or institute in England. The Centre was not just created; the Centre has not only survived as a structure. The Centre has promoted the teaching and research of many areas of commercial law, which had been neglected in England until its appearance. And central in its policy plan— and that is why I mention it here—we also find the study of foreign law and comparative methodology. This is not just a sign of Goode seeing comparative methodology as being essential to commercial lawyers and practitioners. It is also a sign of vision, coming as it did at a time when the old universities, Cambridge in particular, was willing to let its own (ad hominem) chair lie dormant for 15 years as its last holder, Tony Jolowicz, retired in the mid-1980s.

116 See his own assessment in 'L'Italie en tête' (1995) *RIDC*, 131.

117 On the other hand, and in accordance with what was said earlier on, Cappelletti, having written extensively in English, dwarfs Sacco in citations in the American literature.

118 *Fairchild v Glenhaven Funeral Services Ltd* [2002] 3 WLR 89.

119 In Annelise Riles (ed), *Rethinking the Masters of Comparative Law* (2001) 256. We were originally tempted to attribute the tendency to exaggerate to the Mediterranean predilection for well-intended hyperbole. The phenomenon, however, like so many other patterns of human behaviour, is nowadays also encountered with increased frequency in this country, so stereotypical accusations must be avoided. Thus, to give one example, Nicholas' obituary in *The Times* of 7 March 2002 referred to his student textbook on *The French Law of Contract* as showing comparative law 'at its best.' Even allowing for some latitude given the nature of the piece, the statement still conveys a picture which not all full-time comparatists would recognise. Yet even greater praise is reserved for Nicholas' *Introduction to Roman Law* which is described as 'quite simply the best introduction to law that has ever been written.' Again, it could be argued that the obituarist might have achieved his aim more plausibly had he at least added the word 'Roman' before the word 'law.' Talking to me, the country's leading Roman lawyer seemed even more reserved. The statistics in this chapter could be seen as supporting him.

[120] Here, in another sense, my text represents an over-simplification, for one at least of Gorla's disciples, Professor Maurizio Lupoi, has published two major works in English—*The Origins of the European Legal Order* (1994) and *Trusts: A Comparative Study* (2000), which have earned him both in his own country and abroad a formidable reputation.

[121] The country used is not necessarily the country of origin but the country in which is located the university of the author at the time of writing.

[122] *The American Tort Process* (1988).

[123] 'Impracticability and Impossibility in the UN Convention on Contracts for the International Sales of Goods' in Galston and Smit (eds), *International Sales* (1984).

[124] In Bianca and Bonell, *Commentary on the International Sales Law* (1987).

[125] *Deliktsrecht* (various edns) = 3; *Münchner Kommentar zum Bürgerlichen Gesetzbuch, Allgemeine Geschäftsbedingungen* (1984, 1993) = 46; others = 4.

[126] A contribution to von Caemmerer (ed), *Vorschläge und Gutachten zur Reform des deutschen internationalen Privatrechts der außervertraglichen Schuldverhältnisse* (1983).

[127] Of which 31 citations refer to Lorenz' contribution to Staudinger, *Kommentar zum Bürgerlichen Gesetzbuch* (1999).

[128] There are no citations of 'Marcus Lutter.' 'Lutter' is cited in 127 cases, of which 125 deal with German law only (mostly company law) and 2 with EC law.

[129] *Festschrift für Rheinstein* (1969) = 2 and *Festschrift für von Caemmerer* (1978) = 2.

[130] Citations in the context of CISG.

[131] Of which 17 citations refer to Jauernig and Schlechtriem, *Bürgerliches Gesetzbuch* (10th edn, 2003).

[132] Cited on comparative Swiss, Austrian, English and French international private law.

[133] Staudinger and von Bar, in von Standinger's *Kommentar zum Bürgerlichen Gesetzbuch mit Einfuhrungsgesetz und Nebensgesetzen* (13th ed, 1996) (EGBGB) 4; *Internationales Privatrecht* (vols 1 and 2) = 8; *Europäisches Gemeinschaftsrecht und Internationales Privatrecht* (1991) = 1; others = 6.

[134] There are no hits for 'Reinhard Zimmermann'; 'Zimmermann' is cited in 50 cases, of which only one citation is comparative (Swiss law).

[135] Both citations refer to Möhring, Schulze, Ulmer and Zweigert, *Quellen des Urheberrechts, Länderberichte* (Stand 30.VI.1971).

[136] See, eg, Brox, *Allgemeiner Teil des BGB* (25th edn, 2001) 38–44; von Münch, *Staatsrecht I* (6th edn, 2000) 11–13.

[137] Zweigert, 'Rechtsvergleichung als universale Interpretationsmethode' (inaugural lecture in Tübingen) (1949/1950) 15 *RabelsZ* 5–21.

[138] Häberle, *Rechtsvergleichung im Kraftfeld des Verfassungsstaates* (1992) 27 ff.

[139] Drobnig, 'Rechtsvergleichung in der Deutschen Rechtsprechung' (1986) 50 *RabelsZ* 610 at 611.

[140] Kötz, 'Der Bundesgerichtshof und die Rechtsvergleichung' in Heldrich and Hopt (eds), *50 Jahre Bundesgerichtshof, Festgabe der Wissenschaft, Band II* (2000) 842.

[141] Lutter, 'Die Auslegung angeglichenen Rechts' *JZ* 1992, 593 at 604; Mansel, 'Rechtsvergleichung und europäische Rechtseinheit' *JZ* 1991, 529 at 531; Odersky, 'Harmonisierende Auslegung und europäische Rechtskultur' *ZEuP* 1994, 1 at 2.

[142] Such as the Warsaw Convention.

[143] Which has been influenced by English contract law.

[144] Drobnig, above n 139, at 615.

[145] Optional or voluntary exercise in ice skating; see Kötz, above n 140, at 832.

[146] Zweigert, above n 137, at 9; Aubin, 'Die Rechtsvergleichende Interpretation autonom-internen Rechts in der deutschen Rechtsprechung' (1970) 34 *RabelsZ* 458–59.

[147] Infringement of personality rights: BGHZ 35, 363 (1961); BGHZ 39, 124 (1963); BGHZ 131, 332 (1995); BVerfGE 34, 269 (1973). Compensation for damage suffered in the course of dangerous sports activities: BGHZ 63, 140 (1974). Wrongful life: BGHZ 86, 240 (1983). Rescue doctrine: BGHZ 101, 215 (1987). Claims based on tort if the requirements of claims based on sales contracts are precluded: BGHZ 101, 337 (1987). Duty of a tortfeasor to pay compensation although the victim continues to be payed by an employer during sick leave on the basis of § 616 BGB: BGHZ 21, 112 (1956).

[148] BVerfGE 36, 146 (1973).

[149] BGHZ 24, 214 (1957).

[150] BGHSt 1, 293 (1951); BGHSt 9, 385 (1956); BGHSt 32, 345 (1984); BGHSt 38, 214 (1992); BGHSt 44, 308 (1998).

[151] BVerwGE 12, 42 (1961).

[152] Aubin, above n 146, at 458 ff.

[153] RGZ 74, 276 (1910); RGZ 77, 152 (1911); RGZ 79, 332 (1912); RGZ 80, 385 (1912); RGZ 82, 116 (1913); RGZ 84, 419 (1915); RGZ 123, 102 (1928).

[154] Mössner, 'Rechtsvergleichung und Verfassungsrechtsprechung' *AöR* 1974, 193 ff.

[155] Parliamentary system: BVerfGE 1, 144 (1952) on parliamentary procedures concerning money bills; BVerfGE 1, 208 (1952) on election principles; OVGE 12, 470 on the participation of cabinet members in parliamentary commissions of inquiry; BVerfGE 4, 144 (1955) and BVerfGE 32, 157 (1971) on the expenses of MPs. Social state principle (*Sozialstaatsprinzip*): BVerfGE 1, 97 (1951). Division of powers: BVerfGE 3, 225 (1953); BGHZ 10, 266 (1953) and LG Lübeck, *NJW* 1953, 907. Definition of political treaties within the meaning of art 59(2) Basic Law: BVerfGE 1, 372 (1952). Prohibition of political parties: BVerfGE 5, 85 (1956). Extradition: BVerfGE 4, 299 (1955) and BVerfGE 18, 112 (1964). Adjudication of law

enacted by the allies during their occupation of Germany after 1945 (*Besatzungsrecht*): BVerfGE 2, 181 (1953). Analogous application of time limits: BVerfGE 4, 31 (1954). Validity of penal judgments pronounced in the absence of the accused: BVerfGE 1, 332 (1952) and BGH, *NJW* 1965, 1146. Right of members of the press to give evidence in criminal procedings concerning treason: BVerfGE 20, 162 (1966). Freedom of expression: BVerfGE 1, 198 (1951). Nature of laws dealing with press delicts (state laws, not federal criminal law): BVerfGE 7, 29 (1957). Family law: BVerfGE 10, 59 (1959). Freedom of artistic opinion: BVerfGE 30, 173 (1971). Freedom of occupation: BVerfGE 7, 377 (1958) and BVerfGE 21, 245 (1967). Constitutional complaint (*Verfassungsbeschwerde*): BVerfGE 1, 97 (1951).

[156] Mössner, above n 154, at 228.

[157] Drobnig, above n 139, at 626.

[158] Mössner has counted 11 unspecified comparative arguments in 29 decisions. These decisions frequently use phrases such as 'the development of this area of law in other countries' or refer to 'international developments.'

[159] One example is the unspecified quotation of Cardozo in the famous Lüth-decision of the Bundesverfassungsgericht (BVerfGE 7, 198 at 208).

[160] BGHZ 86, 240 at 250.

[161] BVerfGE 3, 225 at 244 endorses the use of comparative law in the interpretation of statutes.

[162] BVerfGE 20, 162.

[163] At 220–21.

[164] At 208. The lack of a coherent comparative methodology in court decisions is also noted by Drobnig, above n 139, at 625.

[165] RGZ 91, 269 (1917).

[166] RGZ 109, 243 (1924).

[167] RGZ 99, 105 (1920).

[168] RGZ 103, 359 (1921).

[169] RGZ 120, 205 (1928).

[170] RGZ 123, 102 (1928).

[171] Aubin, above n 146, at 463 ff.

[172] Dölle, 'Der Beitrag der Rechtsvergleichung zum deutschen Recht' in *Hundert Jahre Deutsches Rechtsleben (Festschrift Deutscher Juristentag), Band 2* (1960) 19 at 37; Kötz, above n 140, at 835; Mössner, above n 154, at 220; Aubin, above n 146, at 470.

[173] Dölle, above n 172, at 34.

[174] Odersky, above n 141, at 4; Kötz, above n 140, at 840.

[175] Kötz, above n 140, at 841.

[176] This is noted by Drobnig, above n 139, at 611.

[177] Dölle, above n 172, at 47.

[178] Max-Planck-Institut Hamburg für ausländisches und internationales Privatrecht in Hamburg; Institut für ausländisches und internationales Privat- und Wirtschaftsrecht der Universität Heidelberg; Institut für

ausländisches und internationales Privatrecht der Universität Freiburg; Institut für internationales und ausländisches Privatrecht der Universität zu Köln; Institut für internationales Recht—Rechtsvergleichung—der Universität München; Institut für internationales Recht und Rechtsvergleichung der Universität Osnabrück; Institut für ausländisches und internationales Privatrecht der Universität Passau.

[179] A previous series covers the years 1965–88.

[180] BVerfGE 49, 286. A subsequent legislative initiative relates to the material gathered for the proceedings; see BT-Drucks 8/2947, 13.

[181] BVerfGE 7, 377 at 415–16.

[182] Mössner, above n 154, at 204; Coing, 'Aufgaben der Rechtsvergleichung in unserer Zeit' *NJW* 1981, 2601 at 2603; Mansel, above n 141, at 531.

[183] Dölle, above n 172, at 22–33.

[184] Mössner, above n 154, at 208–11.

[185] Entwurf eines Gesetzes zur Regelung des Rechts der Allgemeinen Geschäftsbedingungen, BR-Drucks 360/75.

[186] Entwurf eines Gesetzes zur Modernisierung des Schuldrechts, BT-Drucks 14/6040.

[187] Entwurf eines Zweiten Gesetzes zur Änderung schadensersatzrechtlicher Vorschriften, BT-Drucks 14/7752.

[188] Eg, Wilhelm Consulting, *Study on the Possible Economic Impact of the Proposal for a Directive on the Sale of Consumer Goods and Associated Guarantees* (1998) and the extensive material published by the Federal Ministry of Justice on the reform of the German law of obligations: *Gutachten und Vorschläge zur Überarbeitung des Schuldrechts* (1981); *Abschlußbericht der Kommission zur Überarbeitung des Schuldrechts* (1992).

[189] BT-Drucks 14/6040, 161–63.

[190] *Ibid* 174–76.

[191] §§ 305–310 BGB.

[192] BT-Drucks 14/6040, 92, 149–60.

[193] *Ibid* 133–37.

[194] *Ibid* 176–78.

[195] *Ibid* 180–89.

[196] *Ibid* 178–80.

[197] *Ibid* 98–125.

[198] *Ibid* 131.

[199] BT-Drucks 14/7752, 15.

[200] *Ibid* 24–26.

[201] *Ibid* 31.

[202] Transforming a number of European directives into German law, the *Schuldrechtsreform* is also a move to secure the position of the BGB as a model for a future European codification.

[203] Authors mentioned in this context include Dölle, Huber, Schlechtriem and Weitnauer.

204 BR-Drucks 360/75,. 11.

205 A good example is *The State v Makwanyane and Mchunu* 1995 (6) BCLR 665 (CC) of 6 June 1995 on the constitutionality of the death penalty, one of the first judgments of the South African Constitutional Court. President Arthur Chaskalson, delivering the unanimous decision of the court, had recourse to German constitutional law in the context of (a) the use of legislative history as an interpretative tool in constitutional disputes (at [16]); (b) the right to human dignity (at [59]); (c) the limitation of fundamental rights (at [108]); and (d) s 33(1)(b) of the Interim Constitution, the so-called 'essential content clause' (at [132–33]).

206 A so-called 'homeland' with its own constitution, regarded as independent by South Africa at the time, though internationally never recognised as such.

207 Wiechers, 'Abhandlung über den südafrikanischen Staat' in *Festschrift für Klaus Stern zum 65. Geburtstag* (1997) 381; Rabie, van der Merwe and Labuschange, 'The Contribution of the Alexander von Humboldt Foundation to the Development of the South African Legal System and Literature' *Tydskrif vir Hedendaagse Romeins-Hollandse Reg* 1993, 608 at 610; Venter, 'Aspects of the South African Constitution of 1996: An African Democratic and Social Rechtsstaat?' *ZaöRV* 1997, 51 at 73.

208 The Konrad Adenauer Stiftung, the Friedrich Ebert Stiftung and the Friedrich Naumann Stiftung were very active in South Africa during the constitution-making process.

209 Among the German universities which established academic ties with South African institutions were, inter alia, Augsburg, Bonn, Köln, Frankfurt, Freiburg, Göttingen, Hamburg, Münster, Regensburg, Saarbrücken and Tübingen.

210 See s 35(1) of the 1994 Constitution and s 39(1)(c) of the 1996 Constitution.

211 Scott, 'Evaluation of Security by Means of Movables: Problems and Possible Solutions. Section C: Codification of the Law of Cession' *Tydskrif vir Hedendaagse Romeins-Hollandse Reg* 1997, 633 at 638.

212 This section draws heavily on Dr Fedtke's exhaustive analysis of this wider topic, above n 8.

213 See, eg, the *Makwanyane* decision of the South African Constitutional Court mentioned earlier (above n 205). In *Makwanyane*, the court referred to the *Grundgesetz* and various judgments of the Bundesverfassungsgericht mainly with the help of two American sources: Kommers, *The Constitutional Jurisprudence of the Federal Republic of Germany* (1989) and Currie, *The Constitution of the Federal Republic of Germany* (1994). Kommers and Currie are thus cited 3 and 5 times respectively by the court. Professor Dieter Grimm (at that time a member of the German Constitutional Court) is also cited twice, but for one of his English publications, namely 'Human Rights and Judicial Review in

Germany' in Beatty (ed), *Human Rights and Judicial Review: A Comparative Perspective* (1994) 267 ff. Original German sources (judicial and academic) are referred to only indirectly. The judgments of the Bundesverfassungsgericht were accessed through the works of Kommers and Currie; and a reference to Maunz and Dürig, *Grundgesetz* (one of the leading commentaries on the German Basic Law) can also be found via Currie. This and other such cases, which we do not cite because of lack of space, confirm the validity of one of the theses of this book: academics can help judges, thus not only ensuring better co-operation between the different parts of the legal profession but also promoting the use of foreign law. Studying these cases can also offer comparatists the opportunity to fine-tune the methodology proposed in this book.

²¹⁴ See the following dictum by Justice Kriegler in *Bernstein and others v Bester NO and others* 1996 (4) BCLR 449 (CC): 'I agree with the identification and the logical analysis of the principle . . . but prefer to express no view on the possible lessons to be learnt from other jurisdictions. That I do, not because of a disregard for section 35(1) of the Constitution, or in a spirit of parochialism. My reason is twofold. First, because the subtleties of foreign jurisdictions, their practices and terminology require more intensive study than I have been able to conduct. Even on a superficial view, there seem to me to be differences of substance between the statutory, jurisprudential and societal contexts prevailing in those countries and in South Africa as to render ostensible analogies dangerous without thorough understanding of the foreign systems. For the present I cannot claim that degree of proficiency. . . . The second reason is that I wish to discourage the frequent—and, I suspect, often facile—resort to foreign 'authorities.' Far too often one sees citation by counsel of, for instance, an American judgment in support of a proposition relating to our Constitution, without any attempt to explain why it is said to be in point. Comparative study is always useful, particularly where the courts in exemplary jurisdictions have grappled with universal issues confronting us. Likewise, where a provision in our Constitution is manifestly modelled on a particular provision in another country's constitution, it would be folly not to ascertain how the jurists of that country have interpreted their precedential provision. The prescripts of section 35(1) of the Constitution are also very clear: where applicable, public international law in the field of human rights must be considered, and regard may be had to comparative foreign case law. But that is a far cry from blithe adoption of alien concepts or inappropriate precedents.'

²¹⁵ See, eg, the frequent references to the Occasional Papers series of the Konrad Adenauer Stiftung.

²¹⁶ See, eg, the frequent citations of Blaauw, 'The Rechtsstaat Idea Compared with the Rule of Law as a Paradigm for Protecting Rights' (1990) *South African Law Journal* 76 ff; de Waal, 'A Comparative Analysis of the Provisions of German Origin in the Interim Bill of Rights' (1995)

South African Journal of Human Rights 1 ff; de Wet, 'Can the Social State Principle in Germany Guide State Action in the Field of Social and Economic Rights?' (1995) *South African Journal of Human Rights* 30 ff.

[217] This is recognised by South African academics such as Professors H A Strydom, André van der Walt and Venter.

[218] The so-called Trento project seems to be the major exception, but then it is run by the very same people who belong to the Sacco/Schlesinger schools.

4

Foreign Law Inspiring National Law: Lessons from *Greatorex v Greatorex*

1. THE THEORY PUT INTO PRACTICE

In this chapter we will not talk of recourse to foreign law because the parties chose it, or because it has to be applied because it is so decreed by the rules of private international law. Nor are we referring to the law coming from such courts as those of Strasbourg or Luxembourg—not least because, nowadays, for most of the systems discussed in this book, this cannot be properly called 'foreign' law. Here we shall, instead, focus only on the voluntary use by judge (or counsel) of foreign law and foreign legal ideas as a means of shaping national law when this is unclear, contradictory, or otherwise in need of reform.

One thing must be made clear from the outset. The number of instances in which this kind of borrowing may happen must, of necessity, be limited—though in intellectual terms, such conscious inspiration from abroad must always be exciting to attempt. Yet in a shrinking world in which increased movement of people and ideas is making the convergence of tastes, habits, and practices more pronounced than ever before, legal convergence in various shapes and forms cannot be that far behind. In this world the incidents of legal borrowing can thus only increase, not decrease.

In *Fairchild v Glenhaven Funeral Services Ltd*,[1] Lord Bingham of Cornhill added two more reasons to those already mentioned, which will prompt such comparative law exercises.

First, he observed that:

> If . . . a decision is given in this country which offends one's basic sense
> of justice, and if consideration of international sources suggests that a
> different and more acceptable decision would be given in most other
> jurisdictions, *whatever their legal tradition*, this must prompt anxious
> review of the decision in question.

The italicised words make the judge's open-mindedness
truly admirable—even though it is not novel, given that he has
given evidence of it already in many extra-judicial pronouncements. But then Lord Bingham gave a second reason, from a
practical point of view potentially more significant than the
first. He put it in this way:

> In a shrinking world (in which the employees of asbestos[2] companies
> may work for those companies in any one or more of several countries)
> there must be some virtue in uniformity of *outcome*[3] whatever the
> diversity of approach in reaching that outcome.

This harmonisation or convergence cannot come without
increased knowledge of foreign law. I would go even further
than that and say, 'sympathetic' knowledge of foreign law. An
open mind is, of course, a pre-requisite for any such process;
but it is not enough. The ability to borrow solutions—'ready
made', so to speak—is, in most cases, simply not possible,
however 'sympathetic' the potential borrower may be. The
problem is that foreign law is unlikely to come in a simple
form, attractively packaged or, to change the metaphor, easily
digestible. Language is by no means the only, or even major,
problem in such attempts to import a foreign idea if not actually transplant the foreign solution. It is certainly beyond the
abilities of a hard pressed practitioner. That is why I came to
advocate a more *co-ordinated* use of the different talents that
judges, practitioners, and academics bring to the process of
creating and interpreting law.[4]

Three decades of teaching foreign law and trying to develop a
workable theory of comparative methodology has had its ups
and downs. When one finds oneself in the final stretch of one's
career such admissions are easy to make. But one of the greatest
obstacles in moving closer to one another has, in my view, been
the result of the attitude adopted by my fellow-comparatists
who have tried to shape wider theories about legal transplants
(or their impossibility). Great names have contributed to this

debate: Watson is one; and to this task he has dedicated his knowledge of history as well as his understanding of many cultures which has been alluded to in earlier chapters. More sceptical, as we have noted, is Legrand; and he has flourished amidst the controversy he has skilfully generated around his theories. My approach, as I explained in the earlier chapters, has steered clear from such grand schemes. It has been pragmatic and judge- and practitioner-oriented rather than trying to capture the imagination of fellow academics. This is not because I am working in a common law environment where the judge is, as it was once said, the 'senior partner in the law creating process.' Watson and Legrand, after all, have also spent much of their time working in the same environment. My methodology has been shaped by the decline experienced by the subject in those classrooms, which attributed to it mainly or exclusively a *mission civilisatrice*. Thus, I always felt and feel, if one could only get judges interested in foreign law, practitioners would have to use it. And they could not use it without some help and preparation from academics. The subject would thus, in a roundabout way, be revived; and its revival would also stimulate another favourite cause of mine: the greater collaboration between academics and practitioners.

I said all this in earlier chapters. But I repeat it here, for in this country my approach seems to have found its best practical illustration yet in the judgment of the High Court in *Greatorex v Greatorex*.[5] This case thus gives me an occasion to speak of my own methodology in a concrete manner, talk of its potential achievements, and pinpoint some areas where further refinement is needed. As pointed out in chapter two above, it also shows how difficult (and certainly time-consuming) it can be for the researcher. But, I think, this offers the chance to argue— and perhaps prove—that the practical orientation of the subject need not deprive it of a purely intellectual appeal. So what was *Greatorex* about?

The facts of the case were relatively simple. In that case a young man, whom as n 7, below, explains we shall henceforth call D2, was injured in an accident caused by his own grossly negligent driving. P, his father, a professional fire officer stationed nearby, suffered serious post-traumatic stress disorder as a result of attending his unconscious son at the scene of the accident. The question was whether the father could claim damages for his harm from the driver/ injured son or, since he was uninsured, from the Motor Insurance Bureau (MIB), which stepped into the gap and became the second defendant in the action. In his judgment for the defendants Mr Justice Cazalet made bold, even interesting, use of foreign law. Yet thus far his judgment has been only the subject of one case note;[6] and from a comparative point of view, it has not received anywhere near the attention given to Lord Goff's opinion in *White v Jones*.[7] Why this is so can, for the time being, be left open to speculation. But without any disrespect to Cazalet J it might be legitimate to ponder whether in law, as in other activities in life, the importance attached to a pronouncement can depend more on the status and profile of its maker than on its own intrinsic value. This is unfortunate, for it means that valuable ideas may be ignored until they are considered or adopted by an appellate court. Whatever the answer to this wider question, the fact remains that in terms of comparative law and methodology Cazalet J's judgment is, in some respects, more significant than Lord Goff's obiter dicta ruminations in *White v Jones*. For, unlike *White*, where foreign law embellished an opinion of a high-profile judge but did not influence it directly,[8] in *Greatorex* foreign law formed an important part of the argument of both counsels' submissions as well as the decision of the judge. The outcome is as interesting as the way it came about. For this decision can be seen as the result of a de facto collaboration between the three sides of the legal profession. That, in my view, is the major interest of the case; and anyone who does not share my approach can, from a comparative point of view, criticise *Greatorex* only in one way, namely by saying that it still very much a minority example.

The discussion will be undertaken under four headings: the German model (2. below); its application to the English case (3. below); unresolved questions (4. below); further ideas from the USA (5. below). The four sub-headings or themes will then be brought together in the form of some tentative conclusions of wider import consistent with the main theses of this book.

2. THE GERMAN MODEL

The case that figured prominently in *Greatorex* was the decision of the German Federal Supreme Court of 11 May 1971.[9] The facts of the case were simple. On 6 March 1965, when he was 64 years old, the plaintiff's husband (henceforth referred to as D2)[10] was fatally injured in a collision with the defendant's motor vehicle caused partly by his fault and partly by that of the defendant (henceforth we shall refer to this 'primary' defendant as D1). The plaintiff in this case (henceforth P) was the 50-year old wife of D2 (the primary victim of the accident). In her suit against the tortfeasor, she claimed damages for the injury to her health, which she suffered when *told*[11] of the death of her husband, D2. The Landgericht allowed the claim in full, the Oberlandesgericht in part. P appealed with permission to the German Federal Court, and her appeal was allowed. The judgment below was vacated, and the case remanded to the Oberlandesgericht.

The case involved a claim for what we now call psychiatric damage in England.[12] Naturally, one is inclined to say, it also touched upon some of the usual questions that we, too, have encountered in this part of the law and, it seems, are unable to solve through the courts.[13] How German law handled the shock aspect of the claim is not the subject of discussion in this essay since the matter has been discussed in detail elsewhere.[14] But the second part of the German case addressed the question of D2's contributory negligence and how this would/ should affect P's claim. The German court's approach need only be reported in its bare essentials and to the extent that it bears on what is the main theme of this article.

Understandably, D1's contention was that P's claim should be reduced to take into account D2's contributory fault. One way to do this was to attempt to rely upon § 846 BGB, which states that:

> If, *in the cases provided by §§ 844, 845,* some fault of the injured party had contributed to cause the damage which the third party has sustained, the provision of § 254 BGB [about contributory negligence] applies to the claim of the third party.

The problem with such an approach, however, lies in the italicised section of this paragraph which refers to what is, in essence, the German equivalent to our Fatal Accident Acts as amended in 1982. In fact, § 846 BGB provides precisely the same kind of answer that we accept in fatal accident claims: the deceased's negligence affects the claims of the dependants. But in this case, so far as the wife's claim for psychiatric injury was concerned, it was *not* a fatal accidents claim but a direct personal claim based on § 823 I BGB. This was a crucial twist. The German court thus took the view—rightly, it is suggested—that the application of § 846 BGB was not available, even for an analogical extension.

With the wife (P) claiming not as dependant but in her own right (for her own psychiatric damage as injury to her health under § 823 I BGB), D1's attempt to mitigate the extent of his liability seemed optimistic. For, if P's claim was original and not derivative—terms hinted at by the German decision but, as we shall note later, excessively relied upon by American cases—her demand that her damages remain undiminished by her husband's (D2's) negligence looked unshakeable. Yet the German court, invoking the catchall clause of good faith contained in the celebrated § 242 BGB, decided to reduce her damages in proportion to D2's fault. Thus, for our purposes, the relevant part of the judgment reads as follows:

> Here the accident to her husband was only able to cause the harm supposedly suffered by the plaintiff because as a result of their close personal relationship his tragedy became hers. One cannot imagine a person suffering in this manner on hearing of a fatal accident to a total stranger; indeed, if it happened, it would be so unusual that one would decline to impute it to the defendant on the ground that it was unforeseeable. But if the critical reason of the plaintiff's suffering this injury to her health was her close personal relationship to her husband, it was thus only fair that her claim should be affected by his fault in contributing to the accident.

This reasoning was further reinforced by (what we would call) an obiter dictum that was to prove crucial in the *Greatorex* litigation.[15] For the German court added that:

> If the husband's death had been solely attributable to his failure to take care of himself, the plaintiff would have had no claim whatever for compensation for the consequent injury to herself. A person is under

no legal duty, whatever the moral position may be, to look after his own life and limb simply in order to save the dependants from the likely psychical effects on them if he is killed or maimed. To impose such a legal duty, except in very peculiar cases, for instance, wherever a person commits suicide in a deliberately shocking manner, would be to restrict a person's self-determination in a manner inconsistent with our legal system.

To the above rule the only exception that some authors[16] are prepared to make is in the context of suicide. Suicide may provoke rescue, especially in a system where the duty to rescue others is recognised by law.[17] Thus they have argued that a person wishing to commit suicide may be under a duty to carry out the suicide in a way which does not 'provoke' any rescue by third parties; otherwise he *may* be liable for any damage suffered during the rescue. But the point does not appear to have been settled by the courts and the above amounts to little more than an academic speculation.[18]

3. THE APPLICATION OF THE GERMAN IDEA TO *GREATOREX*

Prior to *Greatorex* common law courts do not appear to have faced the problem squarely of contributory negligence *in the context of nervous shock*, at any rate in England, though in his judgment Cazalet J alluded to some inconclusive Commonwealth authority.[19] In the context of nervous shock, the picture in the USA may not be much clearer, though *Dillon v Legg* contains some seemingly confused views on the subject.[20] However, the same point about contributory negligence has also arisen in 'rescue' cases, and in those American States which recognise actions for 'loss of consortium or companionship' or loss of 'parental or children's companionship.'[21] In all these triangular situations the same range of legal suits is possible and the abbreviations adopted in this paper (P, D1, D2) are equally appropriate to them, as well. The lessons that can be drawn from the many consortium cases are not insignificant and we shall return to them later on, especially in the light of the paucity of the existing English material and the complexity of the German.

Since all negligence reasoning starts with a discussion of the notion of duty of care, *Greatorex* naturally had to grapple with the question whether a victim of self-inflicted injuries owes a duty of care to a third party not to cause him psychiatric injury. As stated, Cazalet J acknowledged that there was no binding authority on the question of duty. For guidance he was thus directed to German law, among other systems, and his conclusion was, undoubtedly, influenced by a decision of the German Federal Court of 11 May 1971,[22] cited to him by counsel for the Motor Insurance Bureau, which had been joined as second defendants since D2 was not insured while driving the car.[23] It will be recalled that to the question now asked by Cazalet J the BGH had given a negative reply. In the opinion of the Federal Court the imposition of such a duty would unduly restrict the person's (D2's) right to self-determination (though we have noted that an exception might have to be considered where the suicide was committed in a 'deliberately shocking manner'). Cazalet J expressly followed the reasoning of the BGH and regarded the argument derived from the right to self-determination as enunciated in the German case as 'powerful.'[24] Matters would be different where, by harming himself, D2 causes damage other than nervous shock to another person. It would thus seem that in German[25] as well as Scottish[26] and possibly English law, the ethical duty not to harm oneself becomes a legal duty as soon as the self-harming activity also causes *physical* harm to another person. From this perspective D2's immunity from liability for nervous shock (suffered by others) constitutes an exception. In other words, D2's right to self-determination prevails only if we regard this injury as special. Cazalet J's constant reference to 'policy' lends credence to this view and illustrates, once again, our legal system's difficulty to cope with the ramification of nervous shock and emotional injuries.

4. UNRESOLVED QUESTIONS

In the German decision one of the issues that had to be decided by the court was whether the contributory negligence of D2 could be imputed to P and her claim for damages against D1 accordingly reduced. At this stage it is helpful to reconsider the argument in favour of imputing D2's contributory negligence to P in the light of Cazalet J's analysis of the 'primary victim's' (ie D2's) limited or non-existent liability to others for causing harm to himself. For the two issues are interrelated.

The rationale seems to be this. If, generally speaking, a person (D2) does not owe to others (P) a duty of care not to harm himself, then it would appear to be fair that, if a third person (D1) causes physical injury to D2, then D2 should bear his, the primary victim's, causal contribution to the accident. As in the USA so in Germany, this problem has occurred also in other contexts of adjustment among multiple 'debtors' and the BGH has (not always consistently) applied similar considerations.[27] Because of special circumstances, characteristic of the relationship between D2 and P, P does not have a cause of action against D2 (all other conditions of liability being fulfilled). In the nervous shock case this is because such a cause of action would be contrary to D2's right to self-determination.[28] The result is that D2 is no longer seen as a *Mitschuldner* (joint debtor) with D1 since he is immune to any action by P. This immunity (or privilege) enjoyed by D2 by virtue of his relationship with P 'distorts' the normal rules which apply to the internal relationship between joint tortfeasors and which in general law largely follows the pattern of our own law.[29] The Germans thus refer to this problem as *gestörter Gesamtschuldnerausgleich*, a phrase that could be rendered into English as 'disturbed internal settlement between joint debtors.' The composite word is typically Germanic, and even awkward; but its emphasis on 'distortion' and the 'internal adjustment that has to take place between two (possible) debtors' makes it clear what it is trying to address. This 'distortion' of the internal relationship between the possible two joint debtors (D1 and D2) because of the rules that govern the relationship between D2 and P can, in terms of contribution rules, be addressed in one of three ways. First, we could say that P can sue D1, and D1 can then claim contribution from D2. Alternatively, we can take the view that P can sue D1 for all his loss, but D1 cannot claim anything back from D2 because of his privileged position (that is why D2 is, in German law, often referred to as the privileged debtor). Finally we could adopt an altogether different rule, namely say that P can sue D1 but only for his share of P's loss.

We see this unfolding in our case as P is forced to sue D1. If D1 could subsequently claim contribution from the primary victim (D2) then, *in the end*, D2 would be held liable for his causal contribution to the accident.[30] But this result of holding D2 liable was, as we saw in the German judgment, seen to be undesirable (because of D2's right to self-determination). So this avenue seems to be blocked. Therefore, it is held that D1 cannot claim contribution from D2 even if the latter was primarily responsible for the accident.[31] This result may follow logically the reasoning just expounded. Nonetheless, many would regard it as unsatisfactory, for it does not seem fair in such circumstances to impose full liability on D1, especially if his contribution to the harm was in terms of causation and fault very low and that of D2 very high.[32] So in such circumstances why should D1 (rather than P) bear D2's causal contribution to the accident? After all, it is because of special circumstances arising out of the relationship between D2 and P, that D2 cannot be made liable for causing nervous shock. It is therefore plausible to argue that the rationale of § 846 BGB should also be applied to claims of secondary victims (those we have called Ps) in respect of nervous shock and to reduce, accordingly, P's claim against D1. This implies that where D2 is solely answerable for the accident, P cannot recover at all. We are thus back to our point of departure! Given the special—one might say unusual—facts of *Greatorex* (for D2, the primary victim, was solely responsible for his hurt) the point did not have to be resolved in that case. But it could arise in other contexts where the personal autonomy argument is not in play. That is where the German ideas, complex though they are, could, once again, serve as a source of inspiration.

So what will happen where the reason why D2 is not liable to P is due to a family immunity rule such as that found in §§ 1359 or 1664 I BGB, which applies to all cases other than motor car accidents?[33] D1's liability towards P is not in doubt. But will he (D1) then be able to claim a contribution from D2? Or will D2's immunity, which protects him from actions by P, also shield him from a contribution claim brought by D1? To this last question, some 14 years ago, the German Federal Court gave a positive reply,[34] reversing earlier case law[35] and leaving German academic opinion reeling with the unfairness of a result which means that D1 has to carry all the loss. This solution is even more confusing if one bears in mind that the German courts take a different view if the reason for the immunity given to D2 is the result of a *contractual* exemption clause that regulates his relationship with P. For here, the courts allow P to claim his full loss from D1 and then allow the latter to claim a contribution from D2 as a result of an analogical application of § 426 BGB. To this variety of answers we must add one more: German academics, almost in their entirety, prefer a liability rule that limits D1's liability to the amount of the loss due to his fault and avoids all further actions. But in English common law terms such a solution would be contrary to our joint tortfeasors rule, which renders each joint tortfeasor liable for the entire harm of the plaintiff.[36]

This last-mentioned position does not seem to be the position currently taken by most American courts. The loss of consortium claims, frequently litigated in the USA, suggest another approach very similar to that preferred by German *academics* (but not German courts). Thus, the current tendency in the USA seems to treat the claims of P (usually the wife) against D1 as being 'independent,' but to reduce them to take into account the contributory negligence of the physically injured spouse (D2).[37] Since the familial immunities, wherever they are recognised, mean that P cannot sue D2 for his share of the accident, and since the American courts have now, in their majority, come to accept that the action against D1 is limited to his share of the loss, contribution claims between D1 and D2 do not appear to be prevalent.[38] In practice this means that the usual rules of joint tortfeasors (which entail that each of them is liable for the full amount of the plaintiff's loss) are never brought into play—a condition which would probably not be condoned by English law.

5. THE AMERICAN DIMENSION

The American dimension is interesting for a number of reasons. To begin with the paucity of English material has been noted. This means that if we need guidance from within the common law we must turn to the law in the USA since it is well known for its richness. Strangely, the richness is there, though not in the context of nervous shock claims such as the one I have been considering in this essay. Nor, indeed, do we find much guidance within the context of rescue situations where, again, the same issues may arise if rescuer (P) sues tortfeasor (D1) whose fault caused rescuee's (D2) injuries: can D2's fault be put forward to reduce the damages due to P? But the number of decisions found in consortium litigation is so numerous that more than guidance can be found from the study of their many pages. More precisely, what can be found are two things.

First is the lesson mentioned above, namely that D1 pays, but pays only for his contribution to the plaintiff's loss. As stated, this is different to making him liable for everything and then leaving him to assume the risk of obtaining a contribution from D2, the other cause of P's loss. The American solution is thus not just different from the one adopted by German courts; it is also quite close to that advocated by German academics. Clearly, future English courts have a choice; and it is important to know the pros and cons of each alternative. Once again, we will gain if we look abroad for arguments on points, which we have not yet fully addressed. And they should be that much easier to evaluate now that we have tried to set the *Greatorex* discussion against a wider canvass. Bit by bit the pieces of the puzzle fall into place.

But the American cases also hold a further lesson for the foreign observer. Quite simply, they illustrate that the law is a seamless web. In the USA the answer given to our question is to a large extent determined by the rules that apply in other parts of the law of torts. In our type of cases, the rules any particular State adopts towards (a) contributory negligence; (b) joint tortfeasors; and (c) family immunities will influence the solution. The realisation that the law is a seamless web is a valuable one for both the student and the practitioner. However, the difficulties a coincidence of these rules give rise to, also provide a salutary warning about the dangers of comparative law.

Take the well-known case of *Handeland v Brown*.[39] It is a decision of the Supreme Court of Iowa dated 27 March 1974. The *main* action involved the loss of consortium claims brought by the father (P) of a young motorcyclist (D2) injured in a traffic accident as a result of a collision with a motor vehicle (D1) at a road intersection. The jury entered a verdict for D1, rejecting D2's claim because of his own negligence. The plaintiff father requested an instruction to the effect that his son's (D2's) negligence could not be imputed to him (P), but the jury again found for D1. The father appealed and the Supreme Court of Iowa was thus concerned only with this claim. The appeal was successful.

What strikes the reader of this decision is how focused the majority judgment was in its attempts to reject the argument that the father's (P) action was derivative. Like other courts before it, the Iowa court was keen to show that:

> the gist of the parental action . . . is a wrong done to the parent [P] in consequence of injury to his child [D2] by the actionable negligence of another [D1].[40]

The result was that the damages claimable would not/should not be reduced to take into account D2's fault. An interesting dissent questioned this view to the extent that it would allow a parent (P) of a child (D2) injured largely by its own fault to claim full damages from the tortfeasor (D1) whose fault had, say, contributed only 10 per cent to the child's harm. It is only here, in a mere three lines,[41] that we find any reference to the contributory negligence rule as a possible reason for this construction. But this sentence, almost a throwaway line, made my American students and me review the judgment and the law in Iowa at the time of the *Handeland* decision. And the prevailing rule then was the old rule of contributory negligence. If that had been applied in *Handeland*, the court would have been compelled to reject the father's claim as being contaminated by his son's fault.

Seen in this light, the decision is thus not really about whether the parents' claim is independent (which it is) or derivative, but how one can ensure that it is not defeated by the child's fault and the old rule about contributory negligence. The problem with such an interpretation, however, is that (a) though it is arguably the true reason for the judgment, it finds few clues in the majority opinion to support it, and (b) if few students or practitioners—at any rate foreigners—notice this, much effort will be diverted towards arguing whether the claim is independent or derivative. This is an arid attempt to define an essentially meaningless term. Yet the size of the American literature and the pages found in American decisional law on this subject,[42] suggest that even American lawyers have fallen into this trap and carried out the definitional debate.

Another case that had proceeded in precisely the same manner was *Rollins v General American Transportation Corp.*[43] There, too, the court was confronted by two actions: one by a physically injured man (D2), who had contributed through his negligence to his hurt; and the other a consortium claim by his spouse (P). Both were rejected because of the fault of D2. In that case also the discussion had centred on the independent or derivative nature of P's claim, saying little of the real issue that must have worried the court. The reasoning was, yet again, essentially adopted in *Plocar v Dunkin Donuts of America Inc,*[44] another loss of consortium case. But by now Illinois, as most States in the late 1970s and 1980s, was moving towards the comparative negligence rule.[45] Our cases missed the significance of the shift, perhaps because the consortium rule had never been openly linked to the contributory negligence rule but had, instead, been obscured by the debate over the independent or derivative nature of the claim. Then, 10 years later, came *Blagg v Illinois F.W.D. Truck and Equipment Co,*[46] where the court had to revisit the consortium rule. Happily it did; and did so in an open way when it said:

> The aforementioned cases [*Rollins* and *Plocar*] . . . were decided prior to *Alvis* and thus were based on contributory negligence principles. Today the absolute bar to recovery for loss of consortium that formerly existed must be reviewed under comparative negligence principles.

The result of the change, however, was obvious; and in line with the bulk of American States[47] where:

> the loss of consortium award [is] reduced by the comparative negligence of the physically injured spouse.

To re-assert what had thus far been kept (almost) under wraps, the court concluded with the statement:

> The *Alvis* decision, and the advent of comparative negligence principles, has subsequently reduced the harsh effects of contributory negligence by the physically injured spouse, as the loss-of-consortium plaintiff is no longer barred from recovery.[48]

The discussion about independent or derivative claims is thus now for all intents and purposes *dépassé*. So, if this were the only lesson to be derived from these American decisions, it would be of limited value. On the educational front, its interest would lie in the need to remind students (and sometimes practitioners) that the answer in one part of the law (consortium claims) is determined by the position adopted in another (joint tortfeasors rules). On the practical front, however, the lesson derived from these decisions remains valid if definitively unresolved. And it consists in the decision de facto to set aside the rules about joint tortfeasors and, as already stated, reduce P's entitlement against D1 *by the comparative negligence of D2*.[49] To English (and continental European) eyes this may look like a replacement of the 'full liability' that applies to joint tortfeasors by a 'proportionality rule.' But, given that in this case there is a special relationship between plaintiff and primary victim, the departure from the rule may be justified.[50]

6. SOME TENTATIVE CONCLUSIONS

Some academics in this country (notably Sir Roy Goode) have preached all their lives the case for a closer co-operation between judges, practitioners, and academics. I was converted to this creed some 20 years ago, and have since tried to apply it to the study and comparison of legal systems. How well it can work can be seen by *Greatorex*; and this for a number of reasons. Here are eight.

First, German law influenced the English decision because a practitioner (counsel for the MIB) used its ideas to construct his own argument before the English court. The practitioner was, in turn, able to access and evaluate positively this foreign material because it was made available to him by an academic lawyer in a form that was useable on this side of the Channel. This, incidentally, may also explain why German (instead of French or Italian law) served here as a model: no French or Italian material on the subject is available in English so the experience of neither of these systems could be used as a source of ideas.

Secondly, German law became attractive because it was served to the English 'consumers' in an easily digestible way.

For the material came in the form of a judicial decision which had litigated facts that bore considerable resemblance to those of the English litigation and thus cried out for comparison to all but the most narrow-minded. Luck determines the outcome of every human enterprise; and as luck would have it, the protagonists in the *Greatorex* case were willing to take ideas irrespective of their national origin. But there is no denying the fact that another counsel or another judge might not have been so diligent in his research or open-minded towards foreign products.

Thirdly, in *Greatorex* luck favoured the comparatist in yet another way. The inspiration or transplantation of the foreign thinking was not hindered by one of those Germanic terms that are untranslatable and thus so off-putting to those unaccustomed to the demands that the Germanic culture makes on the intellect of the potential borrower! To be sure, as the theory of 'transferred loss' shows (in German: *Schadensverlagerung*), even such notions, provided that they are intrinsically valuable, can penetrate a foreign legal system. Some help from academic quarters can, again, help overcome problems associated with their abstract nature. If another illustration is needed, think of *Drittwirkung*. Ten years ago there was hardly an English lawyer who was alive to the problem let alone the concept. Now, the literature it is generating is almost excessive. But let us return to the German decision. There the Federal Court had refused to hold that a person was under a duty not to injure or kill himself since such a duty would infringe his autonomy.[51] Such language could easily slide into the English legal reasoning as it began its search for a duty of care as a basis for a tortious obligation to make amends. Indeed, reading *Greatorex* one is left with the feeling that it did so without any jarring, linguistic or conceptual. This is an immensely significant observation for anyone translating foreign legal documents and then hoping to use them in our courts.

Yet, fourthly, the English court looked only at one side of German law; indeed, it could not have done more since counsel drew the judge's attention to the German decision but nothing more. The English court was thus not made aware that the German result might, in some instances, have also been reached by utilising the immunity conferred by § 1359 BGB.[52] This alludes to the policy reasons, which also weighed heavily in Cazalet J's mind (family relationships) and militate against allowing a legal action. Why did the German court refuse to go down that path? We can only speculate; but at least three reasons spring to the mind of an outside observer. First, as already stated, § 1359 BGB does not apply to car accident cases for the reasons that we know from our law as well. Secondly, the accident in the 1971 nervous shock case was caused by D2's gross negligence and this would have defeated the immunity given by § 1359 BGB. Finally, the court might have wished to create in such cases an immunity that went beyond the family relationships covered by § 1359 BGB.[53] If it did, the result would be that facts such as those encountered in the Australian case *FAI General Insurance Co Ltd v Lucre*[54] would receive the same answer: no duty and hence no liability. Since *Greatorex* followed the (wider) court reasoning, does the same result now hold true for English law? Would a claim by P, who was unrelated to D2, likewise fail? On the other hand, would the outcome be affected by the fact that Cazalet J's policy points would be inapplicable to my hypothetical? *Greatorex*, as we keep saying, has left a number of points open, even though it has done a good job in alerting us to new ways of looking at them. If the Germans have discovered too many (subtly different) ways of solving this problem we, in England, have not even addressed it!

Fifthly, all of the above could not have been undertaken, and the chances of the German ideas influencing the case would have been slim, had the attempt at legal borrowing gone through Codes or academic writings. For even the briefest consultation of the German treatises reveals the discussion in Germany to be theoretical and conceptual in the extreme.[55] Had English counsel chosen that course he would have found it bewildering both to himself and to the court. The fact that parts of German law were still left unused and unexplored does not matter. Further research may produce even more fruits next time around.

Sixthly, the above would not, of course, preclude recourse to American law as an alternative source of inspiration. But here, again, without appropriate academic preparation, the American material might reveal only part of the picture and thus make suitable inspiration dubious. If the hint that our highest courts cannot manage American law without the occasional assistance of academics were to be seen as disrespectful towards them, one must remind the reader of how the House of Lords in *Murphy*[56] 'misunderstood' the law in the USA. It was a cosmopolitan judge[57] who pointed this out in no uncertain terms in an academic article; and as fate would have it, he was later to join their lordships as a judge. The moral of this is that the fact that foreign legal material is accessible to us in linguistic terms does not mean that it can be transplanted into our system without thought, caution, and preparation. In my view we are on the verge of forgetting this warning if we go on looking at the theology of the First Amendment in an uncritical manner. But that is for another day!

The seventh point places the case against the wider contemporary discussions about comparative law. Its literature is growing; and Europe, one way or another, is the greatest stimulus. Directives, case law from Luxembourg and Strasbourg, private initiatives to formulate general principles (or soft law as it is sometimes called): we have it all these days. And yet at the lowest level of a single case that could arise in any country of the so-called Western world, we find an illustration which shows how types of reasoning can travel easily if they are packaged in user-friendly ways to those that matter and solve practical problems. Our example also shows that some systems have studied the underlying issues more deeply than others. In this instance, the Germans were ahead of the English (though their thought processess are highly complex). On a different matter, for instance a problem of commercial law such as securitisation, English law might be seen to be more flexible than, say, its French counterpart. The borrowing at specific, pragmatic levels might not have the allure that comes with grand theories; but *Greatorex* suggests that the methodology here advocated not only works: it works well enough to offer an efficient spring-board for further study and understanding of foreign law. And at this stage the endeavour is not only a practical one; it also acquires a worthwhile intellectual component. Those who think that a cosmopolitan approach to law is bound to lack in depth are, I believe, proved to be utterly wrong by the *Greatorex* case study. And so are those who fear that the 'functional specificity' sacrifices wider cultural studies on the altar of a narrow fact-based problem. For this approach does not hinder such wider studies; it simply allows the expositor to bring them in bit by bit as the research fans out to encompass other things. My studies on privacy and the wider right of personality have shown how this can be done.[58] And what will be said in the next chapter will, I think, show that the same approach works in the area of public law and enables us to move from comparing specific situations to understanding them better by seeing them against the wider background of their particular societies.

Finally, has the work started by *Greatorex* come to a conclusion? We have already alluded to the fact that the point seems to be open if in the next case P and D2 are not related. German academics also seem to be divided as to the ambit of the 1988[59] decision, which decided on the contribution claim between tortfeasors and, it will be remembered, held[60] that D1 had to carry all the cost to P. The successful completion of the work started by Cazalet J might, once again, be aided by the proper consideration of foreign law. This is the eighth and last point that emerges from *Greatorex*. For though the case made a good start in addressing the complex kind of legal problems that arise in these triangular situations, it did not completely finish the job it started. The tail end of the judgment, where the extent of liability of the potential defendant is considered, is thus notably 'hurried,' and the only legitimate and convincing explanation one can offer for this is that the resolution of this problem was not necessary to the facts of *Greatorex*. Future courts will thus have to consider whether the same rules apply to cases where D2 is, for other reasons, immune to an action from the secondary victim or, alternatively, protected by an exemption clause.[61] More importantly, our courts will also have to mull over the question whether it is better to allow P to sue D1 for all the loss (and then leave it to D1 to obtain contribution from D2 if he can) or only obtain from D1 the amount which is due to his share of the blame. This author's preference is for the second option, which is also favoured by German academe and many of the more recent American decisions, ie 'proportional liability.' But the study of German and American law also suggests that there are other solutions (though the theoretical merits of each option seem to have been studied only by German academics). In the light of the above, the English practitioner can only benefit by dwelling further on foreign, especially German, law. And if this time the dip is into complex German theory and not just case law, it can at least be done with greater confidence since *Greatorex* has successfully broken new ground in the area of comparative law in English courts. To put it differently and in wider terms, the comparative approach to common problems rarely if ever runs out of interesting variations, disproving the narrow-minded conviction of many national lawyers that theirs is the only way of doing things. But if one translated case can give rise to so much thought, imagine what could happen if the other 150 decisions found in the English book on German tort law which provided the translation for *Greatorex* were subjected to the same kind of scrutiny in search for new ideas and directions. The author of the book, if no one else, must surely be allowed the hope that this may happen.

Notes

¹ [2002] 3 WLR 89 at 119.

² And, of course, why not other companies as well? Pharmaceutical companies spring to mind. But see below n 3.

³ I have italicised the word 'outcome' because I think it requires explaining. I confidently assume that his Lordship was *not* implying equality of damages across national borders, for the quantification process is determined by a myriad of factors which fully justify the idea that the same injury, caused by the same product, manufactured by the same company, may nonetheless justify different levels of compensation. These factors can be economic (different levels of national earnings), structural (presence or absence of social security systems covering part of the harm), legal (use or not of the jury system; presence or absence of a contingent fee system etc), and sociological or anthropological (eg, a particular culture's aversion to litigation or preference for conciliation). Recent attempts in the USA to devise worldwide class action compromises confirm the above (as well as the complexity of the underlying issues which, clearly, are only touched upon lightly by these observations).

⁴ A beautifully phrased but not entirely convincing formulation can be found in Sir Robert Megarry's judgment in *Cordell v Second Clanfield Properties* [1969] 2 Ch 9 at 16 ff.

⁵ [2000] 1 WLR 1970.

⁶ Peter Handford, 'Psychiatric Damage Where the Defendant is the Immediate Victim' (2001) 117 *LQR* 397, comparing the result with the more generous Australian law.

⁷ [1995] 2 AC 207 at 252 ff.

⁸ For doubts about the practical utility of the foreign law references in Lord Goff's judgment, see Lord Rodger of Earlsferry, 'Savigny in the Strand' in *The Maurice Kelly Memorial Lecture 1995*, esp at 24–25; Neil Duxbury, *Jurists and Judges* (Oxford 2001) 107. This, incidentally, is one reason why the subsequent decision of the House of Lords in *Fairchild v Glenhaven Funeral Services Ltd* [2002] 3 WLR 89 will prove a more durable model for practical comparative law by the courts than *White v Jones*. For, unlike *White*, which used much space to discuss foreign legal doctrine, *Fairchild* largely focused on litigated factual equivalents (and the true policies behind their outcomes) to show how foreign law buttressed the solution their Lordships favoured. In this context, the citation of Palandt, the most practitioner-oriented book of German legal literature, is indicative.

⁹ BGHZ 56, 163 = NJW 1971, 1883 = VersR 1971, 905 at 1140; taken from the 3rd edn of Markesinis, *The German Law of Torts: A Comparative Introduction* (1994) (translation by Weir). In the 4th edn (with Unberath) the case can be found at 115 ff. The German decision is still the subject of controversy not so much for its result but for the way it chose to justify it. Its status as 'good law' has also been thrown into doubt after the decision of the Federal Court of 1 March 1988, BGHZ 103, 338, which is mentioned several times in the discussion that follows. For a summary of the academic views, see Staudinger and Hager, *Kommentar zum BGB, Unerlaubte Handlungen*, B39 (13th edn, 1999).

¹⁰ D2 is the primary victim of the accident; but because he may, through his own negligence, also have contributed to his hurt and the loss of P (secondary victim), he may be sued by the main tortfeasor (D1) for a contribution or an indemnity. In Germany D2 can also be referred to as the 'privileged defendant,' for he may benefit from an exemption clause arising from his relations with the plaintiff or he may enjoy an immunity *ex lege* because of his family relationship with P. As we shall note later, one of the questions that may arise in such cases is whether D2's 'immunity' from action by P can also protect him against an action brought by D1, the joint tortfeasor.

¹¹ In principle, German law allows recovery for 'distant' psychiatric injury. In practice, however, such claims are kept under control by judges—no juries exist in German law—rigorously checking their standard requirement that the 'shock be an appropriate and understandable consequence' of the accident that befell the primary victim. In practice a close relationship (*Schicksalsgemeinschaft*) between the plaintiff and the primary victim is of paramount importance. A further restriction can be seen from the reasoning of the court given below.

¹² *Attia v British Gas Plc* [1988] QB 304 at 317 per Bingham LJ (as he then was).

¹³ This, at least, seems to be the view of Lord Steyn who argued that the subject might have now passed the stage of redemption by the courts

and needs legislative intervention. See his opinion in *Frost v Chief Constable of South Yorkshire Police* [1999] 2 AC 455 at 500. It is submitted that *W v Essex County Council* [2001] 2 AC 592 has compounded the uncertainty.

[14] Markesinis, *The German Law of Torts: A Comparative Treatise* (4th edn by Basil Markesinis and Hannes Unberath, Oxford, 2002) 45 ff. Note, however, that this was a case of 'distant shock' which would thus not be compensated by English and (most) American courts.

[15] In such factual situations the court can normally rely on § 1359 BGB to bar any action by the wife against her husband (or, in this case, his estate). This is because § 1359 BGB states that one spouse is liable to the other only if he (or she) failed to attain 'the degree of care which they are accustomed to exercise in their own affairs.' So the spouse sued can avoid liability if he can show that in his own affairs he would have displayed a lower standard of care than that required by ordinary negligence (a similar rule can be found in § 1664 1 BGB dealing with the parent/child relations). The rationale of both provisions is to avoid legal disputes between persons who are in such close family relationships and in many respects draws on the policy reasons, which were also touched upon by Cazalet J in *Greatorex*. The immunity rule just described does not, however, apply where D2's fault amounted to gross negligence. Another limitation on this rule is that it is not applicable in car accident cases (on this constant case law see BGHZ 53, 352 of 11 March 1970; BGHZ 61, 101 of 18 June 1973; and BGHZ 63, 51 of 10 July 1974) For these points and the effect they may have had on the reasoning of the German court, see below.

[16] See Medicus, *Schuldrecht, Besonderer Teil* (9th edn, Munich, 1999) 302.

[17] So long as the rescue can be rendered without any danger to the rescuer: § 323c German Criminal Code (*Strafgesetzbuch*).

[18] Presumably, the same argument could be advanced in other systems (such as the French) which also recognise affirmative duties of rescue but, to my knowledge, the point has not been settled by their courts. The Scottish case of *A v B's Trustees* (1906) 13 SLT 830 allowed a claim in very similar circumstances, but the successful claim has been generally seen to be based on breach of contract. See Lord Johnston's words at 831, apparently thus interpreted by Lord Porter in *Bourhill v Young* [1943] AC 92 at 120. In *R v Criminal Injuries Compensation Board, ex parte Webb* [1986] QB 184 at 196, Watkins LJ also appeared to take the view that a 'person attempting to commit suicide may well be in breach of a duty of care owed to [others].' But the observation was obiter; and in *Greatorex* Cazalet J brushed the point aside as irrelevant on the facts before him. An American case has, however, held that a mentally distressed man who tried to commit suicide in his garage is under a duty towards his son who came to his rescue and was, in the process, *physically* injured: *Talbert v Talbert* 199 N.Y.S. 2d 212 (1960).

¹⁹ But see Handford's note, above n 6. In English law, the most interesting obiter dicta come from Lord Oliver's opinion in *Alcock v Chief Constable of South Yorkshire Police* [1992] 1 AC 310 at 418.

²⁰ 441 P. 2d 912 (1968). In *Dillon* the majority (at 916) asked the question whether the contributory negligence of the victim *and* the plaintiffs should affect their claims; whereas the minority (at 928) asked the very different question whether the deceased child's negligence can affect the living plaintiffs' claims.

²¹ In Germany, we have noted that the rescue variant has been considered in the context of suicide. Since loss of consortium claims are not known in German law, the most litigated type of American case finds no parallel in Germany.

²² Above n 9.

²³ The owner of the car was also joined as a defendant by the second defendant, the MIB, on the grounds that he had allowed his friend, the first defendant (D1), to drive the car without insurance. But neither the owner of the car nor the first defendant appeared in court or were represented by counsel.

²⁴ See also the Law Commission's report on *Liability for Psychiatric Illness* (Law Com No 249, 1998) paras 5.34–5.44.

²⁵ Similarly, in BGH ZIP 1990, 1485 the court held that as a general rule a lessor did not owe a contractual duty to the lessee not to commit suicide and as a result the estate was not answerable for the termination of the lease. To impose such a duty would have amounted to an unjustifiable intrusion upon the right to self-determination of the lessor.

²⁶ Above n 18.

²⁷ Thus see BGH JR 1989, 60 and cf BGHZ 12, 213.

²⁸ Approximately the same considerations apply easily if we replace the legal immunity with an exclusion clause contained in a contract between D2 and P.

²⁹ See § 421 BGB.

³⁰ Albeit the risk of insolvency of the primary victim (D2) would be transferred from P to D1.

³¹ Cf *Alcock v Chief Constable of South Yorkshire Police* [1992] 1 AC 310 at 418 per Lord Oliver.

³² The point made by Lord Oliver, *ibid*, but rejected (obiter) by Cazalet J in *Greatorex*.

³³ As already stated, it is here that we find an abundance of cases in the USA.

³⁴ Decision of 1 March 1988, BGHZ 103, 338, 346 ff; Palandt, *Bürgerliches Gesetzbuch* (60th edn, Munich, 2001) no 426.

³⁵ Decision of 27 June 1961, BGHZ 35, 317 at 323–24 (though this earlier case law may still apply to other factual instances).

³⁶ This may be the reason why the Law Commission took a somewhat negative position in the context of psychiatric injury; see Law Commission

Report on *Liability for Psychiatric Illness* (Law Com No 249, 1998) para 5.39. But the Law Commission does not appear to have considered the various alternatives canvassed in Germany on this point.

[37] For a review of the case law, see *Blagg v Illinois F.W.D. Truck and Equipment Company* 572 NE 2d, 920 (1991), with references at 925. See, also, *Mallett v Dunn* [1949] 2 KB 180 (England); *Feltch v General Rental Co*, 383 Mass. 603, 421 NE 2d 67 (1981), reviewing the contradictory American case law; and *Handeland v Brown*, 216 NW 2d 574 (Iowa, 1974), where the conflicting views of the majority and the dissent repay careful reading and reveal that many of the problems in American law may be linked with the differing views adopted towards contributory and comparative negligence. Imputed contributory negligence is discussed in detail in Gregory, Kalven and Epstein, *Cases and Materials on Torts*, 3rd edn (1977) (716 ff, esp 730 ff), and Harper, Fleming James Jr and Gray, *The Law of Torts*, (2nd edn, 1986), vol II, ch 8.8 and 8.9.

[38] For references see below n 49. But like all such statements about American law this, too, has to be qualified by mentioning the fact that decisions do exist suggesting that the tortfeasor (main defendant) can sue the primary victim for his share of the plaintiff's harm. See, eg, *American Motorcycle Assn v Superior Court* 20 Cal. 3r 578, 591, 578 P. 2d 899 (1978) and *Lantis v Condon* 95 Cal. App. 3r 152, 157 Cal. Rptr.22 (1979). The *Lantis* facts, with the primary victim being 80 per cent responsible for his injuries, illustrate the need to shield the tortfeasor from the risk of carrying the entire loss. But as stated in the text, the solution of sharing the cost with the primary victim may not be the best since it, essentially, defeats any immunity that the law (or contract) may have given him towards the secondary victim. For an American case that makes precisely this point see *Feltch v General Rental Co* 421 NE 2d 67, 92 (1981, Mass).

[39] 216 NW 2d 574 (1974).

[40] *Ibid* at 578.

[41] 'Such a result seems unjust. Application of comparative negligence would most adequately rectify the injustice, but we do not have comparative negligence *in such cases.*' I have deliberately italicised the last few words of the quotation because to a foreign reader they seem to be confusing insofar as they imply that in the early 1970s Iowa knew the rule of comparative negligence *in other types of cases.* So far as I know, this was not the case, so the end of the judicial dictum seems unfortunately phrased.

[42] Conveniently collected in ALR 4th, vol 25. Michael DiSabatino, the author of the annotation, thus remarks at 9 that: 'The reason *most often advanced* for denying a spouse or parent recovery for loss of consortium where the physically injured spouse or child has been contributorily negligent is that the consortium action is derived from the physically injured spouse or child's cause of action' (italics supplied). The ALR annotation is up to date to September 2000.

[43] 46 Ill App.2d 266, 197 NE 2d 68 (1964).

44 103 Ill. App.3rd 740, 748, 431 NE2d 1175.

45 *Alvis v Ribar* 85 Ill.2d 1, 421 NE 2d 886 (1981).

46 143 Ill.2d 188, 572 NE 2d 920 (1991).

47 Conveniently collected by the court at 925 of its judgment.

48 *Ibid* at 926. A similar statement, significantly tucked away in a footnote, can be found in the judgment of the Supreme Court of Colorado in *Lee v Colorado Department of Health* 718 P. 2d 221, 231, text and note 8 (Colo. 1986).

49 See, eg, *Eggert v Working* 599 P. 2d. 1389 (Alaska 1979); *Turnbow v Wasden* 608 F. Supp. 237 (D.Nev. 1985); *Lee v Colorado Department of Health* 718 P. 2d 221 (Colo. 1986); *Quadrone v Pasco Petroleum Co* 156 Ariz. 415, 752 P. 2d 504. (1988); *Blagg v Illinois F.W.D. Truck and Equipment Co* 572 NE 2d 920 (Ill. 1991). But cf the cases cited above n 38.

50 The shift from the full liability to a 'proportional liability' rule was considered and rejected by the Law Commission in a paper it presented in 1966 for the DTI entitled *Feasibility Investigation of Joint and Several Liability*.

51 It will be remembered from above n 15 that § 1359 BGB could, in some instances, have served as another way of ensuring the immunity of D2 towards P, this immunity being based on the policy reasons appropriate to the D2/P relationship. These reasons figured in Cazalet J's judgment; but not in the German judgment, which chose to justify the non-liability rule by reference to human autonomy. One (further) consequence of this justification is that it ensures that the non-liability rule applies even where there is no family relationship between D2 and P. This is exactly what happened in the Australian case of *FAI General Insurance Co v Lucre* [2000] NSWCA 346 (decision of 29 November 2000); and the verdict there was for the plaintiff.

52 See above n 15. There is a problem, however, with the immunity rule contained in § 1359 BGB: its application depends on the status of marriage and not the closeness of the relationship between P and D2.

53 My German friends, however, warn me that this is not the kind of reasoning that would appeal to a German judge.

54 Above n 51. In the Australian case the car accident between D1 and D2 was, again, entirely due to D2's fault. In this case, however, there was no family or other relationship between P and D2; P's claim for his post-traumatic stress disorder succeeded.

55 See, eg, Larenz, *Lehrbuch des Schuldrechts I* (13th edn, Munich, 1982) § 37; Thiele, 'Gesamtschuld und Gesamtschuldnerausgleich' *Juristische Schulung* 1968, 149; Medicus, 'Haftungsbefreiung und Gesamtschuldnerausgleich' *JZ* 1967, 398; Medicus, *Schuldrecht I, Allgemeiner Teil* (10th edn, Munich, 1998) Rn. 793.

56 [1991] 1 AC 398.

57 Sir Robin (now Lord) Cooke in his 'An Impossible Distinction' (1991) 107 *LQR* 46 ff.

[58] See, eg, chs 7, 8 and 11 in my collection of essays entitled *Always on the Same Path; Essays on Foreign Law and Comparative Methodology*, vol 2 (2001).

[59] BGHZ 103, 338.

[60] Contrary to the early decision of BGHZ 35, 317, which had allowed D1 to claim a contribution against D2. It must be remembered that BGHZ 56, 163 (the 1971 nervous shock case that guided the English decision) was decided against the background of BGHZ 35, 317 decided in 1961.

[61] Which was not the case in *Greatorex*, but was considered by the German Federal Court in BGHZ 12, 213 = NJW 1972, 942.

5

The Focused Approach in Public Law

Denn nur durch Vergleichung unterscheidet man sich und erfährt was man ist, um ganz zu werden, was man sein soll.

(For only by comparison does man distinguish and learn what he is in order to become what he should be.)

Thomas Mann, *Josef und Seine Brüder*, vol III, *Josef in Ägypten* (trans by HT Lowe-Porter, Minerva edn, 1936) 754–55

1. INTRODUCTION

In public law the wider political setting has a deep and obvious impact on the legal problem before a court and in some respects this may accentuate the differences over the similarities that exist between different legal systems. In my view, however, the focused approach which I have been advocating again presents an important benefit. Put simply, it is that the study of a foreign legal system, especially through decisional law rather than through doctrinal writings, has the advantage of putting one initially at ease. For invariably in such studies one is starting the discovery journey by looking at litigated situations that are the same in most countries. Teaching and understanding law through cases also offers the inestimable advantage of making the student's experience of the world deepen as his study progresses in sophistication. Of course, the product of such research can, initially, be quite fragmented, resembling a painting of the pointilliste school that has to be admired by standing somewhat back and slowly taking in the whole. The contrast with the world of geometry, architecture, and consistency, which academics so like to construct, could not be greater. Yet the comparative juxtaposition of factually

similar cases makes one feel at home. For the observer is comparing familiar situations and not confused by structures,
terminology or concepts that are either untranslatable or, if
apparently easy to translate, misleading. The study of French
or German administrative law reveals many such terms which
do not yield to an obvious translation or, more troublesome, to
one translation but must be slightly mutated to accommodate
the circumstances. So the reality (or illusion) of similarity is
shattered once we move to concepts, which is how comparative law has often been taught. The comparison of two systems
through their concepts is thus, at first instance at least, off-
putting. This is because, look as you will, you cannot find the
concept, notion, or architecture[1] you are looking for, and which
is so self-evident to your foreign colleague.[2] By contrast, the
two systems come much closer when you look at litigated cases
and discover that the differences in result are diminished. That
neither system functions as purely as it is meant to do is
inevitable since the neatness that can exist in the world of ideas
is rarely found in the real world of litigation. But discovering
this on one's own through detailed research has its own
rewards.

2. A STUDY IN PARALLEL

In accordance with the above methodology, in this sub-section
we shall look at one factual variant in two legal systems: the
English and the French. Lack of space prevents us from including the German counterpart; though the conclusions that one
can draw from this system are not that different from those
applicable to French law.[3] The aim is to show how one can
compare different systems at a level of considerable specificity
and then, as one fans out, begin to get a wide picture of the foreign legal system. Here we shall apply my method to public
law. And the factual variant we shall look at deals with claims
for negligent exercise of powers vested in social services meant
to protect children in danger or with special needs.

X *(Minors) v Bedfordshire County Council*[4] was one of two
'child-abuse' actions (consolidated and heard together with
three other cases not discussed in this chapter). It arose in con-

nection with a claim that a local authority negligently and in breach of its statutory obligations failed to exercise its powers to institute care proceedings after it had received serious reports that the plaintiff/child had been the subject of parental abuse and neglect. The second case, *M (A Minor) v Newham London Borough Council*, was the mirror image of the first, for here the complaint was based on the negligent removal of a child from maternal care on the basis of an unfounded belief that the abuse had taken place by the mother's cohabitee and the conclusion that the mother was unable to protect her child. The cases were tried on a matter of law ie on the basis that the facts were assumed to be as pleaded; and the House of Lords held that no action lay against the local authority either for its alleged violation of statute or for the tort of negligence.

In the French equivalent of *X v Bedfordshire*, the social services were held liable because of their negligence in the exercise of the powers vested in them for the purposes of protecting children in danger of family abuse (this administrative duty is called *protection maternelle et infantile*). In *Epoux Quaras*[5] a three-year-old girl had been sent, with the agreement of her parents, to stay with a foster family for three months. The foster family, which was not French, had been selected by an association devoted to children care. The child was seriously maltreated. Her parents were granted compensation. The Conseil d'Etat considered that the administration was at fault for not having verified the reliability of the foster family carefully.

Another French case offers a possible comparison with *Newham*. In *M et Mme Pillon*[6] the Conseil d'Etat held that a social service had committed no fault in not warning the authority able to institute care proceedings about the threat posed to the health of children entrusted in the care of a particular family (information collected by the agency pointed to such dangers, and the concern should have been even greater given that the family had refused permission to the social workers to enter their house and talk to the children). It follows from these facts that had fault been found, liability would have ensued. To an English lawyer the facts as given would indicate the presence of fault, but we cannot labour this point too much given that the finding of fault depended on the facts in each case, and we do not have them before us as the court did. The outcome of the litigation, however, clearly shows how the controlling device of fault works in practice. However, one must also note the dangers that may arise from the fact that such determinations may only be possible *after* litigation has taken place. To an English lawyer this observation will not just be crucial, but also, arguably, a reinforcement for his view to dispose of such disputes without the cost and delays of a full trial. Nevertheless, one must also repeat—perhaps with some degree of surprise—the paucity of French litigated examples, something which must indicate that *in practice* the potential liability rule has not opened the floodgates of litigation.

The factual examples I have chosen could not be narrower. Yet as will be shown, the true value of my example lies not so much in money, in which human interest, of course, is great. It rather lies in the fact that the arguments used in these cases for and against liability are broadly applicable over a wide range of state liability situations. This means two things. First, I can draw—and in this chapter have drawn—supporting statements from cases dealing with factual permutations of my chosen example. Secondly, it means that if at some stage I reach a point where the systems diverge despite the factual similarity of the instances considered, I have to start looking into other areas of the law for explanations. Which area it is does not really matter. What matters is that the search (and the knowledge that comes with it) has now been broadened to include such topics as the law of damages, the law of social security, the law of procedure. Equally noteworthy is the fact that, equipped with the sense of security acquired by the knowledge that I am dealing with a familiar problem, I feel courageous enough to venture into these others areas of foreign law which, had I tried to tackle *de nuovo*, I might have found forbidding. It is my submission therefore that my proposed methodology draws you into the foreign system rather than allowing different conceptualism to put you off its study.

So let us proceed with my experiment. How did the French and English courts deal with my problem?

3. THE REASONING OF THE COURTS

In the *Bedfordshire* decision the 'technical,' legal arguments connected with tort liability[7] were limited to the enquiry whether the local authority owed a direct duty of care to the children.[8] Lord Browne-Wilkinson's remarks are brief on two of the usual requirements of liability, foreseeability and proximity, largely because the local authority (wisely) chose not to challenge the fact that they were satisfied in this case. Instead, he asserted (without discussion[9] and, some might argue, not so convincingly) that the requirement of 'fair, just and reasonable,' essentially introduced into our system by the *Peabody*[10] and *Caparo*[11] judgments, also applied to cases involving physical harm to the person. This meant that if the court did not think that it was 'fair, just and reasonable' to discover a duty of care there would be no primary liability. To decide this issue Lord Browne-Wilkinson then switched his discussion to the policy arguments, which in his view negated the presence of any duty. In his Lordship's view these were basically four. First, imposing liability on the public bodies in question would make bad economic sense. Secondly, liability would inhibit the freedom of action of these bodies. Thirdly, it would be inappropriate for the courts to control elected bodies and tell them how to exercise their discretionary powers. Finally, the victims in these cases had alternative remedies, which make a tort remedy not only dangerous but also superfluous. This part of the judgment is the most crucial for present purposes.

What about the French motivation? In *M et Mme Pillon*[12] the exact nature of the duty that should have made the social service more careful in the placement of children was not specified. On the contrary, in *Epoux Quaras*,[13] the Conseil d'Etat referred to certain provisions, which, in the Public Health Code (*Code de la Santé Publique*) require that social services supervise the health of all children under a certain age. In short, almost the same brevity encountered in the reasoning of the judgments of the Cour de cassation is, again, the hallmark of the administrative jurisdiction, especially if its products are compared to the much longer and fuller judgments of the highest

English courts. If the search for similarities is to proceed, one must begin to consult additional sources.

4. IN SEARCH OF A RAPPROCHEMENT

In one sense what is most remarkable about the comparison of these two systems is not that they (a) reach different results in these factually equivalent situations but (b) that they choose to motivate their judgments in such a patently different way. The English allusion to policy, with all its attractions and weaknesses (if it is attempted without empirical evidence to support it),[14] is thus notably absent from the French decisions. Closer examination of the systems, however, reveals that the second assertion, (b), is only partially correct. This becomes clear once one moves away from the decisions themselves and starts looking at their supporting official as well as academic literature.[15] Here one finds evidence to support two observations. First, the English concerns can be found duplicated in France and can even be traced (though more tenuously) to judicial decisions. This, however, is a crucial assertion. For the more one can substantiate this point, the closer one can bring the two systems and challenge the illusion of difference and separateness. Secondly, further study of these policy arguments also reveals that, at the end of the day, they have faired differently in the two systems. The (final) rejection by French law of the English policy concerns thus leads us to the question why this has happened? The answer will be found at a different and deeper level of enquiry. And revealing as it does a different socio-political philosophy, once again leads us to assert a divergence and then to try to understand it. The absence of overt discussions, however, again makes the search difficult and any conclusion speculative. But one thing is clear. At this last stage (and deeper level) of our enquiry we are no longer comparing legal or legalistic arguments but competing philosophies about the role of the state in modern society. We shall deal with this aspect of the problem later on in section 6 below. Here suffice it to note that such core political, moral, or philosophical issues may be incapable of a right answer let alone one answer. Equally, one must note that what works for the specific prob-

lem discussed in this chapter also works for other legal problems subjected to a similar kind of analysis.

(a) Policy Reasons and Concepts in Decisions Involving the Liability of Public Bodies

As already stated, what most distinguishes common law judgments from French ones is not just their greater length but also
their increasing willingness to confront *openly* the underlying
policy issues. This makes the reading of common law decisions
not only more attractive but also more informative as to what
is really happening not only during the secret judicial deliber-
ations but also in the mind of the judge, himself. Last but not
least, such greater frankness could make the argument of
future cases more meaningful as counsel confront openly and
with increasing evidence of an interdisciplinary nature the
issues that lie at the core of the dispute. For instance, the
emphasis that the causation issue[16] has received in the French
cases of wrongful life as a result of the recent *Perruche* decision[17] is a good illustration as any. And it contrasts sharply
with the parallel American[18] and German[19] judgments which
state quite clearly that they will not allow conceptual debates
to interfere with the pursuit of justice.

This (apparent) absence of policy factors in French decisions
is even more obvious in the group of cases, which deal with the
potential liability of the state and other bodies operating under
statutory authorisation. Once again, the disputes I have in mind
find factual parallels in both countries, so by studying them one
can see how the two systems have dealt with similar problems.
These cases involve such varied matters as the potential liability of the police for failing to prevent the commission of a crime
or the negligent failure of the social security services to remove
a sexually abused child from the care of its abusing relatives.
Another example of contemporary significance is the possible
liability of a school authority for failing to diagnose the learning problems of one of the children in its care and thus failing
to provide it with the appropriate kind of training.[20] In all these
cases Anglo-American and French law takes different views;
the English—until very recently—denied liability almost

systematically; the French have not only allowed it—they also give the impression of taking it almost for granted. The difference in results is matched by a difference in motivation of the judgments. Once again, the Anglo-American judgments are replete with allusions to policy reasons justifying their results, while their French counterparts resort to a myriad of concepts, some known to English law (eg, causation and contributory negligence) and others unknown (such a *faute lourde* or *égalité devans les charges publics*). Yet, once again, the true picture is not what appears to the naked eye but what is discovered after painstaking research hidden under the surface of a published decision. My general thesis thus remains unaltered even in the area of public law. It is what happens under the surface—what I later on call the 'core' of the problem—that really matters, and it is this that shows whether the systems can converge or are destined to remain divergent until the underlying philosophy is re-assessed. A remarkable dissertation by my former pupil Dr Duncan Fairgrieve, entitled *A Comparative Study of State Tortious and Delictual Liability in Damages in English and French Law*, has recently shed new light on the issue at hand. It also provides additional supporting evidence for a thesis that I have been promoting for over 30 years. I am grateful to him for allowing me to draw here on his material and on his ideas in advance of their publication in book form.[21]

Thus, in the factual scenarios here considered, two arguments have, above all, carried weight with English judges when deciding against liability. First is the fear that liability would impose a crushing financial burden on the state and, secondly, is the danger that the threat of legal action would make officials hesitant to act. We could almost call these English arguments since they do not figure in the French judgments. Yet both of them can, in fact, be found in France as well, though they must be sought in the interstices of the academic literature and not in the motivation of the judgments. With regard to the second of these arguments, for instance Professor Pierre Chapus has admitted that:

> administrative authorities might be held back from acting with the speed that is sometimes required for fear of committing a fault and thus being the cause of damages liability. In other words, the risk of too frequent an imposition of liability would translate into a certain reluctance to act.[22]

Likewise, many argued that the easy imposition of liability would seriously deplete the reserves of the public purse. This view has thus been shared by Professors Alex Weil,[23] Maurice Hauriou[24] and Touchard;[25] though it has been countered by other, equally eminent experts[26] as an illegitimate consideration, which should be ignored by the judge. Yet another group of commentators has claimed that, good or bad, these academic preoccupations have actually influenced judges and thus determined judicial outcomes whether we like this or not. An unpublished (but widely influential) thesis by J C Hélin[27] has thus maintained that:

> it is difficult to deny that the financial argument, invoked by the doctrine in order to restrict the ambit of liability, has been taken into account in the case law itself.

Equally fascinating are two other points.

The first is how these policy reasons (against the imposition of liability) have surfaced in the French judgments in legal, conceptual clothes but are not immediately apparent to anyone who does not know what he is looking for. Fairgrieve, for instance, a common lawyer by training, applied common law techniques in analysing his raw French material. And what he has revealed is as remarkable as it is encouraging for all those who like myself have for decades now[28] been arguing that the systems are very similar once you scratch below their surface of juridical reasoning and search for policy. The point must be emphasised over and over again; for decades of prejudice—legal and political—have been erected on the notions of separateness, difference, and ethnicity. Secondly, what gives the Fairgrieve thesis an extra dimension is the fact that the raw material it uses is widely available in France and yet, in another sense, little used by French administrative lawyers and entirely unexploited by French public law comparatists. It thus took a common lawyer's mind to draw it out and demonstrate its significance, especially for the purposes of comparative methodology. In the long run, this kind of work could, however, encourage French lawyers to apply the method to their own material. And this, not only as a way of testing the viability of their answers, but also as a way of demonstrating to outside observers of French law the system's richness and sophistication which can often be concealed behind its blandly-phrased judgments.

Thus, the requirement that state liability be engaged only if there is a *faute lourde* is, very likely, one of these surreptitiously controlling devices based on the kind of policy reasons that have been openly invoked by the English courts. No wonder, those who condemn such defensive attitudes as something of a by-gone era seriously doubt whether 'the administrative judge [should be allowed to] prioritise systematically and protect the finances of the State.'[29] This, it must be noted in passing, is a fascinating approach, for it turns on its head Lord Hoffmann's very same argument used (in England) to achieve the opposite result, namely to allow the judge to use economic arguments to protect the state.[30] Be that as it may, this French use of the notion of *faute lourde* has led other influential commentators to express the hope 'that, in due course, the requirement . . . will cease to be part of the law.'[31] But, once again, whether one adopts or deplores the philosophy that allows judges to act as protectors of state finances, one cannot deny that Professor M Deguergue[32] sounds convincing when she argues that:

> all authors agree that the principal function of *faute lourde* is to lighten the liability of public bodies.

And, even if the use of this notion, *faute lourde*, were to weaken or it were to be seriously eliminated from some of the areas where it has been used, French law still has ways for, essentially, reintroducing it in some oblique form in order to keep liability within reasonable bounds. Thus, it is already accepted that not every minor malpractice (such as simple errors) constitutes *faute simple*; and that this distinction between *faute simple* and *erreur*, if properly applied, can avert a tidal wave of cases or an obliteration of public finances.[33] One specialist author[34] has thus expressed this thought in the following manner:

> Finally, it is fairly clear in our country that the judicial mind is increasingly uncomfortable with the raising of the threshold of public liability achieved through the notion of administrative gross negligence. Since the protection that this notion accords to public authorities has been judged excessive, it will be up to the judge to decide whether to

rely on it or not, without, however, either provoking a tidal wave of litigation or burdening public finances. For in that case the fault/ error duo would supplant the ordinary negligence/ gross negligence alternative.

In French administrative law this wide-ranging discussion over the ambit and purpose of the notion of *faute lourde* shows, in my view, that the legal concepts in that country are as pliable as their English counterparts and can be made to bend to judicial views on policy. More importantly, the citations that I have given show that the French authors, themselves, accept this point. In my opinion, it requires only a small step further to accept that, in the light of the above, the concepts should be accorded some—but not total—respect or reverence. They are, as I keep saying, the tools that formulate judgments but not the reasons for them.

The same observations (about policy behind concepts) can, I submit, be made of the notion of causative theories in administrative law. To the extent that this is supportable by evidence it reaffirms my view, expressed in the context of the *Perruche* affair, that one should not take legal concepts too seriously.[35]

We thus note, in the context of the problem examined in this chapter, the frank and illuminating observation of Chapus who, referring to the use of the *théorie de causalité adéquate* in the context of (French) administrative law, states that its:

> judicial assessment is not mechanical. It is undertaken with a good deal of freedom and is influenced by common sense and subjectivity.[36]

Chapus continues with the observation that this is also the reason why the potentially more expansive theory of *équilvalence des conditions* has, on the whole, met with less favour with French administrative courts, and, one could add, German courts, as well. Yet other authors have maintained that overall causative theories have received a restrictive application in order to minimise the burden on public finances.[37] Fairgrieve, in his aforementioned work, has gone further than repeat such statements. He has thus meticulously collected case law and references that show that 'the test of causation has been used to ward off large liabilities in sensitive areas such as planning, travaux publics, tax and regulatory activities.'[38]

The same protective philosophy can be found in other causative-related devices such as an act of a third party or *faute de la victime*. Thus, where it can be proved that the third party conduct—some say *faute*—contributed to the injury suffered by the plaintiff, the administration will be expected to pay only the share of the damage which is due to them (there being nothing equivalent to the English notion of joint and several liability).[39] And where children have contributed to their hurt, their damages seem often to be reduced substantially, the apportionment process often, apparently, over-favouring the administration.[40]

(b) A Divergence in Fundamental Philosophy?

So, approaching the case law of different countries in the above way leads us to a number of conclusions.

First, legal systems when compared through their decisional law reveal a considerable similarity of factual litigated instances. Beginning the comparison by using such material (instead of the *doctrine*) has the advantage of putting the reader at ease since he feels he is on familiar terrain and not lost in a jungle of legal notions and concepts. On the minus side, however, it must be admitted that this approach presents the drawback of having to do much original research before finding the obvious objects for comparison. No judge has the time to do that; but that is where academics can be of assistance both to their students as well as to their courts in helping them bridge the gap.

Secondly, when the comparison is pursued further, differences of concepts and reasoning become obvious. The need to explain them then becomes pressing and the researcher is pushed into a different and deeper level of enquiry that requires him to search for the policy reasons of a particular judicial solution rather than for the verbal devices used to formulate them. This search, eventually, reveals that the policy debates that have dominated one system can also be found in the other; indeed, the little that has been cited above suggests a quite remarkable degree of duplication of ideas. But this material is discovered at different levels or in different sources, eg, academic writings (often in inaccessible journals rather than in the main treatises), preparatory papers leading to legislation, or conclusions by advocates general. The one place from which they are missing are the judicial opinions, themselves. The art of discovering the equivalent material is thus one which must be mastered but is not easily learnt. Even more intriguing (and difficult) is the task of tracing the impact that this material has had on the case law since the latter pretends to ignore it. The discovery of conclusive answers is by no means guaranteed; and, often, can only be attempted by talking to the real protagonists of litigation: judges and practitioners. But, at the very least, the pursuit of these aims gives the foreign observer a deeper and, it is submitted, more satisfying understanding of his own case law as he grapples with the difficulties of the foreign solutions.

Thirdly, intelligent questioning of this similar, policy-impregnated material leads one to the final and deeper level where one has to confront the core issues. At this level, legal arguments become subservient to political, economic, or moral ones, which now come to the fore. Inevitably, the key issues that have to be resolved here are not always susceptible to one answer; nor, indeed, are they always capable of receiving a right answer and certainly this cannot come from lawyers acting on their own. I have always felt this to be true of our system and was thus delighted when I came across the same idea expressed by some eminent French colleagues while criticising the over-legalistic dissection to which the important *Perruche*[41] decision was subjected by most French jurists. These three French colleagues were thus, in my view, right when they said that:[42]

> the jurist cannot make use of the law and claim that it can solve [problems] by itself when, in reality, he can only (and does only) opt for an ontological, logical, or moral stance without being any more qualified than anyone else to do so. On the other hand, it falls upon him to create the tools and the techniques which make practicable in law the political solution he has decided to adopt. And that is no mean feat.

It is thus at this final and third level that our illustrations from the Anglo-French administrative law finally find the reason for the diverging answers. The fear, for instance, of financially crushing deserving defendants, though genuinely entertained by both systems, in France gave way to a broader philosophical consideration. This underlying broader philosophy was not always different in France and England. The divergence developed[43] as the French state, in the late 1960s, was progressively seduced by the idea of equality, socialisation of risks, and social solidarity. Under this newer French philosophy the law tends to admit that when citizens suffer damage of a certain type and size it is the duty of the state to compensate them. This is so even if it is not possible to link them with something, which could be called maladministration. This vision explains why, in the recent past, several pieces of regulatory legislation were put into place in order to grant people compensation—from the state budget—for damages having sometimes no relation[44] to any administrative action or omission. The 1990 Act for victims of terrorist acts as well as the 1991 Act concerning people affected by transfusions of blood contaminated by the AIDS virus fall under this category.

Once the above 'philosophical stance' is noted—even if not accepted—one can see why French judges are likely to disregard the cost that a liability rule might entail for public authorities. More interestingly, the idea, so obvious in some English judgments, that such resources might be better used in another 'public' context, becomes equally irrelevant. For, in the kind of consumerist vision of public liability which has become predominant in French law since the late 1960s, compensating the damages suffered by citizens because of administrative activities can never be a wrong use of public money. On the contrary, it may even be seen as the best possible use of public money when it is viewed as serving the principle of equality by avoiding a result that means that people who have randomly been affected by administrative action remain without compensation.

The reader digesting the thoughts in the previous section may accept them as explaining the outcome of the French decisions. But the superficial reader—and for present purposes even educated English lawyers might fall into this category—may precipitously dismiss them as *totally* alien to the role of the state as it has come to be seen in England during the last 20 years. Certainly the views of some judges (such as Lord

Hoffmann) and some academics (such as Weir) would seem to espouse such a 'conservative' philosophy that is prepared to allow (if not encourage) judges to act primarily with the view of shielding the finances of the state. Yet something that comes close to the (new) French philosophy can also be found in England when one reads such documents as the First Report of the Select Committee on the Parliamentary Commissioner for Administration[45] or the views of other leading judges such as Lord Bingham.[46] So, what really matters is not to realise that the prevailing view is different in France and in England; even less, to exercise the political decision and choose between them. For the jurist, certainly the comparative jurist, what is much more important is to realise that these views and debates have, despite misleading appearances caused by different concepts and notions, their *exact* equivalents in England, France (and, indeed, Germany and Italy). A no less significant realisation would lie in the fact that the answer to this 'core' question is not one that can be given by lawyers, or lawyers acting and thinking on their own. The previously quoted views of de Beschillon[47] and his colleagues thus come back to one's mind as containing a truth that is equally valid on both sides of the Channel and thus proves how similar we really are.

A not dissimilar kind of attitude would colour the view of a French judge towards the so-called inhibition argument.[48] For though it is not unknown in French theory of public liability, it certainly plays a secondary part. This is so because, apart from its fundamental compensatory function, public liability is also viewed as a way of disciplining the administration. In that role, it complements judicial review, by imposing payment of compensation, whereas the former provides for the annulment of illegal decisions.

Finally, would a French administrative judge refrain from imposing public liability because he thinks that it would mean that he has second-guessed the public body in the exercise of its discretion? Such an approach, which has found such an appeal in England, would hardly strike a French judge as a natural one. The reason is the following. In practice, in a large majority of cases in which the administration is held liable, the fault which has been identified is an illegality. Illegality, in other words, is the most ordinary form of administrative fault.

This strong relation between fault and illegality has the consequence that the adjudication of administrative liability largely mirrors judicial review of administrative legality. The judges' attitude, when faced with questions of discretion, is the same in both cases. This means that judges have no reason to think that accepting liability would especially impinge upon administrative discretion: they respect it, and review it to the same extent that they would otherwise do when reviewing questions of legality.

5. WIDER CONCLUSIONS

Looking at foreign law the way I have in this chapter[49] is, as I have readily admitted, both difficult and time-consuming. It takes time to read decisions in order to find factual equivalents that lend themselves to comparison. It takes even more of an effort to ensure that, having delved deeper into the procedural, constitutional and political peculiarities of each system, you feel confident enough to emphasise their similarities and explain their differences. Finally, it takes Jovian patience to remain faithful to the overall cause of searching for and emphasising similarities in order to facilitate greater European integration without distorting the raw material you have discovered. This is particularly so as one becomes conscious of the difficulties of imparting this expertise to those who really matter, namely the judges and the practitioners. For academics, with few exceptions, have both in England and France approached comparative law in an excessively theoretical and abstract manner, unwittingly making it of little interest in the classroom and of even less use in the courtroom. The high priests of my subject bear a great responsibility for this sorry state of affairs.

If, despite the above, one perseveres, one realises that the core issues that confront our European systems are the same even though the answers they receive may be different. The next realisation is that if the answers differ it is not really because of the concepts or even the arguments used on the surface, but because of understandable and legitimate divergences at the core. As stated, however, at the core we do not find legal, certainly not legalistic, arguments. On the contrary, we here encounter political, moral, social, and economic issues. Because these issues are of wider import, lawyers alone cannot solve them. Moreover, and this is just as important, they are not issues that can be described as typically French, German, or English, since they appear across borders and thus by their very nature encourage comparison. Finally, individual systems, for instance the French, can and have themselves vacillated over what kind of answers are appropriate to these fundamental questions. Thus, as swings and changes have taken place, so have the results of the judicial decisions altered.[50]

So the real differences between the systems do not lie at the surface where sets of similar facts lead to litigation (I call this the first circle) but at the core (and I call this the third circle). But what stops us from realising this phenomenon and, where necessary, addressing it in an intelligent way (especially if harmonisation of laws is our aim), are the arguments that take place in the second circle, where concepts, notions, and legal reasoning reign supreme. Unfortunately, it is here that most jurists have focused most of their energies. In keeping with nineteenth century ideas of state sovereignty, this has led them to a state-based case law. This, in turn, has led the same jurists to over-emphasise (undoubted) differences rather than stress equally important similarities, and to stick jealously to the tools that their system has bequeathed them. But this is not what the twenty-first century requires, given the move towards transnational legal regimes, be they in the human rights area or in the domain of commercial law. This emerging, new, and interdependent world cannot work with a legal science that is over-attached to parochial structures or local ways of doing business. It needs broad and flexible legal minds to import what is useful and to export what they, in their own countries, have done best. To do this, one must identify and confront the core issues and realise that they cut across national borders, offering great opportunities for a traffic in legal ideas.

The proper understanding of the systems thus requires us to reduce the importance of the second circle and find and define the real issues that lurk in the third. In the controversial *Perruche* decision, where the plenum of the Cour de cassation had to decide whether to give *any* kind of damages in a wrongful life claim, the dominant theme was that of life, itself. However affected and diminished, our current thinking cannot accept it as 'damage' or as a 'harm.' And for as long as this remains true, compensation for 'being born' cannot and will not be sanctioned anywhere in the world. This is true and philosophically tenable, though not as incontrovertible as courts functioning in a politically correct age would like us to believe.[51] At the same time, the same public opinion is not prepared to allow impaired children to suffer because eminent jurists such as Dean Carbonnier have argued that 'life, even if affected by misfortune, is always preferable to nothingness.'[52] As I argued in my article in the *Revue trimestrielle*,[53] the *opinion savante* has no better claim to our loyalty than the *opinion souffrante*. Only academics, it seems to me, can aspire to such levels of intellectual arrogance. So, what *Perruche* did was to make sure—without entering the major philosophical debate—that the affected child had its extra needs taken care of in an adequate way.[54] Provided its damages are not (eventually) duplicated with those already given to the parents by the Court of Appeal which will finally put an end to this protracted litigation, the dignity of the French legal system will not be affected. I think this is the true meaning of the *Assemblée Plénière* of 17 November 2000. It is also the interpretation that brings the case, in its ultimate result, in line with American and German law because it looks at the core of the problem and is not distracted by the biased use of concepts. In France this dimension has, in my view, been missed. For most lawyers used the causation debate to block out of sight the fact that the court was trying to take care of the child and, at the same time, remain faithful to the prevailing view that impaired life was not less valuable than a healthy one.

The examples of tortious liability of statutory bodies, which have provided the main theme of this chapter, must be approached in the same way, as the simple juxtaposition of English and French law will only reveal a false picture. For the equation made by French (but not English) law between illegality and fault makes French law appear doctrinally different and philosophically pro-plaintiff in a most extreme manner. Yet this is precisely the kind of opening statement which, though correct in one sense, does great disservice both to French and English lawyers. For, on the grounds that the differences between the two systems are so great, the statement almost inevitably implies that their further comparison is meaningless. It thus takes the works of Fairgrieve and his French counterparts (such as Hélin) to alter the first impression and show how the normative use of a multitude of concepts, such as *faute lourde, causalité, faute de la victime* etc, go a long way towards reducing the differences which on paper seem so glaring. But this is still only the beginning of the kind of enquiry we need in order to make comparative law attractive as a discipline and useful to our courts. For the fact remains that in the eyes of those who have fashioned French administrative law, the economic concerns, which troubled their English counterparts, were only one part of the equation. What, in a sense, was paramount in their minds was to make a philosophical stand and subordinate economic expediency to it. This stand was founded on the ideas of equality, risk-socialisation, and social solidarity: activities which benefit us all must also spread their costs among us all. Though we know that in France fashions change, one suspects that this edifice could become unstable only if the level of damages seriously endangered the financial viability of the 'deserving pockets' that meet these bills. My theory, however, works only on the basis of an *unproven* assumption that in this type of case,[55] unlike those involving medical malpractice, the level of damages awarded by French administrative courts is much lower than those that might be reached by English courts if they ever became sympathetic to these claims. I stress, however, *unproven*, for the collection of raw data on damage awards is an extraordinarily difficult task in French law and is still incomplete. And the assumption that my co-authors and I made in our *Tortious Liability of Statutory Bodies* was, in fact, the opposite, suggesting that the level of damages awarded in these cases could be equated to those found in personal injury litigation where some kind of parity can be established between English and French law.[56]

This (as yet unquantified) moderation of French law, coupled with the more concrete data one can collect from German law, might hold out some lessons for English law as it contemplates a more liberal stance in its post *Barett* and *Phelps* phases. In one sentence this is: compensate but do not go overboard! Certainly, a number of dicta from *Phelps* could be collected to suggest that such a development of the law of damages might not be unwelcome to their Lordships.[57] Yet French law might make an even more important contribution to our legal theory if its underlying philosophy were ever to be adopted by our judges. For some, such ideas as that of social solidarity could well provide the underlying theme that could bring together the patchwork of remedies—given by ombudsmen, criminal injuries compensation boards, common law etc—that are slowly being crafted in the penumbra of public law proper in our country. Of course, such a suggestion runs counter to common law incrementalism, especially the English variant, and the system's aversion to fashioning wide and unifying principles. Yet is this not what happened to our private law of unjustified enrichment thanks to the combined tenacity of judge and jurist? And if it happened in one part of the law, and happened in the short space of twenty-five years or so, why cannot it also happen in the troublesome area where public law and tort overlap with such confusion? But this is as much as one can say at this moment and I leave the issue to be reviewed again some time in the future.

In any event, my main concern as a Professor of Comparative Law has not been to theorise in the borderline of tort and administrative law but to promote a better way of bringing together the different legal systems. For over 30 years in academic life I have tried to apply the approach I sketched here to the entire area of the law of obligations and, most recently, to expand it to include some areas of human rights. It is my belief, but not yet supported by adequate personal research, that this methodology can be applied successfully across the various areas of the law and across national borders. And if it can, it will, I think, suggest that despite formidable differences, the similarities that exist in the contemporary European systems are growing by the day. More importantly, the similarities are growing not because of Directives, model laws, or international treaties, which are regulating more and more of our life, but because growing urbanisation, industrialisation, interstate commerce and travel are attenuating local differences of behaviour and thought, and are assimilating human tastes, attitudes and values. In short, they are affecting the core or third circle; and this, sooner or later, will force our lawyers to make their reasoning more open, more susceptible to interdisciplinary data, and more user-friendly. Such an approach will not only ensure greater mutual understanding; it will also ensure that good ideas, be they English or French, will travel faster and further. And the true comparatist can ask for nothing more.

Notes

[1] By this I mean the systematic arrangement of the subjects. Thus the English tort of nuisance appears as part of the French law of property (and related rights) and a search for it in a French tort treatise would produce little of interest to a common lawyer. It is only when one reflects on the generic rubric of *troubles de voisinage* that one realises that what one system sees as rights another can, equally sensibly, examine under the heading of wrongs. History is, of course, responsible for this different optic which, however, does not affect the similarity of litigated cases nor of their outcome.

[2] The same is, of course, true if one compares French and English law. The cardinal common law notion of 'duty of care' is thus totally absent from art 1382 CC though many decades ago Planiol and Savatier came close to recreating it for French law. See Marcel Planiol, *Traité élémentaire de droit civil* (11th edn, Paris, 1948–9) no 863; René Savatier, *Traité de la reponsabilité civile* (2nd edn, Paris, 1951) 56–134. Examples such as these are particularly important since they show how close the different systems can be and that if they have come to follow different paths this does not mean that their differences are deep-rooted or insurmountable.

[3] The next few sections make use of material contributed by Professor Jean Bernard Auby (and to a lesser extent myself) to a book we co-authored with Professor Dagmar Coester-Waltjen and Dr Simon Deakin entitled *Tortious Liability of Statutory Bodies* (1999).

[4] [1995] 3 WLR 152.

[5] Conseil d'Etat, 23 September 1987, *Recueil des arrêts du Conseil d'Etat*, 290.

[6] Conseil d'Etat, 4 May 1983, no 22811.

[7] It would involve too great a digression into English administrative law rules to discuss the local authority's liability for breach of statute, so the discussion in the text is limited to the tort of negligence.

[8] The question of vicarious liability for the torts of its employees was, initially, left open. But it was finally decided in favour of the plaintiffs in *Phelps v Hillingdon London Borough Council* [2001] 2 AC 619, a decision of the House of Lords which, however, still left open the question whether the local authority could be *primarily* liable.

⁹ [1995] 3 WLR 152 at 183. This was, indeed, accepted by the majority in *Marc Rich & Co A G v Bishop Rock Marine Co Ltd* [1996] 1 AC 211, a case involving property damage. Two years later an attempt was made to transport this reasoning to cases of physical injury in *Perret v Collins* [1998] 2 Lloyd's Rep 255, but it was boldly repulsed by an unanimous Court of Appeal. Lord Justice Hobhouse (as he then was) had this to say on this crucial issue (at 258): 'What the second and third defendants seek to achieve in this case is to extend decisions upon "economic" loss to cases of personal injury. It represents a fundamental attack upon the principle of tortious liability for negligent conduct, which had caused foreseeable personal injury to others. That such a point should be considered to be even arguable shows how far some of the fundamental principles of the law of negligence have come to be eroded. The arguments advanced in this case [*viz* that the kind of wider policy considerations used in *Marc Rich* to justify the majority decision should also be used in this case and absolve the defendants from all liability] illustrate the dangers of substituting for clear criteria, criteria which are incapable of precise definition and involve what can only be described as an element of subjective assessment by the Court; such ultimately subjective assessments tend inevitably to lead to uncertainty and anomaly which can be avoided by a more principled approach.'

¹⁰ *Governors of the Peabody Donation Fund v Sir Lindsay Parkinson & Co Ltd* [1985] AC 210 at 241C, per Lord Keith. The idea can, however, be traced back to Lord Morris' judgment in the *Dorset Yacht* case of [1970] AC 1004.

¹¹ *Caparo Industries Plc v Dickman* [1990] 2 AC 605.

¹² Above n 6.

¹³ Above n 5.

¹⁴ This author at least thus has much respect for Lord Justice Buxton's reaction when, presented by counsel with some policy concerns, he retorted that '[t]here is no evidence to support any of these contentions. . . . In my respectful view, the Court should be very cautious before reaching or acting on any conclusions that are not argued before it in the way in which technical issues are usually approached, with the assistance of expert evidence.' See *Perrett v Collins* [1998] 2 Lloyd's Rep at 255, 276–77.

¹⁵ Whenever it is published, for, unfortunately, the conclusions of the *Avocat général* and the *Commissaire du Gouvernement* are not always easily available.

¹⁶ At its barest the argument is this: the doctor's negligence in failing to diagnose the mother's rubella did not cause the child's impairment but only allowed it to be born. Therefore the doctor should not be liable for anything towards the child. The best reply to this argument, suitable to the way the case was pleaded in French law, has come from Professor Michelle Gobert in 'La Cour de cassation méritait-elle le pilori?' *Les Petites Affiches*, 8 December 2000, 4.

[17] Decision of the *Assemblée Plénière* of 17 November 2000 published in *La Semaine Juridique*, No 50, 13 December 2000, 2293 ff.

[18] *Procanik v Cillo* 478 A 2d 755 (1984) at 763: 'The philosophical problem of finding that such a defective life is worth less than no life at all has perplexed [many] distinguished members of this Court. We need not become preoccupied, however, with these metaphysical considerations. Our decision to allow the recovery [by the child] of extraordinary medical expenses is not premised on the concept that non-life is preferable to an impaired life, but is predicated on the needs of the living.'

[19] See, eg, BGHZ 3, 261 (23 October 1951) where the court, after reviewing the various German theories about causation, said: 'The search is for [a] corrective that restricts the scope of the purely logical consequences to produce an equitable result. . . . Only if the courts are conscious of the fact that it is a question here not really of causation but of the fixing of the limits within which the originator of a condition can be equitably presumed liable for its consequences . . . will the danger of schematisation . . . be avoided and the correct results be guaranteed.'

[20] The leading English decision is *Phelps v Hillingdon London Borough Council*, above n 8. For a factually parallel German decision see OLG Hamm, 11th Civil Senate, 23 March 1990, 11 U 108/89.

[21] The English translations of the French quotations are likewise his, unless otherwise stated.

[22] P Chapus, *Droit Administratif Général*, vol I (13th edn, 1999) 1463.

[23] A Weil, *Les Conséquences de l' Annulation de l' Acte Admininstratif Pour Excès de Pouvoir* (1952) 255.

[24] M Hauriou, Case note on CE 29 May 1903, *Le Berre*, Sirrey 1904.3.121.

[25] The latter even going as far as suggesting that the judge should protect public funds. See Touchard, 'A propos de la responsabilité pour faute de l'Administration Fiscale' *RDP* 1992, 785 at 806.

[26] Such as Georges Vedel, *Droit Administratif* (2nd edn, Paris, 1961) 281. Likewise, Clinquennois, 'Essai sur la responsabilité de l' Etat du fait de ses activités de contrôle et de tutelle' *Les Petites Affiches* No 98, 16 August 1995, 4.

[27] *Faute de Service et Préjudice dans le Contentieux de la Responsabilité pour Illégalité* (Nantes, 1969) 63. I owe this reference to Fairgrieve's thesis.

[28] Thus, 20 years ago von Bar and I tried to do this for English and German law; see *Richterliche Rechtspolitik im Haftungsrecht* (CB Mohr, Tübingen, 1981).

[29] Clinquennois, above n 26.

[30] For instance in *Stovin v Wise* [1996] AC 923 at 952 ff. Yet, one must also bear in mind that the Hoffmann approach can also be found in France. See, eg, the views of Touchard, above n 25.

[31] Roger Errera [1990] *Public Law* 571.

[32] Deguergue, *Jurisprudence et Doctrine dans l'Elaboration du Droit de la Responsabilité Administrative* (1994) 638.

³³ This has been admitted even by some *Commissaire du Gouvernment.* See, eg, CE 29 June 1997, *RFDA* 1998, 87.

³⁴ Michel Paillet, *Responsabilité Administrative* (Paris, 1996) para 259 (my translation).

³⁵ I stressed this point in my article 'Réflexions d'un comparatiste anglais sur et à partir de l'arrêt Perruche' *RTD civ.* 2001, 77–102.

³⁶ Above n 22, para 1414. Likewise M Deguergue, above n 32, para 147.

³⁷ C Guettier, *La Responsabilité Administrative* (Paris, 1996) 127.

³⁸ Unpublished thesis, at 162; citations omitted.

³⁹ CE 28 October 1977, Commune de Flumet (1977) Rec 412; CE 14 May 1986, Commune de Cilaos (1986) Rec 716.

⁴⁰ S Rials, *Le Juge Administratif Francais et la Technique du Standard* (Paris, 1980) 331.

⁴¹ The *Perruche* decision of the *Assemblée Plénière* of the Cour de cassation of 17 November 2000, dealing with a wrongful birth claim by a seriously handicapped child; above n 17.

⁴² Article published in *Le Monde,* 21 December 2000, by Professor de Béchillon, Olivier Cayla and Yan Thomas, both *directeurs d' études à l'Ecole des hautes études en sciences sociales* (my translation).

⁴³ While the underlying philosophy and concerns were similar, the legal solutions were likewise closer than they are today. Thus, see P Weil, above n 23, at 255.

⁴⁴ Or at least without the need of demonstrating any relation.

⁴⁵ 1994–1995, HC 112, para 70: 'We agree that the priority in expenditure should be the improvement of services. Effective redress is itself a service improvement. It may be unfortunate that funds are spent in compensation. It cannot, however, be right to use such argument against schemes which justly reimburse the complainant for financial loss. The answer is not to avoid compensation but to avoid the original failure of service.'

⁴⁶ '[S]ave in clear cases, it is not for the courts to decide how public money is best spent nor to balance the risk that money will be wasted on litigation against the hope that the possibility of suit may contribute towards the maintenance of the highest standards.'

⁴⁷ Above n 42.

⁴⁸ Namely, that the imposition of civil liability will make civil servants reluctant to act.

⁴⁹ And with greater tenacity in the rest of my writings. Thus, see *Foreign Law and Comparative Methodology: A Subject and a Thesis* (1997) and *Always on the Same Path: Essays on Foreign Law and Comparative Methodology* (2001).

⁵⁰ Think of the *concubinage* cases that divided the civil and criminal sections of the Cour de cassation throughout the 1950s and 1960s and how the Cour de cassation changed its stance in the 1970s, and you will understand my point in addition to discovering another example of how legal

concepts—there the notion of *dommage légitime*—were distorted by policy considerations.

⁵¹ Writers such Herodutus, Sophocles, Shakespeare, and Nietzsche, to mention but a few, never managed to solve this underlying issue, so how can we expect a judge to do this for us? For fuller references see my article, above n 35.

⁵² Quoted by *l'Avocat général* Sainte-Rose in his conclusions in the *Perruche* case, above n 17, at 2307.

⁵³ Above n 35.

⁵⁴ *M le Conseiller rapporteur* Sargos makes, I think, this clear in his report to the court. See *SJ*, above n 17, para no 49, p 2302.

⁵⁵ Such as *X (Minors) v Bedfordshire County Council* [1995] 2 AC 633, *Barrett v Enfield London Borough Council* [2001] 2 AC 550, or *Phelps*, above n 8.

⁵⁶ These 'second thoughts' I am entertaining here about French law are personal and in no way bind my co-authors of *Tortious Liability of Statutory Bodies* (above n 3). They also do not alter the validity of our (combined) thesis with regard to German law. For the German examples we quoted in our book show that the German awards, though not huge (especially by American standards), are not insignificant.

⁵⁷ Though how, for instance, a dyslectic child should be compensated for not having been given a proper education remains to be worked out.

6

Reflecting on the Future: An Epilogue

Life is a long discovery, isn't it?
You only get your wisdom bit by bit,
If you have luck you find in early youth
How dangerous it is to tell the truth;
And next you learn how dignity and peace
Are the ripe fruits of patient avarice.

Hilaire Belloc: Discovery

During my 35 years as an academic teacher I have witnessed great changes in the academic world and also the real world around it. I recall, for instance, that in my early Cambridge days—in the late 1960s—the entire law faculty possessed one primitive, old-fashioned photocopier which was positioned at the top entrance to the Squire Law Library; it first had to be fed some pink paper and then produced what, by today's standards, would be considered unacceptable copies which would fade very quickly. A far cry from today when most leading faculties are planning to make computer equipment extensively available to their computer literate students. Paris, where I also spent time during the 1970s, lacked even a photocopier. And one had to climb endless steps to reach Tunc's *pigeonnière* off the *Gallerie Dumas* in the building off *la vraie Sorbonne* in order to find the one and only available secretary to all and sundry working in the area of comparative law. Nearby was also an extremely modest collection of English law books, mainly gifts from Tunc's friends from outside France. Waiting for books in the main library in the rue Cujas could take the better part of the day, unless you were a professor—and I was not—in which case you had access to the most untidy book stacks I have ever seen (which I once did, escorted by Tunc). Books about foreign law, were, as I have already said in chapter one above, a scarcity; and exchange programmes were, quite literally, unimaginable, the United Kingdom of course not yet being a member of the European Community. The late Hamson[1] (Cambridge) and William Parker (Exeter) were among the very few who would try to attract lawyers from different countries to their Strasbourg courses, then run by Regina, the elderly widow of David's Catalonian friend Felipe de Solà Cañizares. In the United Kingdom, the truest example of professionalism was to be found in John Mitchell's (Edinburgh) persistent efforts to bring in European (in the sense of Community) law as part of our constitutional law courses, while on the Continent of Europe the Max Planck Institutes were the only professionally organised and well-equipped bodies devoted to the study of comparative law, not to mention regional institutes like that of the University of Munich, then ably run by Lorenz. But the well-known English Germanophobia kept them clearly out of the minds of most English lawyers. In retrospect, I can only think of one British colleague, Jonathan Mance, now Lord Justice Mance, who spent some time in Germany working with the late Zweigert. The only other jurist whom I recall as being proficient in German law, was Konrad (now Lord Justice) Schiemann; but since he was the great, great, grandson of the first President of the Reichsgericht, Eduard von Simson,[2] one would almost expect this. The world of yesterday had something primitive and yet also something endearing about it. But only those who lived through it can ever fully understand (let alone miss) this 'world of yesterday.'

Our contemporary world could not be more different; and as far as books, exchanges, teacher mobility, and new schools are concerned, I have already said something in the earlier chapters and need not cover the same ground again. The change is great; in most respects, I would call it re-orientation of energies, even progress. Progress, I think, has also been made on the language front, which is clearly a plus as far as the study of foreign law is concerned. Again, in my view, much of the credit for these changes must be linked to the proliferation of student exchanges, which the European Commission has encouraged through a multiplicity of programmes. Finally, one must not forget that some kind of academic legal training, as a prerequisite for a law career, became obligatory in England during the period of time which I have been describing in this book. These are all changes that will encourage greater interest in foreign law; and they have been accompanied by the means and the opportunities that will make it easier to satisfy this interest. In my opinion, some of the changes which I have described, particularly the growing tendency of judges to show an interest in foreign law, can be linked to these changes in the wider environment in which they operate. The growing impact of Luxembourg and Strasbourg on our law and on the minds of our judges represents the coping stone of this change which makes 2003 very different to 1968, the year I began my legal career in England. And yet what still remains an obstacle in the great legal convergence which I see as happening and which I strongly favour, especially in the educational field, is that unquantifiable factor: mentality. It is with this that I think all of us who wish for more give and take with the continental legal systems will continue to face the greatest difficulties.

It is strange that an 'introverted mentality' remains such a formidable block, for in the last 35 years England in general and London in particular have become more multicultural, multiracial, multidenominational than ever in their entire history. Tastes have also changed dramatically as the 'cappuccino' has edged out the 'tea' break—even in the Underground stations—and the television culture has transformed, and to a large extent made uniform, our views about the world. But with law, and despite the combined effects of enhanced travel and work abroad as well as the institutional influx of European legal ideas, a great number of lawyers remain parochial. This, I think, is the truth; and dangerous to proclaim it if you are at the beginning of your career. Happily, I am at the end of mine.

In one sense such parochialism is understandable. The bulk of legal disputes involve minor (for all but those who are caught up in them) local problems, which the legal system has to resolve routinely and quickly. In such disputes, exercises in comparative law have no place. In more important cases, the needs are different; but here, at the highest echelons of the judicial profession, many of the actors of the law, by virtue of their age, are also accustomed to a different frame of mind. I know many judges and even more practising lawyers who still regret, and if they could they would reject, this growing internationalisation of the law. Since, for them, this new world is a challenge to the world they know, one has much genuine sympathy for their predicament. Nor, it has to be said, are their German or French counterparts fundamentally different. Yet the impact of Luxembourg and Strasbourg is growing incessantly; and as I have pointed out in other writings, there is hardly an area of domestic law that is now escaping their effect. This is what makes our era so different from that of the previous generation. If we do not embrace this transformation with a plan, we will fail to preserve some of the strong features of the world of yesterday. We will also fail to export something of our own ideas to others whom we might influence to our advantage.

Many younger scholars are doing just the kind of work I am advocating; but being young sometimes means that they are not yet noticed. More importantly, however, one also finds innovators among the top judiciary. Lord Bingham, Lord Woolf, Lord Steyn, Lord Clyde (and not that long ago Lord Goff) are some examples. And there is another stream of judges, such as Lord Justices Auld, Laws, and Sedley, to mention but a few, who are toying with the new and are not afraid of it. Many, in various seminars that I[3] and others[4] have organised, have expressed their views about growing convergence in a way which their predecessors would never have done, even 20 years ago. Even more have used foreign law in their extra-judicial utterings. And all seem to me open to more of the same if it is properly presented to them. The recent decision of the House of Lords in *Fairchild v Glenhaven Funeral Services Ltd*[5] must surely mark a kind of high water mark in the use of foreign law by the highest court of the land. Even Palandt, the bible of the German private law practitioners, and the examples given under § 830 BGB, figured in the opinion of the Senior Law Lord while Lord Rodger of Earlsferry even cited the *Motive*—the supporting explanations that accompanied the 1896 version of the BGB—in order to determine the policy pursued by the relevant paragraph of the Code. This can only happen if the academic packages the foreign product in an attractive way, the practitioner is willing to make use of it, and the judge is broad-minded enough to do so. The battle for the soul of the latter is, I think, slowly won; and when this receptiveness to foreign ideas becomes widely accepted, as I think it is in countries like Canada and South Africa who are pioneering the use of foreign law in their judgments, the practitioners will fall into line. In this sense it is noteworthy that the practitioners in the *Fairchild* case had not, of their own volition, addressed their Lordships on European law; they were asked to do so. The climate is changing, albeit slowly.

I might be excused for claiming that this change is partly due to the method I have been urging upon my English colleagues throughout my career. And if this sounds immodest and un-English, I plead in my support Montaigne, an author not known for pomposity. For he wrote:[6]

> A man of straight and elevated mind who judges surely and soundly employs in all circumstances examples taken from himself as well as from others, and frankly cites himself as witness as well as third parties. We should jump over those plebeian rules of etiquette in favour of truth and freedom.

Still, for greater effect, let me cite Lord Justice Sedley. Referring to my *German Law of Torts: A Comparative Treatise*, he wrote:[7]

> [This book] has already been cited in the judgments of anglophone courts from Australia to Canada to South Africa, as well as those of England and Wales. This is its great and growing value. *It no longer represents, as comparative law used to represent, an absorbing academic pursuit. It represents a body of working jurisprudence developed by able lawyers to cope with problems common to both our jurisdictions, and doing so on a largely shared foundation of basic rights and norms.*

Those critically inclined might well be quick to comment that, naturally, the learned judge was bound to write something flattering since he was, after all, writing a foreword to the fourth edition of my book. Yet the italicised words are for me the most significant part of his statement, for they reveal *the form* which the learned Justice felt was most appropriate to express his support for the venture. And, just as importantly, they echo precisely the sentiments of Lords Goff and Bingham when they had contributed forewords to earlier editions. And if this still seems unconvincing, one should be allowed to feel some satisfaction that the fourth edition was cited in the *Fairchild* decision, a mere week after it found its way into the bookshops. This is not pride for the success of one's work,

though it would be human to feel such sentiments and hypo-
critical to try to hide them. It is pride that a *methodology* laboriously developed over 35 years (and derived from the teachings
of a great man) is finally producing some fruits for the benefit
of the entire profession. The day when an electronic search may
be desirable to show how the citations of European law (and I
include here Luxembourg and Strasbourg law) are beginning
to match in numbers those of American and Commonwealth
law may not be that far away. I can make this claim now even
though many may contest it. But had I made it in the mid-1960s
I would not have gained a foothold even at the bottom of the
academic ladder.

Yet I still see in what I call 'mentality blocks' the greatest
difficulties ahead. So how are they likely to be manifested in
practice? In my experience they will take different forms, from
the most crude to the very plausible. Here are some in ascend-
ing order of importance (or difficulty).

The Europeans are 'Huns' or 'Frogs' who will dilute and
spoil our culture. This is tabloid language forgetting the long
pedigree of the continental legal culture; and in my view has
caused much harm to our political relations with other countries. For the jealousy towards the Germans can, in a different
setting, easily become contempt for the Italians or the Greeks;
and both are unproductive. No one can change such unnecessarily destructive attitudes easily; but, equally, no serious
person takes them seriously. Nonetheless, they poison the
atmosphere of co-operation and interchange.

Next comes the well-intended misunderstanding of contemporary European law. Great jurists, academics and judges
(and there is no need to give names) have made sweeping
pronouncements about French or German law which display
a degree of ignorance that is no longer acceptable among
educated lawyers operating within an ever-shrinking Europe.
The broadsheets have also their share of sin as they have
spread erroneous information about the French *juge d'instruction*, the (apparently detrimental) effect of the German law of
privacy on free speech, and that classic of all misstatements,
that in France one is guilty until proved innocent!

Language is the third obstacle; and it is not an unimportant
one. But this is not only a real problem. In a strange sort of way

it is also imaginary; and it is one shared by our neighbours. Take, for instance, what we said about the German legislator's habit of consulting foreign law but doing so through German writings. My impression is that the Germans are better linguists than the English, certainly at the educational and social level we are talking about. Their preference for German texts is thus not due to the fact that they cannot read an English textbook but due to the belief—to a large extent understandable—that going through the German version means that a fellow German has distilled this material first and made it safe and more usable. Language is a problem; but with increased travel and joint degree programmes it will get less formidable. And coupled with this, one has an ever-growing amount of foreign material reproduced in the English language through websites, books or specialised journals.

Translating is not the only problem; packaging the foreign ideas in a usable form is another and far more important hurdle that must be overcome. I have addressed this in chapter four above (and elsewhere), so little more need be said about it except to repeat the refrain of this book: that it is here that much of the comparatists' effort should go, not the fluffy, politically correct literature that is so ephemeral and sensationalist.

With the growing volume of legal material neither the national judge nor the practitioner can keep himself up to date without a huge effort. That is where the academic enters into the picture. He can assemble, package, explain the foreign material and direct the attention of the practitioners in the way they wish to go. Time, or rather lack of it, is often put forward against such an attempt to create an ambience of combination of talents to serve the cause of justice. But time can be found if people know how to ration it. The following illustration supports my view; and it comes from a panel discussion organised by the British Institute of International and Comparative Law in London in March 2002.

The topic was some recent English cases concerning the problem of wrongful conception, which lead to healthy or impaired children. Among the participants were Lord Justice Brooke, Lady Justice Hale, Professor Michael Coester of the University of Munich, Miss Elizabeth-Ann Gumbel QC, and the present author. The two judges had been involved in the case of *Angela Parkinson v St James and Seacroft University Hospital NHS Trust*,[8] a case of an impaired child being born from a failed sterilisation operation. Judging from the tone of the judgment of the senior judge, he felt he had to skirt around Lord Steyn's judgment in *MacFarlane v Tayside Health Board (Scotland)*,[9] where the House of Lords had denied damages to a healthily born child. Lord Brooke, apparently, decided to confront the invocation of the Aristotelian notion of distributive justice used judicially (and, subsequently, extra-judicially)[10] by Lord Steyn. So he asked counsel to conduct a computer search and find out how often Aristotle and his theory had previously figured in English judgments. The result of the search was poor; only in one tax case, apparently, had the idea ever appeared in print in an English judgment. One may regret Aristotle's low citation rate! But the real point I am making is not how familiar British jurists are with Aristotelian ethics, but whether it would have been better if Lord Brooke had instituted a search that could reveal whether other major courts had dealt with the same problem elsewhere with a view to finding some transplantable crumbs of thought. This is not intended to be unfair to the learned Justice for whom I, like others in my profession, have a high regard. It is only meant to imply how much more instructive the final result might have been if the Court of Appeal had, as the House of Lords did in the *Fairchild* case, asked counsel to address them on continental European law. For, as it happens, the German Constitutional Court,[11] the German Federal Court,[12] the Austrian Supreme Court,[13] the Dutch Supreme Court[14] and the French Cour de cassation[15] have all, *within the last two or three years*, delivered major judgments on this issue. Would not the time used to search for Aristotle been better spent doing the kind of comparative search I am suggesting? Is there any reason why one should not have looked at the experience of our major European partners—especially on an issue such as this, which touches upon wider political, moral, and philosophical issues and is not dependent on codal provisions? I think we should and could do this, especially in cases such as *MacFarlane*, where the transplantability of legal ideas is easy and not prevented by institutional impediments. I am confident that the problem that had to be addressed in the *Parkinson* case will, sooner rather than later, return to the House of Lords, which will be asked to complete its ruling in *MacFarlane*. In the light of *Fairchild*, the chances of my plea being accepted must be fair. Thus, what has hindered us so far, in my view, is the mentality of little Englanders—a mentality which the globalisation climate of our times will soon put an end to.

The long and the short of it is that if people wish to avoid taking advantage of foreign experience they will always find ways to make their resistance sound plausible. My own view is that such narrow-mindedness is unprofitable in academic as well as practical terms, and I honestly think that modern circumstances of trade and globalisation will defeat it in the end. This, however, is a prediction and we shall have to wait and see if time proves me right.

But for anyone who is an eclectic my world must be attractive. And it emphatically does not mean substituting new friends for old, but only making lawyers aware that on a growing number of issues there is a wider choice of answers and models than the ones they were taught in their school days. The wrongful conception cases reveal these alternatives; and other instances can be given to show, through diversity, the richness of available solutions. The American model of free speech is thus not the only one; there is also the tempered model found in countries such as Germany. And it is not just me saying this but the doyen of British judges, Lord Wilberforce.[16] Likewise, there is not only the American model of federalism but also a Canadian, an Australian, a German and an Italian variation, which must be considered as well. We, in Britain, fear the word 'federalism'; but could not our brand of emerging regionalism learn something from these various models? And in tort law there is scope for compromise between the American generosity (made necessary, in my view, because of the lack of an efficient social security system) and the, at times exaggerated, European parsimony. Thus, in my view, in a host of cases the answer to the question 'why do some systems appear more generous than others to plaintiffs of a certain kind'[17] may lie in an increased willingness to find liability, coupled with sophistication in keeping the measure of damages to manageable limits. But the different legal rules that govern the liability of auditors in German and American law is not the only example where the 'practice on damages' can explain the differences 'in liability.' Many others can be cited, and all support the fascinating lesson that when comparing systems we may start by looking at their decisions but we must then try to set them against their wider background. I am here thinking of civil liability for maladministration of different kinds, which cannot be solved, I think, in the old way of denying a remedy altogether. Thus I, and I think no other jurist, can better Lord Nicholls' dictum that 'denial of the existence of a cause of action is seldom, if ever, the appropriate response to fear of its abuse.'[18]

Those who share my optimism about promoting the cause of greater intellectual interchange in such a way must thus focus their efforts on five things, rather than be wistful about the past or enticed by trendy ideas of the present with an ephemeral appeal.

First we must continue to make available in the English language important legal materials from major legal systems such as the German, French and Italian. This is not born out of a desire to put down other languages but out of the belief that we must make other legal cultures better known by exploiting the universality of the English language. My website[19] aims to promote just such a cause. And I hope that after we have expanded it to include leading French material, we can then slowly spread our umbrella to include Italy, which has traditionally enjoyed a very rich academic and judicial legal culture but which has sadly been neglected in this country. How important this exercise can be, in political as well as cultural terms, can be seen by the use that South African judges made of German material 'packaged' for them by American jurists. 'Packaging,' as the attentive reader of this book will have noticed, is an important part of my method. But the one type of 'packaging' that I have suggested, in chapter four above for instance, and which consists of presenting the foreign law through litigated factual situations which have close parallels in two or more countries, is neither the only one possible nor, indeed, the only one indicated for all cases. Another way of packaging, still consistent with the functional approach to comparative law, may consist in analysing carefully a notion or concept found in one system and then discovering what notion or concept performs its functions in another system. To be precise, in an earlier piece[20] I tried to suggest that it was fruitless to compare the notions of cause and consideration since the function that the first performs for French law are, in the common law, performed by a multitude of concepts and institutions such as common mistake, consideration, frustration, failure of consideration and illegality. Another way of packaging can be found in Honoré's fascinating but as yet unpublished piece entitled 'On Fitting Trusts into Civil Law Jurisdictions.'[21] And here the suggestion is that one should search for the core or absolutely essential feature of an institution and then see how this can be fitted into the new environment. For as Honoré puts it, 'To compare institutions in different jurisdictions it is important to attend to both structure and function.'

Secondly, we should encourage the gradual annotation of this material. This should be undertaken by teams of jurists from the countries involved, and it should aim to bring out the true utility of the foreign material by pointing out its difficulties, its peculiarities and its most attractive features. Students reading foreign law should be major users; but the prime market should be that of judges, practitioners and, where appropriate, law reformers. I know there is a such a 'market' and the most recent illustration I can give is that of the firm of solicitors who were preparing (at the time of writing of this book) the appeal in the *Naomi Campbell* case and felt it was in their interest to commission the translation of two of the *Caroline* decisions for use in the Court of Appeal hearings. Such incidents are still too few to be called a trend; but full-time comparatists should try to turn them into one. To these private initiatives, I should add government departments and, of course, the Law Commission, which are beginning to need a steady stream of advice about foreign law.

Thirdly, the growing number of institutes or centres of comparative law in this country should try to develop a coherent policy aiming to promote this greater knowledge and the dissemination of this material rather than rival each other for points in the next research assessment exercise. I experienced the same fragmentation of effort in my Dutch days when I saw all Dutch law faculties, which had ambitions in the foreign and comparative law field, suffer from the sub-divisions of limited resources. In this context, we (and here I certainly include the Dutch with whom I worked for nearly 20 years) might consider drawing some lessons from the German experience, which has chosen to locate these institutes in different cities and universities, each assuming a leading role in some branch of the law. As far as England is concerned, Cambridge, for instance, could assume the leadership in public law, international law, criminology, and legal history. Oxford could take the leading role in European Union and labour law. London could exploit its position as the nation's capital and give a lead in private, commercial, and trade law. Southampton could play a part in shipping law and so on. This is only an off-the-cuff distribution of tasks; and having created three institutes and been on the board of management of a fourth, I know perfectly well how unlikely it is that there would ever be voluntary agreement among institutions of high learning to such a rationalisation of scarce resources. But someone has to get the ball rolling by suggesting the idea; and HEFCE might even wish to provide financial incentives for such an original and resource-conserving new initiative.

Fourthly, we should attempt to enlist the help of the Inns of Court (and their equivalents in other countries) as well as the multinational firms of solicitors in the *training* of the lawyers of tomorrow, rather than just turning to them for periodic refilling of our war chests. This task of preparing the lawyers of tomorrow has become too complex and too important to be left to university professors alone, especially those who are content to devote their entire life in the publication of the odd piece about foreign law. The talent that exists must be brought out of the cloisters and put to the service of the real world. And, reciprocally, we should involve more practitioners in shared teaching with full-time academics. We have seen how modern high technology companies have, through the links they have built with science departments, profited the entire university structure. Luckily, lawyers are in the same category of 'usable' academics. Incidentally, this is not just a move for self-preservation; for here, again, we see how the flourishing of some university faculties can indirectly also help sister faculties who, unlike law and science departments, are less able to attract funds themselves. As far as law is concerned, my feeling is that the Inns of Court would welcome any co-operation initiatives that revived their old teaching roles and helped remove the unfair but commonly voiced criticism that they are just sitting on a great deal of money which they only use for feasts. And here, as well, there are many talented people, able and—despite their busy lives—willing to help sharpen the skills of our lawyers.

Finally, with the assistance perhaps of the Judicial Studies Board and the Lord Chancellor's Department (and, on the Continent of Europe, other Ministries of Justice) we should explore ways of institutionalising judicial exchanges. Again, I speak with some experience since I have a hand in organising one or two of these sessions. But I also feel that they are too important to continue to be left to the initiatives of individuals, be they judges or academics. The aim, again, should be the greater knowledge and understanding of each other's legal systems and the furthering of more networking.

These, then, are the kind of ideas I would like to see developed more and, I readily admit, this is quite an agenda. For England in particular, it offers a unifying and harmonising purpose; it could avoid duplication of effort and save public money; it actually serves the needs of our time; it is already being implemented, albeit in an unplanned manner; and, it is submitted, it is beginning to prove its worth. Last and by no means least, however, it is an agenda, which, with some modification, all comparatists could adopt. For it is not designed to give a lead to one individual or his institution but to encourage all to work together in a pragmatic way which would help make comparative law relevant and encourage an organic co-operation between the different parts of the legal profession. Engaging the real world of private enterprise and the professions would also help ensure that our universities remain great centres of learning, something which may be less assured at the beginning of the twenty-first century than was the case during the last century, which saw such an explosion in numbers. Finally, I would add that, having followed with some disappointment the current centralised and state-oriented proposals which have been put forward in France to revive the flagging fortunes of the subject in that country, I feel the ideas contained in this book could provide an alternative way forward. Time, alone, will show if any of them are adopted. For my part, however, I am prepared to wait in the knowledge that I did what I could to help my students gaze at these new horizons.

Notes

[1] Hamson spent most of the war years in a German prison camp, first overcoming a deep personal depression and then, with the help of the Red Cross, coaching his fellow inmates for the bar exams. When he came out he was in many respects a 'broken' man; and he repeatedly told me that the prison years had seriously affected his 'confidence' to write. As a result, he turned down an offer to take over Salmond's tort treatise, which was then given to R F V Heuston, a true polymath of 'the old school.' By the mid-1950s, Hamson had reasonably recovered to publish some mainly short but beautifully written pieces and to start his own crusade of reconciliation. Setting up his summer course in Cambridge was his way of promoting European co-operation by getting students from different countries together; supporting the Strasbourg effort of de Solà was another. His deep and yet at times rebellious Catholicism can be glimpsed in the diaries he kept while in the prison camp, which were published posthumously (1989) by Trinity College Cambridge under the title *Liber in Vinculis*, edited by his friend of later years Helena Shire and Weir. Hamson was exceptionally loyal to his pupils, and they repaid his loyalty to the full.

[2] Simson's successful career, sketched in *Juristen. Ein Biographisches Lexikon* (1995) 567, was of Jewish extraction. Another Jewish jurist, who rose to high office, was Sigfried Sommer; and he, as well, was destined to acquire an interesting link with England since his grandson was to become England's greatest Tudor historian. His name was Geoffrey Elton.

[3] Eg, see the essays included in Markesinis (ed), *The Millenium Lectures* (2000).

[4] Like Dr Mads Andenas in his days at Kings College London.

[5] [2002] 3 WLR 89.

[6] 'On the Art of Conversation' in *The Complete Essays* (trans by M A Screech) 1067.

[7] Co-authored with Unberath (4th edn, 2002).

[8] [2001] 3 All ER 97.

[9] [2002] AC 728.

[10] Since the *MacFarlane* judgment. See his John Maurice Kelly Memorial Lecture published by the Faculty of Law of University College Dublin in 2002 and entitled 'Perspectives of Corrective and Distributive Justice in Tort Law.'

[11] Two major decisions in fact, BVerfGE 88, 203 and BVerfGE 96, 375. An attempt to allow the *Plenum* of the court to resolve the diverging views was turned down; see BVerfG NJW 1998, 523.

[12] Eg, BGH NJW 1995, 1609 (23 March 1995).

[13] OGH JBl 1999, 593 (25 May 1999).

[14] Hoge Raad NJ 1999, 145 (21 February 1997).

[15] Ass. Plén. 17 November 2000, JCP 13 December 2000, no 50, p 2293. Two further decisions, following broadly the same line, followed in the course of 2001.

[16] See his foreword to my collection of essays entitled *Always on the Same Path: Essays on Foreign Law and Comparative Methodology*, vol II (2001).

[17] For one illustration (among many) see Coester and Markesinis 'Liability of Financial Experts in German and American Law: An Exercise in Comparative Methodology' (2003) 51 *Amer J Comp Law* (forthcoming).

[18] *Phelps v Hillingdon London Borough Council* [2000] 3 WLR 776 at 792.

[19] Its address is http://www.ucl.ac.uk/laws/global_law

[20] 'Cause and Consideration: A Study in Parallel' (1978) *CLJ* 53, reprinted in my *Foreign Law and Comparative Methodology: A Subject and a Thesis* (1997) ch 4.

[21] But it can be found in his website: tony.honore@all-souls.ox.ac.uk

Appendix 1

Correspondence Between Lord Atkin and Professor HC Gutteridge

Confidential

The Rydings
Sylvester Road
Cambridge

27th November 1932

Dear Lord Atkin,

I enclose M's letter. I agree with most of his statements, but I think that he is unduly pessimistic.

He is troubled by a state of affairs which I have always regarded as a great misfortune, namely, the almost complete lack of contact between the practitioner and the academic lawyer in England. The gulf between the two is very wide—much wider than it is in America or on the Continent. The reason for this is no doubt the historical development of the teaching of English law and the fact that the Universities were late in the field, but it has led to the development of an inferiority complex on the part of the teacher which is bad for the teaching of law and also inimical to the future of English law. There is so much that the Judge and the practitioner cannot do because they have not got the time to spare, but which ought to be done and can only be done by the academic lawyer. I mean such tasks as the production of legal treatises: the study and development of certain departments of the law which are unremunerative to a practitioner e.g. Public and Private International Lawyers. There are only five in the Institute of International Law: Brierly, Pearce, Higgins, McNair and Fischer Williams. The result is that we cannot make our weight felt in any of the discussions which are constantly taking place, and the French have dug themselves in so thoroughly that it will be difficult to turn them out. English law is losing ground on the Continent because we cannot conduct the necessary propaganda: the Germans are hard at work trying to push it out of the Corn Trade and the other bulk trades as they pushed it out of Japan. I regard this movement as being somewhat serious for us now that we are no longer in a position of economic predominance.

It cannot be disputed that the University lawyer is regarded with benevolent contempt in England. This seems to be due to the following causes:—

a) The difficulty of recruiting first rate men as law teachers;
b) The absence of contact between the teacher and the practitioner;
c) The prevalence of the erroneous idea that there is something which is to be termed 'practical' as opposed to theoretical law.

As regards a) and b) the situation is improving. The law faculties at Oxford and Cambridge are growing in strength and have great influence in their Universities. London is also on the upgrade. I doubt if much can be done at the provincial Universities for financial reasons. The teaching staffs are very small and they are constantly losing their best men because the stipends only provide a base livelihood. We have nearly a thousand students at Oxford and Cambridge doing law in some form or other, which is several times more than all the other Universities combined, if one leaves out the articled clerks. We can give a man a good prospect of making £1,000 a year or so before he is too old. But even with us it is difficult to hold the right type of man. The reason is not money but the lack of prestige attaching to law reading. The remedy seems to me to be a wider recognition of the importance of the work which is being done by teachers. Several of us 'quorum pars minima fui' have received the honour of silk and this has helped a very great deal. I often wonder if it would not be a good thing if each Inn of

Court appointed a teacher to the Bench if the right kind of man of sufficient standing were available. This should be an exception to the convention that only persons actively engaged in practice are eligible, and would only be adopted in the case of a very small number of teachers of real eminence. This would bring teachers and practitioners into contact and would much improve the status of the law teacher without causing any serious dislocation of existing traditions.

I must also feel that the moribund rule that the works of legal authors must not be cited in argument unless they are defunct is rather derogatory to academic lawyers. It is more honoured in the breach than otherwise but its formal abrogation would be a step towards the recognition of the work of academic lawyers.

Academic lawyers might also be made more use of by Government Departments than at present. As Committee men and investigators they have the advantage of being able to devote more time to their duties, and they are independent of vested interests such as Trade Organisations and the like. But above all, the recognition of some part of University examinations as exempting from the professional tests would do more than anything else to close the gulf, and this brings me to point c).

c) It is true that law can and should be taught as a living thing and not as an abstraction. This does not mean however that there is such a thing as practical law, unless one applies the term as one of reproach to certain topics where the law is entirely a matter of detail without any principle behind it. The law teacher, whether he be a practitioner or a don, must teach principles and given the right type of teacher the result will be the same in both cases except perhaps in the case of certain technical subjects which are not taught by the Universities. I think that every law teacher should have practical experience as early in his career and as much of it as possible, but I do not think that it is necessary for him to be actually in practice when he teaches. I am convinced of this as the result of my experience in London University where some of the teachers devoted the majority of their time to practice, whilst others made teaching their chief duty. It is not difficult for a teacher to find out what is going on, and sometimes he is more up to date than a busy advocate who cannot spare the time to investigate certain movements in the law.

Some subjects are best taught by practitioners e.g. Procedure Probate and Divorce, certain branches of Commercial law etc. I feel that such subjects are the peculiar province of the professional law schools and should not be attempted except in bare outline by the Universities. But Contract, Tort, Property, Criminal Law can really be dealt with best by an experienced teacher who knows how to present the matter. The Council of Legal Education have recognised this in appointing Holdsworth for instance as one of their readers. If we could only get rid of this idea that University lecturers teach something which is different in kind from what the legal apprentice ought to know, a very great step in advance will have been made. It may have been true in the past that University teaching was unsuitable but it is certainly not so now.

Lastly, if something could be done to bring judges, practitioners and teachers together in a body charged with proposals for the reform and improvement of the law, we should have still further bridged over the gulf. Next to increased recognition of University examinations this seems to me to be the most likely method of counteracting the present—very unfortunate—isolation of the University teacher from the rest of the legal community.

I hope I have not bored you, but as M. very truly says you are the one person to whom one can unbosom oneself on this matter.

Yours very sincerely,
H. C. Gutteridge

4 Verulam Buildings
Gray's Inn
WC1

Dec. 4 1932

My dear Gutteridge,

It was kind of you to write to me fully on the subject of [. . .]'s letter. I agree with both of you in a good many respects. I think with you that the position is improving. One thing that is doing English law harm is the absence of public criticism by men who know: and the abundance of criticism by the ill-informed. It is largely due to the rule which prevents practising barristers from efforts which appear to be self-advertising, and prevents judges from writing at all. It seems to me to be particularly within the province of law teachers. I would include suggestions on and criticisms of the existing body of the law, the administrations of the law from time to time, refutation of all ill-informed criticism and suggestions for reform based on comparative law.

It would help the position of teachers very much if some of them showed up at times as discriminating champions of the profession.

As to the difference between academic teaching and practice I quite agree that ideally there should be none. In fact there is. You with your own experience don't feel it; but one only has to look at some articles and notes in the law magazines to see how impractical the writers are. Personally I am inclined to think that [. . .]'s is one of them. However I quite agree that many or perhaps I should say some teachers with only academic experience have a lively enough imagination or sympathy to be admirable guides in the appreciation of principles.

We can more fully discuss these and other topics at another time. I only sat down to thank you for your valuable letter.

With best wishes.

Always yours,
Atkin

Appendix 2

The German Approach

11 MAY 1971[1]

BGHZ 56, 163 = NJW 1971, 1883 = VersR 1971, 905, 1140

On 6 March 1965, when he was 64 years old, the plaintiff's husband was fatally injured in a collision with the defendant's motor vehicle. The plaintiff was 50 years old at the time. In this suit she claims damages for the injury to her health which she suffered through the death of her husband.

The Landgericht allowed the claim in full, the Oberlandesgericht in part. The defendant appealed with permission, and his appeal was allowed. The judgments below were vacated, and the case remanded to the Court of Appeal.

REASONS

A ...

2 (a) ...

(b) The Court of Appeal was wrong to find that the plaintiff suffered any real injury to her health as a result of hearing of the accident (see BGH VersR 1966, 283, 285 ff; OLG Freiburg, JZ 1953, 705, 709).

Apart from a few special instances not here in point, our law consciously rejects any claim for harm due to psychical pain unless it results from injury to the plaintiff's own body or health. This is a policy decision of the legislator. It does not, however, prevent our granting an independent claim to the exceptional person who is 'traumatised' by being involved in an accident, or hearing of one, and who in consequence suffers real damage to body or mind. Nor, if we leave aside the cases of 'purposive neuroses' and supervening causes, for which special rules have been developed, is it an objection to granting such a claim that the only reason the victim's reaction was so severe was that he had a pre-existing organic or psychical weakness which was triggered by the accident. The opposite view is taken by Stoll in his paper for the 45th German Juristentag 1964, 20, but we cannot agree with it, if only because such an unusual reaction normally lies outside the victim's control as well as the defendant's.

On the other hand it is a matter of common knowledge that the pain, grief, and fright arising from a very negative experience can have a very marked effect on one's physiological system and one's ability to cope. Yet to treat such disturbances as invasions of health in the sense of § 823 I BGB would be inconsistent with the binding decision of the legislator (Stoll, *idem*, 19 ff). Except in cases where the injury was intended by the actor, liability for harm psychically occasioned, even though it may be adequately caused according to the traditional formula, must be limited to cases where the man in the street, and not only a medical practitioner, would describe it as injury to body and health [*reference omitted*]. Under certain circumstances, therefore, injuries which are medically ascertainable but do not amount to a 'shock' to the system will go uncompensated. Accordingly, no claim can be made in the normal case of deeply felt grief, which, as everybody knows, may have quite serious effects on a person's general well-being.

(c) In the light of these principles, the opinion of the Court of Appeal cannot stand.

The Court of Appeal laid weight on the expert's finding that 'the plaintiff naturally suffered severe psychic shock on first hearing of the death of her husband.' But the court read too much into this. The Court had formally asked the expert to report on whether the plaintiff had suffered 'a severe psychic shock which altered her personality and made her depressed, unduly excitable, sleepless, tearful, and apt to shiver on the slightest occasion', taking these terms from the written evidence of Dr C, the plaintiff's general practitioner, evidence of which the expert was somewhat critical. In his reply the expert simply confirmed in general terms that there had been a 'severe psychical shock,' though it is doubtful, in view of what he said immediately thereafter, whether he intended this to constitute a medical finding. As to the other symptoms about which he was asked, he made no positive finding, but rather indicated that he himself had not observed them. It would require stronger evidence than this before the Court of Appeal could properly hold that the plaintiff had suffered an injury to health sufficient to ground a claim.

In everyday speech the phrase 'severe psychical shock' denotes a violent temperamental reaction which may have nothing in common with an illness of any kind. Medical men do not use the notion of shock to describe a psychopathological condition. Used to describe a pathological condition (apart from the special case of shock therapy) 'shock' denotes simply an acute disturbance of the circulation [reference omitted] which can result from experiencing an accident or, more rarely, hearing of one. This is naturally of a transitory nature, though it can lead to lasting organic damage. It is by no means clear that the expert believed this to have occurred. A person who experiences an accident, and less often a person who hears of one, may also suffer psychopathological effects. Doctors call this 'neurosis' (not necessarily a purposive neurosis of the kind for which no compensation may be given) or in serious cases even 'psychosis' [*reference omitted*]. The expert's affidavit does not suggest that he was testifying to any illness of this kind. It is not enough that he did not say there was none: a positive finding is necessary or the plaintiff will fail to meet her burden of proof.

IV. To the extent, therefore, that it grants the plaintiff a claim for damages on her own account, the judgment under appeal cannot be sustained.

When the Court of Appeal re-examines the matter it will need to be convinced, before it can allow the plaintiff's claim even in part, that on hearing of the accident she not only experienced the normal reactions of pain, grief, and depression, but directly suffered a 'traumatic' injury to her physical and psychical health. Further expert evidence may be required, and if the expert testifies to such a condition, it will be necessary to ask to what extent he is relying on the evidence of the general practitioner, which is inadmissible in its present form.

B. I. If, after further investigation, the Court of Appeal holds that the claim should be admitted, the question of the deceased husband's contributory fault will arise. This must be dealt with in a different manner.

1. The Court of Appeal held that in cases like the present one cannot apply § 846 BGB by analogy, and in so holding it was consciously deviating from a view laid down by the Reichsgericht (RGZ 157, 11; RG DR 1940, 163) and supported by some scholars [*reference omitted*]. We agree with the Court of Appeal on this point: the opinion of the Reichsgericht is unacceptable in the form in which it was expressed. It was certainly right to emphasise that the basic rule of law is that only the direct victim of a tort may sue, a rule to which exceptions are made by §§ 844 and 845 BGB in favour of surviving dependants and persons entitled to services. But it was in error to treat the claim by a third party who suffers injury to his own health when someone else is injured or killed as if this were another case of 'indirect injury to a third party' and to apply § 846 BGB to it by analogy. The difference between this case and those in §§ 844, 845 BGB is essentially that here the third party is affected in one of the legal interests specified in § 823 I BGB and that he is therefore a direct victim with an independent claim of his own under that section. Claims by the indirect victim under §§ 844, 845 BGB presuppose that the primary victim's harm resulted from a tort done to him (BGH VersR 1961, 846, 847) and that is why § 846 BGB provides that any fault on the part of the primary victim which contributed to the harm suffered by the third party must be taken into account in any claim the third party may bring under §§ 844, 845 BGB. This provision is perfectly sensible in relation to claims brought under §§ 844, 845 BGB, but it cannot apply to an independent claim brought under § 823 I BGB, for it must be irrelevant to a claim for harm done directly to the third party that it occurred by means of an injury to someone else. Indeed, the third party's rights may arise regardless of whether the primary victim of the accident had or has any claim for damages at all [OLG Munich NJW 1959, 819d; *other reference omitted*].

2. Yet we must agree with the result reached by the Reichsgericht, at least in cases of the kind before us, that in con-

sidering the personal claim of the indirectly injured widow one must take account of any contributory fault of the deceased husband. This, however, results from an analogical application of § 254 BGB, itself a specific application of the more general principle of law contained in § 242 BGB (BGHZ 4, 355).

(a) This is quite clear in relation to a claim for damages for *pain and suffering* (*Schmerzensgeld*; § 847 BGB), to which equitable principles apply. The Bundesgerichtshof has held (VersR 1962, 93) that a claim for damages for pain and suffering, unlike a claim for material damage, may be reduced because the victim was especially vulnerable to harm by reason of his bodily or psychical constitution, and that the *personal* contributory fault of the victim, which does not arise in this case, is only one of the factors to be taken into account in estimating the damages which are equitable in the circumstances (BGHZ 18, 149, 157). The same must be true of other factors in the victim's area of responsibility which contribute to the harm, such as a close personal relationship to the primary accident victim, as in this case.

(b) But even in cases of *material harm* the result reached by the Reichsgericht is correct. Where, as here, injury to health is caused at a distance, so to speak, the contributory fault of the damaged must be laid to the plaintiff's account. For here the accident to her husband was only able to cause the harm supposedly suffered by the plaintiff because as a result of their close personal relationship his tragedy became hers. One cannot imagine a person suffering in this manner on hearing of a fatal accident to a total stranger; indeed, if it happened, it would be so unusual that one would decline to impute it to the defendant on the ground that it was unforeseeable. But if the critical reason for the plaintiff's suffering this injury to her health was her close personal relationship to her husband, it is only fair that her claim should be affected by his fault in contributing to the accident. We must apply by analogy the basic idea of § 254 BGB, that a person's claim for damages must be reduced to the extent that the occurrence of the harm was due to a contributory factor from the plaintiff's sphere of responsibility. In this connection we must make a further observation. If the husband's death had been *solely* attributable to his failure to take care of himself, the plaintiff would have had no claim whatever for compensation for the consequent injury to herself. A person is under no legal duty, whatever the moral position may be, to look after his own life and limb simply in order to save his dependants from the likely psychical effects on them if he is killed or maimed: to impose such a legal duty, except in very peculiar cases, for instance, wherever a person commits suicide in a deliberately shocking manner, would be to restrict a person's self-determination in a manner inconsistent with our legal system.

It will be seen from this that unsatisfactory results follow from the view adopted by the Court of Appeal and some writers, that the primary victim's contributory fault is not to be taken into account when shock damage is caused at a distance. We have seen that, contrary to the view expressed by the Reichsgericht (RGZ 157, 11, 14) and by some of the writers, a tortfeasor cannot claim contribution under §§ 840, 254 BGB from the heirs of the primary victim, since the primary victim is not liable to the shock victim at all, much less as a common debtor. It follows that unless our present view is adopted, the tortfeasor would owe the shocked widow a full indemnity for her lost earnings even if the husband was so much more to blame for his own death than the tortfeasor that in a suit by the husband the tortfeasor would be wholly exonerated under § 254 BGB. This would be quite unacceptable.

Now it is true that in principle when a tortfeasor is sued he bears the risk of there being no solvent joint tortfeasor from whom he can claim contribution. But there are exceptions. For example, the courts have held that if, by reason of personal relationship with him, the victim releases one tortfeasor from liability in advance, the other tortfeasor should be protected (BGHZ 12, 213). In our case the third party has not been exonerated by release or by capricious conduct on the part of the creditor, but it is none the less true that the primary victim has, though involuntarily, had an adverse effect on the health of the shock victim in respect of which he is not liable. Once again, in these peculiar cases, the harm is caused only because of the very close personal relationship between the plaintiff and the primary victim, thanks to which the plaintiff adopts as her own the harm done to another, and the loss of his life becomes a loss, a serious loss, to her. In such a case, where it would be wrong to require the primary victim or his heirs to make contribution to the tortfeasor, it is only fair that the primary victim's causal contribution to the accident should be borne not by the stranger who triggered the harm but by the dependant who was hurt only because of her personal relationship with the primary victim and her identification with him. It was equitable considerations such as these that led the legislator to enact § 846 BGB though, as we have said, it covers a different case. In relation to that paragraph the *Protokolle* (vol 2, II, 638 ff) explain that to treat the third party's claim against the tortfeasor as entirely independent is too theoretical and logically extreme, and that to apply that view strictly would lead to unjust and inequitable results; the claims of a dead man's survivors result from his death, and if his careless conduct conduced to or accelerated his death, it is only right, in view of their relations with him, that the survivors should have to bear the consequences.

The claim for shock damage which arises in this distinctive manner is a judge-made claim, and though the Court of Appeal would like to extend it beyond the limits set by the Reichsgericht, we are not persuaded by any of the objections which its position on this question has elicited. It only remains to say that, contrary to what is stated in a number of the books, the Reichsgericht was always perfectly clear (see RGZ 162, 321) that cases of shock damage are cases of direct injury to a legal interest protected by § 823 I BGB and not simply instances of indirect harm of the kind covered by §§ 844, 845 BGB.

(c) The present case does not raise the issue of how the decision would be if the occurrence of the harm was wholly or partly independent of any personal relationship, or indeed how far a tortfeasor might be liable at all if the persons suffering the damaging reaction were third parties in no way related to the primary victim.

BGHZ 103, 396

Zum Sachverhalt:

Der damals 1 Jahr 10 Monate alte Kläger erlitt am 17. 5. 1985 auf einem öffentlichen, von der bekl. Stadt unterhaltenen

Kinderspielplatz in M. erhebliche Verletzungen an Kopf und Schultern, als er von dem Podest einer dort aufgestellten Rutsche zu Boden stürzte. Das Podest der Rutsche lag mindestens 1,50 m über dem Boden, der an dieser Stelle aus Asphaltbeton bestand. An den Seiten des Podestes befand sich jeweils ein Holm mit weit ausgelegten Seitenräumen. Zu dem Unfall war es nach Darstellung des Klägers gekommen, als er sich zum Rutschen auf das Podest gesetzt, das linke Bein vorgestreckt habe und—während sein Vater an der Rutsche links neben ihm gestanden habe—in einem unbewachten Moment plötzlich nach rechts rücklings unter den Holm gerutscht und auf den Boden gefallen sei.

Der Kläger hat die Beklagte wegen Verletzung der Verkehrssicherungspflicht auf Zahlung eines angemessenen Schmerzensgeldes sowie auf Feststellung des Ersatzes aller weiteren Schäden in Anspruch genommen, soweit diese nicht auf Sozialversicherungsträger übergegangen sind. Die Beklagte ist dem Klagebegehren entgegengetreten. Sie hat darauf verwiesen, daß das Spielgerät schon seit 1964 aufgestellt gewesen sei und vergleichbare Unfälle in der Vergangenheit nicht aufgetreten seien. Auch müsse sich der Kläger das Mitverschulden seines Vaters aus der Verletzung der ihm obliegenden Aufsichtspflicht entgegenhalten lassen.

Das Landgericht hat dem Kläger ein Schmerzensgeld in Höhe von 10.000 DM zugesprochen und den Feststellungsantrag für begründet erklärt. Auf die Berufung der Beklagten hat das Oberlandesgericht das Schmerzensgeld auf 8.000 DM ermäßigt, die weitergehende Berufung aber als unbegründet zurückgewiesen. Die (zugelassene) Revision der Beklagten blieb erfolglos.

Aus den Gründen:

I. Das Berufungsgericht geht von einer Verletzung der Verkehrssicherungspflichten durch die Beklagte aus. Sie habe die Benutzung der Rutsche, die an den seitlichen Holmen keine ausreichende Absturzsicherung für kleinere Kinder aufgewiesen habe, nicht mit einem Asphaltbeton als Bodenbelag im Bereich der Standfläche zulassen dürfen. Da es immer wieder

vorkomme, daß Kinder von Spielgeräten abstürzten, bedürfe
es nur dann keiner besonderen Sicherungsmaßnahmen, wenn
das Gerät verhältnismäßig niedrig sei. Andernfalls sei, um
Verletzungen zu vermeiden, ein aufprallhemmender
Unterboden zu wählen. Demgemäß sehe die bereits 1979
erlassene DIN-Norm 7926 für Spielgeräte mit Handlauf und
einer Fallhöhe von 1 m bis 2 m als Bodenbeläge nur Rasen,
Kunststoff, Fallschutzplatten oder Sand bzw. Feinkies in einer
Höhe von 200 mm vor. Ein etwaiges Mitverschulden seines
Vaters an dem Unfall könne dem Kläger nicht angerechnet
werden.

II. Das Berufungsurteil hält der rechtlichen Nachprüfung
stand.

1. Zutreffend hat das Berufungsgericht die aus § 823 I BGB
folgenden Sicherungspflichten bestimmt, die der beklagten
Stadt M. aus der Verkehrseröffnung auf dem Spielplatz, auf
dem der Kläger den Unfall erlitten hat, erwachsen sind.

a) Nach dem Grundsatz, daß jeder, der Gefahren schafft,
auch die notwendigen Vorkehrungen zur Sicherheit Dritter zu
treffen hat, mußte die Beklagte die Sicherungsmaßnahmen
ergreifen, die der Verkehr für diesen Gefahrenkreis für
erforderlich hält. Der Senat folgt dem Berufungsgericht darin,
daß sich Inhalt und Umfang der Verkehrssicherungspflichten
für einen öffentlichen Spielplatz aus der Notwendigkeit
ergeben, den Spielplatz möglichst gefahrlos zu gestalten und
zu erhalten, und daß dabei das einzuhaltende Ausmaß der
Sicherheit sich an dem Alter der jüngsten Kinder auszurichten
hat, die für die Benutzung des betreffenden Spielgeräts in
Frage kommen (so schon Hußla, VersR 1971, 877 f.). Wenn das
Berufungsgericht, weil gerade auch bei kleineren Kindern
Übermut, Neugier oder Unerfahrenheit zu einem gefahrvollen
Fehlverhalten führen können und Stürze von Spielgeräten
infolge einer unglücklichen Bewegung, einer Störung des
Gleichgewichts oder aufgrund der Einwirkung durch andere
Kinder immer wieder vorkommen, von der Beklagten fordert,
für Spielgeräte mit einer Fallhöhe wie hier von 1,50 m einen
Untergrund mit aufprallhemmender Beschaffenheit im
Bereich des Standorts des Geräts zu wählen, so ist dagegen aus
Rechtsgründen nichts zu erinnern. An die Sicherheit der

Spielgeräte eines Kinderspielplatzes sind besonders strenge Anforderungen zu stellen. Grundsätzlich müssen Kinder und ihre Eltern uneingeschränkt darauf vertrauen dürfen, daß sich die Kinder gefahrlos der Spielgeräte bedienen können und insb. nicht so schwere Verletzungen erleiden können wie hier (vgl. Senatsurt., NJW 1988, 48 = VersR 1987, 891 (892)). Wegen der bei Kindern immer vorhandenen Gefahr des Sturzes von Spielgeräten ist jedenfalls bei Spielgeräten mit einer Fallhöhe von 1,50 m die Forderung nach einem geeigneten Bodenbelag, der Absturzunfälle weniger gefährlich macht, als elementare Sicherheitsforderung zu bezeichnen.

Dieser Maßstab für die einzuhaltenden Verkehrssicherungs- pflichten steht—im Gegensatz zur Ansicht der Revision—auch nicht in Widerspruch damit, daß auch Spielplätze und darauf befindliche Geräte nicht frei von allen Risiken sein müssen. Dabei kann es aber nur um überschaubare und kalkulierbare Risiken gehen, die für das Kind ihren erzieherischen Wert haben (vgl. Senat, VersR 1978, 739 und 762; RGRK, 12. Aufl., § 823 Anm. 228). Um solche beherrschbaren Risiken handelt es sich aber nicht, wenn es wie hier um die Beschaffenheit des passenden Bodens zur Vermeidung von Verletzungen bei Abstürzen von Spielgeräten geht. Ob die Verkehrssicherungs- pflichten dann eingeschränkt sind, wenn der Kinderspielplatz bzw. bestimmte Spielgeräte nur für Kinder von einem höheren Lebensalter an zur Benutzung freigegeben sind, kann dahingestellt bleiben. Denn unstreitig war eine Beschränkung auf ein Mindestalter für die Benutzung nicht verfügt; vielmehr war der Spielplatz durch ein entsprechendes Schild zur Benutzung für alle Kinder bis zu 12 Jahren freigegeben. Eine etwaige nach außen nicht erkennbare Erwartung der Beklagten, daß Rutschen der vorliegenden Art erst von Kindern ab drei Jahren benutzt werden würden, beschränkte ihre Verkehrssicherheitspflichten nicht.

b) Es begegnet auch keinen Bedenken, daß das Berufungs- gericht zur Feststellung von Inhalt und Umfang der die Beklagte treffenden Verkehrssicherungspflichten die im Dezember 1976 erlassene DIN-Norm 7926, Teil 1, mit herange- zogen hat, die für ein Spielgerät mit Handlauf und einer Fallhöhe von 1 m bis 2 m als Bodenbeläge nur nicht gebundene Böden nach DIN 18034 wie Naturboden, Rasen oder Sand bzw.

Feinkies vorsieht. Auch wenn es sich bei DIN-Normen nicht um mit Drittwirkung versehene Normen i. S. hoheitlicher Rechtsetzung, sondern um auf freiwillige Anwendung ausgerichtete Empfehlungen des "DIN Deutschen Instituts für Normung e. V." handelt (vgl. Senat, NJW 1987, 2222 = VersR 1987, 783 (784)), so spiegeln sie doch den Stand der für die betroffenen Kreise geltenden anerkannten Regeln der Technik wieder und sind somit zur Bestimmung des nach der Verkehrsauffassung zur Sicherheit Gebotenen in besonderer Weise geeignet (vgl. Senat, NJW 1980, 1219 (1221) = VersR 1980, 380 (382) und VersR 1987, 891). Ob bei Einführung neuer DIN-Normen für eine Übergangszeit die bestehenden Einrichtungen ohne Veränderung weiterbetrieben werden dürfen, kann hier dahingestellt bleiben. Eine solche Anpassungszeit—ließe man sie zu—wäre jedenfalls, wie das Berufungsgericht zu Recht festgestellt hat, längst verstrichen gewesen, als es mehr als acht Jahre nach Erlaß der einschlägigen DIN-Norm zu dem Unfall kam. Soweit die Revision sich darauf beruft, Rutschen der in Rede stehenden Art seien noch nach Inkrafttreten der DIN-Norm überwachungstechnisch nicht beanstandet worden, handelt es sich um erstmals in der Revisionsinstanz gebrauchten und daher unzulässigen Tatsachenvortrag. Im übrigen könnte eine solche Praxis die Beklagte nicht entlasten, da die vom Standort des Spielgeräts ausgehende Gefahr für sie als Träger des Spielplatzes ohne weiteres erkennbar war.

2. Fehl geht auch der Angriff der Revision, der sich gegen die Nichtberücksichtigung eines möglichen Mitverschuldens des Vaters des Klägers bei der Haftung der Beklagten wendet.

a) Auch die Revision zieht nicht in Zweifel, daß sich der Kläger ein Mitverschulden seines Vaters an dem Unfall gem. §§ 254 I, 278 BGB nur im Rahmen eines schon im Augenblick des Unfalls bestehenden Schuldverhältnisses oder eines einem Schuldverhältnis ähnlichen Sonderrechtsverhältnisses zu der Beklagten zurechnen lassen muß (vgl. Senat, NJW 1980, 2090 = VersR 1980, 938 m. w. Nachw.). Sie meint jedoch, eine solche Sonderverbindung habe vorliegend bei Schadenseintritt bestanden, weil die Schildertafel auf dem Spielplatz den zugelassenen Personenkreis bezeichnet und

bestimmte Verhaltensweisen untersagt habe. Damit sei ein
Benutzungsverhältnis begründet worden. Zu Recht hat indes
das Berufungsgericht im Einklang mit der Rechtsprechung des
Senats (vgl. VersR 1975, 133 (134) und NJW 1977, 1392 (1394) =
VersR 1977, 668) diesen Umstand als nicht ausreichend
erachtet, um über die allgemeinen deliktischen Rechte und
Pflichten hinausgehende besondere schuldrechtliche oder
schuldrechtsähnliche Beziehungen zwischen dem Kläger und
der Beklagten entstehen zu lassen. Auch wenn es für
die Benutzung des Spielplatzes eine Satzung gegeben haben
sollte, ließe sich daraus allein nicht die Begründung eines
vertragsähnlichen Benutzungsverhältnisses folgern (vgl.
Senatsurt. NJW 1977, 1392). Insbesondere ist nichts für eine
besondere Interessenlage ersichtlich, die Anlaß zu einer derartigen gesteigerten Rechts- und Pflichtenstellung für
beide Seiten hätte geben können. Vielmehr erscheinen die
Interessen beider Seiten durchaus schon durch die allgemeinen
deliktischen Beziehungen hinreichend gewahrt.

   b) Auch soweit die Revision das Berufungsurteil unter dem
Gesichtspunkt einer Einstandspflicht des Klägers für seinen
Vater nach § 278 BGB bei der Erfüllung von Obliegenheiten zur
Schadensabwendung oder Schadensminderung i. S. des § 254
II 1 BGB zur Überprüfung stellt, weist dieses keinen
Rechtsfehler auf. Richtig ist, daß sich ein Geschädigter im
Rahmen seiner Obliegenheiten zur Abwendung oder
Minderung des Schadens nach § 254 II BGB ein Verschulden
dritter Personen nach § 278 BGB anrechnen lassen muß. Indes
muß dazu die unerlaubte Handlung des Schädigers die
Schadensentwicklung schon auf den Weg gebracht haben
(BGHZ 5, 378 (384 f.) = NJW 1952, 1050). Anderes würde nicht
nur die Beschränkung der Einstandspflicht des Geschädigten
für ein Verschulden Dritter nach § 278 BGB auf
Sonderrechtsverhältnisse gegenstandslos machen, sondern
der Geschädigte stünde auch schlechter da als der Schädiger,
der im Bereich der Schadensentstehung für Dritte grundsätzlich nur nach § 831 BGB deliktisch einzustehen hat. Deshalb
reicht es nicht—wie die Revision meint—aus, daß die durch
die Verletzung der Verkehrssicherungspflichten von der
Beklagten ausgelöste Gefahr schon bestand, als der Kläger die
Rutsche an der Hand seines Vaters bestieg. Ebensowenig

genügt es, daß der gesetzliche Vertreter oder die von ihm mit der Beaufsichtigung betraute Person die Gefahr kannte, die dem Kind von einer Anlage oder einem Zustand drohte (vgl. BGHZ 5, 378 (384 f.) = NJW 1952, 1050; Alff, in: RGRK, 12. Aufl., § 254 Anm. 67). Nur soweit sich ein Mitverschulden für den eingetretenen Schaden auf die Phase bezieht, in der der Verletzungstatbestand bereits verwirklicht ist, kommt demnach eine Zurechnung nach §§ 254 II, 278 BGB in Frage.

Zuzurechnen ist das Verhalten des Vaters dem Klägers darüber hinaus auch nicht unter dem Gesichtspunkt der Haftungseinheit, mit der die Revision eine entsprechende Kürzung der Ersatzverpflichtung der Beklagten zu begründen versucht. Der nicht deliktsfähige Kläger hat den Unfall nicht in zurechenbarer Weise mitverursacht. Er kann daher nicht in einer Zurechnungseinheit mit seinem Vater stehen (vgl. Senat, VersR 1974, 34 (35); OLG Düsseldorf, VersR 1982, 300, (301)).

3. Zu folgen ist dem Berufungsgericht auch darin, daß der Anspruch, den der Kläger gegen die Beklagte besitzt, nicht aus dem Gesichtspunkt des gestörten Innenausgleichs unter Gesamtschuldnern zu kürzen ist. Dabei ist es unerheblich, nach welchem Haftungsmaßstab sich der Vater des Klägers bei der Beaufsichtigung seines Kindes auf dem Spielplatz beurteilen lassen muß und ob er danach bestehende Pflichten tatsächlich schuldhaft verletzt hat. In keiner der möglichen Fallgestaltungen ist das Haftungsverhältnis der Beklagten zum Kläger betroffen.

a) Nach § 840 I BGB haftet jeder von mehreren Schädigern dem Geschädigten für den von ihm zu verantwortenden Schaden ohne Rücksicht auf die Einstandspflicht der übrigen in vollem Umfang. Das Gesetz überläßt es dem Schädiger erst auf einer weiteren Stufe, Ausgleich für seine Inanspruchnahme bei den Mitschädigern zu suchen. Selbst wenn deshalb der Kläger nicht nur von der Beklagten, sondern auch von seinem Vater für seine Unfallverletzungen Ersatz verlangen könnte, würde das ihre volle Haftung ihm gegenüber grundsätzlich nicht berühren.

b) Von diesem Grundsatz hat die Rechtsprechung allerdings Ausnahmen in Fällen zugelassen, in denen dem Schädiger die

Möglichkeit zum Ausgleich bei einem Mitschädiger dadurch genommen ist, daß dieser kraft Gesetzes dem Geschädigten gegenüber von seiner Haftung freigestellt ist. In diesen Fällen kann der Geschädigte den nicht privilegierten Schädiger nur auf den Anteil des Schadens in Anspruch nehmen, mit dem dieser im Innenverhältnis zu dem freigestellten Mitschädiger belastet bliebe, wenn die Möglichkeit zum Innenausgleich nicht durch die Haftungsprivilegierung versperrt wäre (vgl. BGHZ 61, 51 = NJW 1973, 1648; zuletzt Senat, NJW 1987, 2669 = BGH RVO § 636 I—Arbeitnehmer 1). Zugrunde liegt dem die Erwägung, daß es unbillig wäre, den nicht privilegierten Schädiger mit der Haftungsfreistellung seines Mitschädigers zu belasten, die nach ihrem Sinn allein dessen Verhältnis zu dem Geschädigten betreffen soll.

c) Im weiteren Sinne kann auch bei § 1664 I BGB von einem "Haftungsprivileg" gesprochen werden. Nach dieser Vorschrift haben Eltern bei der Ausübung der elterlichen Sorge dem Kinde gegenüber nur für die Sorgfalt einzustehen, die sie in eigenen Angelegenheiten anzuwenden pflegen. Im Vergleich zu Schädigern, die nach dem allgemeinen Sorgfaltsmaßstab des § 276 BGB haften, ist ihre Einstandspflicht für einen von ihnen verursachten Schaden wegen ihrer familienrechtlichen Verbundenheit zu dem Geschädigten eingeschränkt (§ 277 BGB). Im Streitfall war zwar der Vater des Klägers nicht Sorgeberechtigter für diesen. Indes spricht vieles für die im Schrifttum vorherrschende Ansicht, auch dem nicht sorgeberechtigten Elternteil in analoger Anwendung des § 1664 BGB den milderen Haftungsmaßstab jedenfalls dann zuzubilligen, wenn er—wie hier—in Ausübung seines Umgangsrechts (§ 1634 BGB) faktisch Personensorge für sein Kind ausübt (vgl. Adelmann, in: RGRK, 12. Aufl., § 1664 Anm. 4; Soergel-Lang, BGB, 11. Aufl., § 1664 Anm. 3; Hinz, in: MünchKomm, BGB, 2. Aufl., § 1664 Anm. 4; Palandt-Diederichsen, BGB, 47. Aufl., § 1664 Anm. 1). Nach Auffassung des Senats würde der Anwendung des § 1664 BGB im vorliegenden Fall auch nicht schon entgegenstehen, daß es (auch) um deliktische Verhaltenspflichten des Vaters zum Schutz der Gesundheit seines Kindes geht. Jedenfalls wo diese Schutzpflichten in Fallgestaltungen wie hier ganz in der Sorge für die Person des Kindes aufgehen, würde anderes auf eine Einschränkung des § 1664 BGB hinauslaufen, die mit Wortlaut und Sinn der Vorschrift nicht vereinbar wäre. Das besagt selbstverständlich nicht, daß ein für die Eltern so zentrales Schutzgut wie die Gesundheit ihrer Kinder einen besonderen Stellenwert nicht auch für ihre eigenübliche Sorgfalt und damit für ihre Haftungsverantwortung maßgebliche Bedeutung hätte. Dahinstehen kann, ob für den subjektiven Sorgfaltsmaßstab des § 277 BGB dort noch Raum ist, wo die Schutzpflichten der Eltern gegenüber dem Kind von ihren nach dem objektiven Sorgfaltsmaßstab des § 276 BGB zu bemessenden Pflichten gegenüber dem Verkehr kaum sachgerecht zu trennen wären, wie dies insbesonders für den Kreis der Verkehrssicherungspflichten, etwa der Aufsichtspflichten nach § 832 BGB (vgl. RGZ 75, 251 (253, 254); OLG Karlsruhe, VersR 1977, 232; OLG Stuttgart, VersR 1980, 952; Adelmann, in: RGRK, aaO, § 1664 Anm. 13; Hinz, in: MünchKomm, § 1664 Anm. 6; Palandt-Diederichsen, § 1664 Anm. 1; a. A. Soergel-Lange, § 1664 Anm. 4) und für den Bereich der Teilnahme am Straßenverkehr (vgl. BGHZ 63, 51 (57 f.) = NJW 1974, 2124; Adelmann, in: RGRK, Anm. 14; Hinz, in: MünchKomm, § 1664 Anm. 6; Palandt-Diederichsen, § 1664 Anm. 1 m. w. Nachw.) befürwortet wird. Eine solche Fallgestaltung liegt hier jedoch nicht vor.

d) Selbst wenn indes der Vater des Klägers allein wegen des milderen Sorgfaltsmaßstabs des § 1664 BGB von einer Mithaftung für die Verletzungen des Klägers befreit wäre, käme das der Beklagten nicht zugute. Die im Schrifttum vorherrschende Meinung, auch in derartigen Fällen dürfte die gesetzliche "Haftungsprivilegierung" nicht zu Lasten des nicht privilegierten Schädigers gehen, sondern müsse durch eine entsprechende Kürzung der Ersatzansprüche des Geschädigten nach den zur gesetzlichen Haftungsfreistellung von der Rechtsprechung entwickelten Grundsätzen (vgl. die Nachw. bei Weber, in: Kraftverkehrsrecht von A-Z, Stichwort: Ehegatten, B IV. 2. S. 35; ferner Adelmann, in: RGRK, Anm. 18; Soergel-Lange, Anm. 7) oder durch Fingieren eines Innenausgleichs (vgl. OLG Düsseldorf, NJW 1978, 891) aufgefangen werden, vermag der Senat nicht zu teilen. Tragende Gründe, auf denen die Rechtsprechung zum sog. "gestörten Gesamtschuldverhältnis" beruht, fehlen hier.

In jenen Fällen sind zunächst alle Voraussetzungen für ein Gesamtschuldverhältnis nach § 840 I BGB erfüllt; dieses wird erst dadurch "gestört", daß das Gesetz in Abweichung von dem Grundsatz des § 840 BGB den privilegierten Mitschädiger von seiner Haftung freistellt. In den Fällen dagegen, in denen die Mithaftung an § 1664 BGB scheitert, wächst der so "privilegierte" Mitschädiger schon gar nicht in die Regelung des § 840 I BGB hinein; es fehlt schon an den Grundlagen für ein Gesamtschuldverhältnis, das "gestört" werden konnte. Das ist nicht nur ein formaler, äußerlicher Unterschied. Es entspricht Wesen und System der Deliktshaftung, daß der Schädiger einen Mitverursacher des Schadens nur dann an seiner Haftpflicht beteiligen kann, wenn und soweit dieser den Schaden zurechenbar mitgesetzt hat. Nur wo das Haftungsprivileg ihm den Mitschädiger trotz dessen haftungsrechtlicher Mitverantwortung als Ausgleichsschuldner nimmt, ist es gerechtfertigt, von seiner die §§ 840, 426 BGB durchbrechenden Belastung mit dem Haftungsprivileg zu sprechen. Wenn dagegen ein Ausgleich schon am Fehlen einer zurechenbaren Mitbeteiligung des Ausgleichsschuldners scheitert, so ist das eine Folge des Ausgleichssystems, die im Rahmen der Deliktshaftung grundsätzlich allen Schädigern zugemutet wird.

An der Zurechenbarkeit fehlt es jedoch beim Vorliegen der Haftungsfreistellung nach §§ 1664 I, 277 BGB, solange die Pflichtverletzung nicht über die eigenübliche Sorgfalt hinausgeht bzw. sich als grob fahrlässig darstellt. Unterhalb dieser Schwelle besteht die Verantwortung des Elternteils für die Setzung eines Schadensbeitrags nicht. Dem Vater des Klägers ist daher, solange der Haftungsmaßstab der §§ 1664 I, 277 BGB nicht erreicht ist, ein für den eingetretenen Schaden mitursächliches Verhalten nicht zuzurechnen.

Bei Fehlen der Zurechenbarkeit wegen des milderen Sorgfaltsmaßstabs des § 1664 BGB kann das Versagen eines Ausgleichs für einen Mitschädiger ebensowenig als unbillige Sonderbelastung angesehen werden wie in jenen Fällen, in denen es an einer zurechenbaren Mitbeteiligung etwa wegen einer gesetzlich besonders angeordneten Aufgabenverteilung oder wegen der Deliktsunfähigkeit der Mitschädiger fehlt. Schon deshalb sieht der Senat keinen sachlichen Anlaß, nach

Maßgabe seiner zur Haftungsfreistellung durch §§ 636, 637 RVO entwickelten Rechtsprechung im Wege der Rechtsfortbildung die gesetzliche Regelung für die Lastenverteilung bei Mehrbeteiligungen auch in den Fällen zu modifizieren, in denen ein Gesamtschuldverhältnis wegen des milderen Haftungsmaßstabs des § 1664 BGB nicht zustande kommt. Für eine derartige Lösung würde es zudem nicht nur an geeigneten Kriterien fehlen, den Beitrag des schädigenden Elternteils, dem §§ 1664, 277 BGB die Zurechenbarkeit gerade versagt, gleichwohl für eine Kürzung des Ersatzanspruchs zu bemessen. Sie würde auch zu dem schwerlich einleuchtenden Ergebnis führen, daß das geschädigte Kind bei einem Verhalten seiner Eltern, das als leicht fahrlässig i. S. von § 276 BGB die Schwelle des § 277 BGB noch nicht erreicht hat, eine Kürzung seines Ersatzanspruchs hinzunehmen hätte, bei grobem Verschulden seiner Eltern dagegen nicht. Insoweit darf auch nicht vernachlässigt werden, daß in diesen Fällen—anders als im Anwendungsbereich der Haftungsprivilegierung der §§ 636, 637 RVO—dem Geschädigten für den genommenen Ersatzanspruch kein Äquivalent in Gestalt einer anderen Ausgleichslösung zuwächst.

Ebensowenig aber erscheint es dem Senat nach Überprüfung seines in BGHZ 35, 317 = NJW 1961, 1966 vertretenen anderen Standpunktes gerecht, den Schädiger von einem Teil seiner Haftungslast, die ihn wegen seines verantwortlich gesetzten Schadensbeitrages trifft, über die Fiktion eines gesamtschuldnerischen Innenausgleichs zu dem mitbeteiligten Elternteil auf dessen Kosten nur deshalb zu befreien, weil dieser an der Schädigung zwar beteiligt war, ohne aber dazu einen zurechenbaren Beitrag geleistet zu haben; dies um so weniger, als im wirtschaftlichen Ergebnis auch eine derartige Lösung in der Mehrzahl der Fälle auf Kosten letztlich auch des geschädigten Kindes gehen würde. Soweit die Ausführungen des Senats in seinem Urteil vom 27. 6. 1961 (BGHZ 35, 317 (322 f.) = NJW 1961, 1966) zu dem milderen Haftungsmaßstab des § 1359 BGB unter Ehegatten dem entgegenstehen, hält der Senat hieran nicht mehr fest. Insbesondere erscheint ihm der dort angestellte Vergleich mit der Interessenlage bei einer vertraglich vereinbarten Haftungsmilderung als Begründung für die Fiktion eines gesamtschuldnerischen Innenausgleichs auch in den Fällen der gesetzlichen Haftungsmilderung des § 1664 BGB schon deshalb nicht ausreichend, weil diese Haftungsmilderung nicht auf einer den Betroffenen im Rahmen der Vertragsfreiheit überlassenen individuellen Gewichtung und Gestaltung ihrer Interessen mit der Möglichkeit zu entsprechenden Auffanglösungen beruht, sondern auf der gesetzgeberischen Würdigung und Bewertung der Familiengemeinschaft, die auch das "außenstehende" Rechtsverhältnis als solches angeht. Im übrigen hat die Rechtsprechung des BGH die Sachverhalte einer Schädigung im Straßenverkehr, wie sie Gegenstand der genannten Entscheidung in BGHZ 35, 317 = NJW 1961, 1966 gewesen ist, inzwischen einer gerechten Lösung auf andere Weise zugeführt (vgl. BGHZ 53, 352 = NJW 1970, 1271; BGHZ 61, 101 = NJW 1973, 1654; BGHZ 63, 51 = NJW 1974, 2124).

Aus allem folgt, daß die Beklagte im Streitfall sich der Klage gegenüber auch nicht unter Hinweis auf die Rechtsprechungs-grundsätze zum "gestörten Gesamtschuldnerausgleich" auf eine Beteiligung des Vaters des Klägers an dem Unfall berufen kann.

BUNDESGERICHTSHOF (SIXTH CIVIL SENATE), 1 MARCH 1988[2]

BGHZ 103, 338

The claimant, who was one year and 10 months old at the time, suffered substantial injuries to his head and shoulders on 17 May 1985 in an open children's playing area in M, maintained by the defendant city, when he fell to the ground from the platform of a slide erected there. The platform of the slide was at least 1.50 m above the ground, which in this area consisted of asphalt concrete. On the sides of the platform there were rails with wide spaces to the sides. According to the claimant's allegation, the accident happened when, as he was sitting down on the platform to start his slide, he stretched out his left foot, and, while his father stood near him to the left of the slide, in a moment when he was not being watched, suddenly slipped backwards to the right under the rail and fell to the ground.

The claimant claimed from the defendant payment of appropriate damages for pain and suffering for violation of the duty to safeguard the public in general (*Verkehrssicherungspflicht*) as well as a declaration of a duty to compensate for all further harm, in so far as this had not passed to social security agencies. The defendant has opposed the claim. It has referred to the fact that the playing equipment has been in place since 1964 and comparable accidents have not occurred in the past. Also, the contributory fault of the claimant's father arising from breach of the duty of supervision which he owed had to be set against the claimant.

The Landgericht granted the claimant damages for pain and suffering in the sum of DM 10,000 and stated that the application for a declaration was well founded. On the defendant's appeal, the Oberlandesgericht reduced the damages for pain and suffering to DM 8,000, but dismissed the remainder of the appeal as unfounded. The defendant's appeal in law was unsuccessful.

Reasons:

I. The appeal court proceeds on the basis of a violation of the duties to safeguard the public (*Verkehrssicherungspflichten*) by the defendant. It ought not to have permitted the use of the slide which had insufficient protection on its side rails to prevent small children from falling, when the surface of the ground in the area in which it stood was asphalt concrete. As children tend to fall from playing equipment from time to time, no special safety measures were needed only if the equipment was comparatively low. In other cases, an impact absorbing surface had to be selected in order to avoid injuries. Accordingly, the German Industrial Standard Norm 7926 issued in 1979 provides only for grass, synthetic material, safety tiles, sand or fine shingle to a depth of 200 mm as ground surfaces for playing equipment with a handrail and a drop of 1–2 m to the ground. Possible contributory fault on the part of the father in relation to the accident could not be attributed to the claimant.

II. The judgment of the appeal court stands up to legal examination.

1. The appeal court has correctly determined the duties to safeguard arising from § 823 (1) BGB which have accrued to the defendant city M from making the playing area on which the claimant sustained the accident generally available.

a) According to the principle that everyone who creates a danger must also take the necessary precautions for the safety of third parties, the defendant had to take the safety measures which experience of life indicates to be necessary for this area of danger. This Senate endorses the view of the appeal court that the content and scope of the duties to safeguard the public (*Verkehrssicherungspflichten*) for an open playing area arise from the need to construct and maintain the playing area so as to be as free from danger as possible; and that in this connection the degree of safety to be observed has to correspond to the age of the youngest children which might use the playing equipment concerned [*reference omitted*]. There is no legal reason preventing the appeal court from requiring the defendant to chose a surface with impact absorbing qualities below playing equipment with a height from the ground, as here, of 1.50 m. It did so for the simple reason that high spirits, curiosity or inexperience can lead smaller children to dangerous and inappropriate behaviour, and plunges from playing equipment frequently occur as a consequence of some unfortunate movement, disturbance of balance or because of the influence of other children. Especially strict requirements are to be placed on the safety of playing equipment in a children's playing area. In principle, the children and their parents must be allowed to place unlimited trust in the fact that children can use the playing equipment without danger and, in particular, cannot suffer such severe injuries as is the case here [*reference omitted*]. Because of the danger—always present with children—of falling from playing equipment, the requirement of an appropriate surface which makes these accidents less dangerous is, in any case, an elementary safety requirement as far as playing equipment with a height of 1.50 m is concerned.

This standard for the duties to safeguard the public (*Verkehrssicherungspflichten*) to be observed does not, in contrast to the view of the appeal in law, contradict the principle that playing areas and equipment situated on them do not have to be free from all risks. But these can only be easily comprehensible and calculable risks, which have an educational value for the child [*references omitted*]. However, such controllable risks do not include the qualities of a surface suitable to avoid injuries of children who fall off playing equipment, which is the issue here. Whether the duties to safeguard the public (*Verkehrssicherungspflichten*) are limited if the children's playing area or certain playing equipment is only made available for use by children from a certain (higher) age on can be left open. This is because a limitation to a minimum age for use was indisputably not prescribed. Instead, the playing area was made available by an appropriate sign for use by all children up to 12 years of age. Any possible expectation by the defendant, not recognisable by other people, that slides of the kind in use here would only be used by children from three years of age and upwards did not limit their duties to safeguard the public (*Verkehrssicherungspflichten*).

b) There are also no objections to the fact that the appeal court, in order to establish the content and scope of the duties to safeguard the public (*Verkehrssicherungspflichten*) applying to the defendant, has referred to the German Industrial Standard Norm 7926, Part 1, issued in December 1976, which provides, in accordance with German Industrial Standard

18034, only for loose laid surfaces like earth, grass, sand or fine shingle as ground surfaces for playing equipment with a handrail and a drop of 1–2 m to the ground. Even if German Industrial Standard Norms are not norms which have effect against third parties in the sense of authoritative legal requirements, but are rather recommendations of the 'German Industrial Standard/German Institute for Standardisation e.V. (registered association)' aiming at voluntary application [*reference omitted*], they still reflect the state of the recognised rules of technology applying to certain areas. They are therefore especially appropriate for the determination of safety measures which are regarded as necessary according to experience of life [*reference omitted*]. Whether existing installations should be allowed to continue to be used without alteration for a transitional period after the introduction of new German Industrial Standard Norms can be left open here. Such a period of adaptation, if it were permitted, would, in any case, as the appeal court correctly found, have long ago expired, as the accident occurred more than eight years after the issue of the relevant German Industrial Standard Norm. The appeal in law refers to the fact that slides of the kind under consideration had still not been questioned by supervising authorities after the coming into effect of the new German Industrial Standard Norm. But this was a fact first submitted at the appeal in law stage, and therefore not admissible. Besides this, such a practice could not relieve the defendant of its responsibility, as the danger arising from the location of the playing equipment could easily be recognised by it as the body responsible for the playing area.

2. The argument of the appeal in law which is directed against the failure to take the claimant's father's possible contributory fault into account in relation to the defendant's liability also fails.

a) Even the appeal in law does not call into question that the claimant can only have his father's contributory fault attributed to him in respect of the accident in accordance with §§ 254 para 1 and 278 BGB within the framework of an obligation relationship or a similar special legal relationship already existing with the defendant at the moment of the accident [*reference omitted*]. It takes the view, however, that such a special relationship had existed in the present case when the harm occurred, because the notice board at the playing area described the persons permitted, and prohibited certain forms of behaviour. A user relationship (*Benutzungsverhältnis*) had been created by this. However, the appeal court, in harmony with the case law of the Senate [*references omitted*], correctly regarded this fact as insufficient to create special relationships in the law of obligations (or relationships similar to these) between the claimant and the defendant, which go beyond the general rights and duties in tort. Even if there had been a bye-law for the use of the playing area, the creation of a user relationship (*Benutzungsverhältnis*) of a nature similar to a contract could not follow from this alone [*reference omitted*]. In particular, there is no evidence of a special interest which could have given cause for increased rights and duties of this kind for both sides. Instead, the interests of both sides seem already to be sufficiently protected by the general tortious relationships.

b) The appeal in law also places the appeal court judgment under scrutiny from the point of view of the claimant's duty to be answerable for his father in accordance with § 278 BGB, in connection with the obligation to avoid or reduce harm in the sense of § 254(2) sentence 1 BGB. But this reveals no legal error. It is correct that a victim, within the framework of his obligations to avoid or reduce harm in accordance with § 254(2) BGB, must allow a fault of a third person to be taken into account in accordance with § 278 BGB. Nevertheless the tort of the wrongdoer must already have brought about the development of the harm [*reference omitted*]. A different approach would not only make redundant the limitation of the victim's duty to be answerable for a fault of a third party—in accordance with § 278 BGB—to special legal relationships. The victim would also be in a worse position than the wrongdoer who, in principle, is responsible in tort only under § 831 BGB in respect of harm arising for third parties. Therefore it is not, as the appeal in law considers, sufficient that danger triggered by the violation of the defendant's duties to safeguard the public (*Verkehrssicherungspflichten*) already existed when the claimant climbed the slide at his father's hand. Nor is it sufficient that the statutory representative or the person entrusted by it with supervision knew of the danger which threatened the child

Appendix 2

from an installation or a given situation [*references omitted*]. Only in so far as contributory fault for the harm which has occurred applies to the phase in which the actual violation is already realised does an attribution in accordance with §§ 254(2) and 278 BGB come into question. Nor is the father's conduct to be attributed to the claimant over and above this from the point of view of a unity of liability (*Haftungseinheit*). The appeal in law seeks by this means to provide a basis for a corresponding reduction of the defendant's duty to compensate. But the claimant, who is not competent in tort, has not jointly caused the accident in a manner which is attributable to him. He and his father cannot therefore share a unity of attribution [*references omitted*].

3. The view of the appeal court that the claim against the defendant is not be reduced from the point of view of a 'disturbed internal settlement between joint debtors' (*gestörter Innenausgleich unter Gesamtschuldnern* or *gestörter Gesamtschuldnerausgleich*)[3] must also be followed. It is unimportant in this connection which standard of liability the claimant's father must be judged by in the supervision of his child on the playing area, and whether according to it he has actually culpably violated existing duties. The liability relationship of the defendant to the claimant is not affected in any of these possible constellations.

a) According to § 840(1) BGB, each of several tortfeasors is liable to the victim for the harm for which he is responsible to the full extent, without regard to the other's duty to be answerable for it. Statute leaves it to the tortfeasor to seek compensation in respect to his claim from the joint tortfeasors only at a later stage. Even if the claimant could demand compensation for his accident injuries not only from the defendant but also from his father, that would not, in principle, affect the defendant's full liability to him.

b) Case law has admittedly allowed exceptions to this principle in cases in which a tortfeasor does not have the possibility of obtaining compensation from a joint tortfeasor since the latter is released from his liability as against the victim by virtue of statute. In these cases, the victim can claim from the non-privileged tortfeasor compensation only for that part of the harm which would have remained that tortfeasor's responsibility within the internal relationship (with the released joint tortfeasor), if the possibility of an internal settlement had not been barred by privilege against liability [*references omitted*]. This is based on the consideration that it would be unfair to burden the non-privileged tortfeasor with the release of his joint tortfeasor from liability, which according to its meaning should only concern the latter's relationship with the victim.

c) In the wider sense it is possible likewise to speak of a 'liability privilege' in connection with § 1664(1) BGB. According to this provision, parents exercising parental care towards the child are only responsible for the care which they usually apply in their own affairs. In comparison with tortfeasors who are liable according to the general standard of care contained in § 276 BGB, their duty is limited because of their family law obligations to the victim (§ 277 BGB). In the case in question, the claimant's father was admittedly not entitled to custody. However there is much to be said for the prevailing view in the literature of applying the more lenient standard of liability even to the parent who was not entitled to custody by analogous application of § 1664 BGB, if he, as here, in exerting his right of contact (§ 1634 BGB) exercises factual personal care of his child [*references omitted*]. Neither would, according to the view of the Senate, the application of § 1664 BGB in the present case be prevented by the fact that tortious duties of behaviour on the part of the father for the protection of the health of his child are (also) at issue. Anyhow, where these protective duties in cases like this one revolve entirely around the care for the person of the child, any different approach would amount to a limitation of § 1664 BGB, which would not be reconcilable with the wording and meaning of that provision. That is obviously not to say that a protected interest which is as central to parents as the health of their children would not have a special status even for the care they use in their own affairs, and therefore for their liability. It can be left open whether there is still room for the subjective standard of care established by § 277 BGB where the protective duties of the parents towards their children could scarcely be separated objectively from their general duties (to be measured by experience of life in accordance with the objective standard of care established by § 276 BGB). This is accepted in particular for the area of duties to safeguard the public (*Verkehrssicherungspflichten*), for instance duties of supervision under § 832 BGB [*references omitted*] and for the area of involvement in road traffic [*references omitted*]. Such a type of case is however not given here.

d) Nevertheless, even if the claimant's father were freed from joint liability for the claimant's injuries only because of the more lenient standard of care established by § 1664 BGB, that would not benefit the claimant. The prevailing opinion in the literature that, even in such cases, the statutory 'privilege from liability' (*Haftungsprivilegierung*) ought not to disadvantage the non-privileged tortfeasor, but must be counterbalanced by an appropriate reduction of the victim's claims to compensation according to the principles developed by the case law on the statutory release from liability (*gesetzliche Haftungsfreistellung*) [*references omitted*] or by creating an imaginary internal settlement (*Innenausgleich*) [*reference omitted*] cannot be shared by the Senate. The supporting grounds on which the case law on the so-called 'disturbed joint obligation relationship' (*gestörtes Gesamtschuldverhältnis*) rests are absent here. In those cases, to start with, all the prerequisites for a joint obligation relationship (*Gesamtschuldverhältnis*) in accordance with § 840(1) BGB are fulfilled; this is then only 'disturbed' by statute releasing the privileged joint tortfeasor from his liability, in deviation from the principle of § 840 BGB. But in cases in which joint liability is barred because of § 1664 BGB, the joint tortfeasor 'privileged' in this way does not even slot into the regime of § 840 BGB; the foundations for a joint obligation relationship which could be 'disturbed' are thus simply lacking. That is no mere formal and outward difference. It corresponds to the nature and system of tortious liability that a tortfeasor can only involve someone who has jointly caused the harm in his liability if and in so far as this person has jointly created the harm in a way which is attributable. Only where privilege against liability deprives him of the joint tortfeasor as a settlement debtor—in spite of the latter's joint liability in tort—is it justified to speak of the former being burdened with a privilege from liability which runs counter to §§ 840 and 426 BGB. If, on the other hand, a settlement fails because of the absence of attributable involvement on the part of the settlement debtor, that is a consequence of the settlement system which is, in principle, suffered by all tortfeasors within the framework of tortious liability.

Attributability is lacking, however, in the case of a release from liability in accordance with §§ 1664(1) and 277 BGB, as long as the violation of duty does not go beyond the care one uses in one's own affairs or appears to be grossly negligent. Below this threshold, the parent is not responsible for a contribution to harm. Conduct partly causing the harm which has arisen is therefore not to be attributed to the claimant's father as long as the liability standard of §§ 1664(1) and 277 BGB is not reached.

Where there is no attributability because of the more lenient standard of care of § 1664 BGB, the denial of an internal settlement for a joint tortfeasor can no more be regarded as an unfair special burden than in those cases in which there is no attributable involvement because, for instance, of a division of tasks specially prescribed by statute or the lack of tortious capacity of the joint tortfeasor. For that reason alone, the Senate sees no objective cause to modify by way of development of the law—according to the standard set by its case law dealing with the release from liability through §§ 636 and 637 RVO (Imperial Insurance Order)—the statutory regime for the division of burdens in relation to multiple involvement also in those cases in which a joint obligation relationship (*Gesamtschuldverhältnis*) does not come into existence because of the more lenient standard of liability of § 1664 BGB. Furthermore, not only would such a solution lack appropriate criteria for measuring the contribution of the parent causing the harm (to whom §§ 1664 and 277 BGB deny attributability) for the purpose of a reduction of the claim to compensation. It would also lead to the scarcely plausible consequence that a child harmed by conduct of its parents, which (because it is moderately negligent in the sense of § 276 BGB) has not yet reached the threshold of § 277 BGB, would have to accept a reduction of its claim to compensation, but would suffer no such reduction in the case of gross fault on the part of its parents. In this respect it should also not be overlooked that in these cases, as opposed to the area where the privilege against liability on the basis of §§ 636 and 637 RVO is applied, no equivalent for the claim made for compensation accrues to the victim (in the form of an alternative settlement solution).

But neither does it appear just to the Senate, after examination of its other standpoint put forward in BGHZ 35, 317, to release the tortfeasor from part of the liability applying to him (because of the contribution which he made to the harm and for which he is answerable) through the fiction of an internal compensation settlement at the expense of the parent—arising from a joint obligation—just because the parent was involved in the infliction of the harm, but without making an attributable contribution to it. This is all the more so as the economic effect of such a solution would in the majority of cases eventually also be to the detriment of the child harmed. In so far as the statements of this Senate in its judgment of 27 June 1961 (BGHZ 35, 317, 322 ff) on the more lenient standard of liability of § 1359 BGB between spouses contradict this, the Senate no longer adheres to this view. In particular, it considers the comparison developed there between the case of a statutory reduction in liability and the interests of the parties in the case of a contractually agreed reduction in liability to be insufficient as a basis for the fiction of an internal compensation settlement arising from a joint obligation under § 1664 BGB. This is simply because this reduction of liability is not based on an individual weighing and formulation of the participants' interests, left to themselves within the framework of contractual freedom and with the possibility of making corresponding counterbalancing solutions. It is based instead on legislative assessment and evaluation of the family community, which also concerns the 'external' legal relationship as such. Besides this, the Bundesgerichtshof has applied, in its subsequent case law, to situations of harm inflicted in road traffic (like those which were the object of the decision in BGHZ 35, 317 already mentioned) a just solution in a different way [*references omitted*].

From all this it follows that the defendant in this case cannot rely on the involvement of the claimant's father in the accident by reference to the principles of the 'disturbed settlement between joint debtors' (*gestörter Gesamtschuldnerausgleich*) as developed by case law.

Notes

[1] Translated by Tony Weir, Trinity College, Cambridge.

[2] Translated by Raymond Youngs, Senior Research Fellow at the Institute of Global Law, University College London.

[3] See chapter four above for an introduction into this concept.

Appendix 3

Databases Searched

Citations in academic literature (USA): Westlaw JLR—a large database of about 775 law reviews and legal periodicals, mostly American.

Citations by courts (Australia): Westlaw AU-ALLCASES—a database containing the judgments of the High Court of Australia and the Federal Court of Australia, both reported and unreported.

Citations by courts (Canada): Westlaw CAN-ALLCASES—a comprehensive database of judgments of Canadian courts, both federal and provincial from 1979.

Citations by courts (England): Westlaw UK-RPTS-ALL—a comprehensive database of judgments of United Kingdom courts, including *The Law Reports* and many specialised series of reports.

Citations in academic literature and by courts (Germany): beck-online—a new database provided by the publishing house C H Beck in Munich.

Citations by courts (USA): Westlaw ALLCASES—a comprehensive database of federal and state judicial decisions from 1945.

The Search in England

The search in England was limited to five legal journals: *Cambridge Law Journal, International and Comparative Law Quarterly, Law Quarterly Law Review, Modern Law Review* and *Oxford Journal of Legal Studies*. It was done manually by Mr Stephen Underwood of the London School of Economics and limited to the period 1980–2001.

The Search in Germany

Due to the absence of adequate databases, the search in Germany was restricted to the commentaries and journals available at beck-online (a new database of the publishing house C H Beck in Munich) in April 2002. Further limitations result from the fact that authors are not cited with their first names in German legal literature. If the name of the author is common (as is the case with Lutter, Lorenz and Zimmermann), it is thus difficult to identify false positives. Finally, names of German authors that are similar or even identical to terms used in everyday German language (as is the case with von Bar) result in a high number of false hits, invalidating the results. A search by using the function 'by author' will, in turn, only reveal the works themselves, not citations in footnotes. In order to obtain at least some hard data, a limited number of the works of these authors were directly searched for. The most important sources searched by beck-online are the *Neue Juristische Wochenschrift* (1981–2002) and the *Münchner Kommentar zum Bürgerlichen Gesetzbuch*: (1) **Commentaries**: Ascheid, Preis and Schmidt, *Großkommentar zum Kündigungsrecht* (2000); Bamberger and Roth, *Bürgerliches Gesetzbuch* (§§ 241–432, 1589–1921 BGB and SGB VIII) (2001); Bärmann and Pick, *Kommentar zum WEG* (15th edn, 2001); Baumbach and Hopt, *HGB-Kommentar* (30th edn, 2001); Baumbach and Hueck, *GmbHG-Kommentar* (17th edn, 2000); Blank and Börstinghaus, *Miete* (2000); Blank and Börstinghaus, *Neues Mietrecht* (2000); Ebenroth, Boujong and Joost, *HGB-Kommentar* (2001); *Erfurter Kommentar zum Arbeitsrecht* (2nd edn, 2001); Fritz, *Gewerberaummietrecht* (2000); Ganten, Jagenburg and Motzke, *VOB B* (1997); Gramlich, *Mietrecht* (8th edn, 2001); Hartmann, *Kostengesetze* (30th edn, 2001); Hüffer, *AktG-Kommentar* (5th edn, 2002); Jürgens, *Betreuungsrecht* (2nd edn, 2001); Kniffka and Koeble, *Kompendium des Baurechts* (2000); Langenberg, *Betriebskostenrecht* (3rd edn, 2002); Langenfeld, *Handbuch der Eheverträge* (4th edn, 2000); Motzke, Pietzcker and Prieß, *VOB A* (4th edn, 2001); Müller, *Praktische Fragen des Wohnungseigentums*; *Münchener Kommentar zum BGB*: vol 1 = §§ 1–240 AGB-Gesetz (4th edn, 2001), vol 2 §§ 241–432 FernAbs-Gesetz (4th edn, 2001), vol 3 =

§§ 433–606 Finanzierungsleasing, VerbrKrG, HausTWG, MHG (3rd edn, 1995), vol 4 = §§ 607–704 (3rd edn, 1997), vol 5 = §§ 705–853, PartnerschaftsgesellschaftsG, ProdukthaftungsG (3rd edn, 1997), vol 6 = §§ 854–1296 WEG, ErbbaurechtsVO, SachenrechtsbereinigungsG, SchuldrechtsänderungsG (3rd edn, 1997), vol 7 = §§ 1297–1588, Gesetz zur Regelung von Härten im Versorgungsausgleich, Gesetz zur Überleitung des Versorgungsausgleichs auf das Beitrittsgebiet, VAHRG, VAÜG, HausratsVO (4th edn, 2000), vol 8 = §§ 1589–1921 Familienrecht II, SGB VIII (4th edn, 2002), vol 9 = §§ 1922–2385 BeurkG §§ 27–35 (3rd edn, 1997), vol 10 = Art 1 bis 38 EGBGB, IPR (3rd edn, 1998), vol 11 = Arts 50–237 EGBGB, Int Handels- und GesellschaftsR (3rd edn, 1999); *Münchener Handbuch zum Arbeitsrecht* (2nd edn, 2000); Musielak, *ZPO* (2nd edn, 2000); Nicklisch and Weick, *VOB B* (3rd edn, 2001); Roth and Altmeppen, *GmbHG-Kommentar* (3rd edn, 1997); Schaub, *Arbeitsrecht von A-Z* (16th edn, 2001); Schmidt-Futterer, *Großkommentar Mietrecht* (7th edn, 1999); Wendl and Staudigl, *Unterhalt* (5th edn, 2000); Werner, Pastor and Müller, *Baurecht von A-Z* (7th edn, 2000). (2) **Journals**: *Arbeitsrechtliche Praxis* (from 1971–2002); *Bilanzbuchhalter und Controller* (2000–02); *Zeitschrift für Bank- und Kapitalmarktrecht* (2002); *Deutsche Notar-Zeitschrift* (1986–2002); *Deutsches Steuerrecht* (1991–2002); *DStR-Entscheidungsdienst* (1997–2002); *Deutsch-Deutscherechtszeit-schrift* (1990–97); *Europäische Zeitschrift für Wirtschaftsrecht* (2000–02); *Praxis der freiwilligen Gerichtsbarkeit* (2000–02); *Familie Partnerschaft Recht* (2001–02); *Gewerblicher Rechtsschutz und Urheberrecht* (2001–02); *GRUR-Rechtsprechungs-Report* (2001–02); *Internationales Steuerrecht* (2000–02); *Juristische Schulung* (2000–02); *Landes- und Kommunalverwaltung* (1991–2002); *Multimedia und Recht* (1998–2002); *Neue Juristische Online-Zeitschrift* (2001–02); *Neue Juristische Wochenschrift* (1981–2002); *NJW-Entscheidungsdienst Familien- und Erbrecht* (1996–2002); *NJW-Entscheidungsdienst Mietrecht* (1996–97); *NJW-Entscheidungsdienst Versicherungs- und Haftungsrecht* (1996–98); *NJW-Entscheidungsdienst WettbR* (1996–2000); *NJW-Rechtsprechungs-Report* (1986–2002); *Neue Zeitschrift für Strafrecht* (1981–2002); *NStZ-Rechtsprechungs-Report* (1996–2002); *Neue Zeitschrift für Versicherung und Recht* (1998–2002); *Neue Zeitschrift für Verwaltungsrecht* (1982–2002); *NVwZ-Rechtsprechungs-Report*

(1988–2002); *Neue Zeitschrift für Arbeitsrecht* (1984–2002); *NZA-Rechtsprechungs-Report* (1996–2002); *Neue Zeitschrift für Bau- und Vergaberecht* (2000–02); *Neue Zeitschrift für Gesellschaftsrecht* (2000–02); *Neue Zeitschrift für Insolvenzrecht* (1998–2002); *Neue Zeitschrift für Mietrecht* (1998–2002); *Neue Zeitschrift für Sozialrecht* (1998–2002); *Neue Zeitschrift für Verkehrsrecht* (1988–2002); *OLG-Rechtsprechung Neue Länder* (2000–02); *Recht der Arbeit* (2000–02); *Zeitschrift für Vermögens- und Immobilienrecht* (1991–2002); *Wirtschaft und Recht in Osteuropa* (2000–02); *Zeitschrift für Erbrecht und Vermögensnachfolge* (2000–02); *Zeitschrift für Rechtspolitik* (2000–02).

The Search in Italy

Dr Marino manually conducted a search of the following journals for the years 1980–2001: *Contratto e Impressa, Carriera giuridica, Digesto IV sul diritto comparato, Foro Italiano, Revue Internationale de droit comparé, Rivista diritto civile, Rivista diritto processuale civile.*

Formulations of Searches

Because citations use various forms of names, it was necessary to construct searches using all variants of names likely to be found in citations. The following is a list of the formulations of the variants of names used to construct searches.

Guido Alpa
G Alpa

Hans W Baade
Hans Baade
HW Baade
H Baade

John Bell[1]

George A Bermann
George Bermann

GA Bermann
G Bermann

Xavier Blanc-Jouvan
X Blanc-Jouvan

Michael Joachim Bonell
MJ Bonell

Mauro Bussani
M Bussani

Mauro Cappelletti
M Cappelletti

René David
R David

John P Dawson
John Dawson
JP Dawson
J Dawson

Mireille Delmas-Marty
M Delmas-Marty

Ulrich Drobnig
U Drobnig

John G Fleming[2]
John Fleming
JG Fleming

Antonio Gambaro
A Gambaro

Mary Ann Glendon
MA Glendon
M Glendon

James R Gordley
James Gordley
J Gordley

Gino Gorla
G Gorla

Erik Jayme
E Jayme

JA Jolowicz

Otto Kahn-Freund
O Kahn-Freund

Hein Kötz
H Kötz

Frederick H Lawson
FH Lawson

Pierre Legrand
P Legrand

Werner Lorenz
W Lorenz

Maurizio Lupoi
M Lupoi

Marcus Lutter
M Lutter

Frederick A Mann
FA Mann

Basil S Markesinis
BS Markesinis
B Markesinis

Ugo Mattei
U Mattei

John Henry Merryman
John H Merryman
John Merryman
JH Merryman
J Merryman

Horatia Muir-Watt
H Muir-Watt

Peter-Christian Müller-Graff
Peter Müller-Graff
P Müller-Graff

Barry Nicholas
B Nicholas

Mathias Reimann
M Reimann

Bernard Rudden
B Rudden

Rodolfo Sacco
R Sacco

Peter Schlechtriem
P Schlechtriem

Rudolf B Schlesinger
Rudolf Schlesinger
RB Schlesinger
R Schlesinger

Denis Tallon
D Tallon

André Tunc
A Tunc

Christian von Bar
C von Bar

Arthur Taylor von Mehren
Arthur T von Mehren
AT von Mehren
A von Mehren

Alan Watson[3]

JA Weir
Tony Weir
T Weir

Reinhard Zimmermann
R Zimmermann

Konrad Zweigert
K Zweigert

Notes

[1] Because of the number of false positives, it was not possible to search on the name 'J Fleming.' This means that inevitably some true positives were missed.

[2] Because of the number of false positives, it was not possible to search on the name 'A Watson.' This means that inevitably some true positives were missed.

[3] Because of the number of false positives, it was not possible to search on the name 'J Bell.' This means that inevitably some true positives were missed.

Index

Index